ROUGH RIDING

SERIES EDITOR

Sonjah Stanley Niaah

ADVISORY BOARD

Carolyn Cooper
Julian Henriques
David Katz
Deborah Thomas
Jo-Anne Tull

Word, sound and power. This is the definition of the musical vibrations of Jamaican music. The music of Jamaica influences and has been influenced by countless other music forms throughout the Caribbean and worldwide. At the intersection of creation, production, consumption and globalization of Jamaican music, and from an interdisciplinary perspective, Sound Culture begins a long-overdue focus on the history and evolution of sounds, tracing the movement from mento to ska and on to rocksteady, reggae, dub, nyabinghi, dancehall and the various styles of reggae fusion. The series covers all Caribbean music that intersects with Jamaican sounds, and artists in the region who work within the musical genres from Jamaica. It examines those who have blended their national musical forms with Jamaica's and acknowledges that, in addition to shaping culture, social relations, economics and politics, Jamaican music has influenced popular cultural production internationally. In particular, reggae has resonated with the disenfranchised and marginalized all over the world, its rhythm and melody appealing to soul rebels from Japan to South Africa, and Croatia to New Zealand. Sound Culture is intended as a record of the colossal impact that Jamaica has had on the planet through its musical vibrations.

ROUGH RIDING

Tanya Stephens and the Power of Music to Transform Society

EDITED BY
ADWOA NTOZAKE ONUORA
ANNA KASAFI PERKINS
AND
AJAMU NANGWAYA

The University of the West Indies Press
Jamaica • Barbados • Trinidad and Tobago

The University of the West Indies Press
7A Gibraltar Hall Road, Mona
Kingston 7, Jamaica
www.uwipress.com

© 2020 by Adwoa Ntozake Onuora, Anna Kasafi Perkins and Ajamu Nangwaya
All rights reserved. Published 2020
A catalogue record of this book is available from
the National Library of Jamaica.

ISBN: 978-976-640-795-7 (paper)
978-976-640-808-4 (Kindle)
978-976-640-809-1 (Epub)

Cover photograph of Tanya Stephens by Jean-Pierre Kavanaugh
Cover and book design by Robert Harris
Set in Minion Pro 10.5/14.5 x 24

The University of the West Indies Press has no responsibility for the persistence or accuracy of URLs for external or third-party Internet websites referred to in this publication and does not guarantee that any content on such websites is, or will remain, accurate or appropriate.

Printed in the United States of America

Contents

Foreword: Dancehall Culture Upsetting Delicate Sensibilities   *vii*
CAROLYN COOPER

Preface: Be Bold for Change: On Violence against Women and Girls   *ix*
VIVIENNE (TANYA STEPHENS) STEPHENSON

Acknowledgements   *xiii*

Prologue: Rough Riding: Tanya Stephens and the Power of Music to Transform Society   *1*
ADWOA NTOZAKE ONUORA, ANNA KASAFI PERKINS AND AJAMU NANGWAYA

Part 1: Who Is Tanya?

1. Tanya Stephens as a Black Feminist Organic Intellectual of Dancehall and Reggae   *23*
AJAMU NANGWAYA

2. The Tenderness of Tanya, Vulnerability of Vivienne: Reassessing Dancehall's Ruff Rider   *49*
MELVILLE COOKE

3. The Gangsta as Feminist in the Lyrics of Tanya Stephens   *64*
TANYA BATSON-SAVAGE

Part 2: "Still #1 with a #2 Pencil": Producing and Disseminating Knowledge

4. "The Sound of My Tears": Tanya Stephens and the Meanings of Crying   *79*
ANNA KASAFI PERKINS

5   Tanya Stephens as Apostle of Critical Literacy   *93*
    ADWOA NTOZAKE ONUORA AND AJAMU NANGWAYA

6   "Yuh Cyaan Hangle di Ride": Tanya Stephens's Critique of
    Societal Inefficiency   *113*
    ELSA CALLIARD-BURTON

7   The Call to Resistance: The Weaponization of Language
    in the Music of Tanya Stephens   *127*
    NICOLE PLUMMER

Part 3: "Put It on You": Tanya Stephens's Erotic Playbook

8   A Lyrical Juxtaposition of Tanya Stephens and
    Fay-Ann Lyons-Alvarez   *155*
    ALPHA OBIKA

9   Collision of RastafarI and the Erotic in the Work of
    Tanya Stephens   *179*
    SARA SULIMAN

10 "It's a Pity Yuh Already Ave a Wife": The Possibilities and
    Pitfalls of Tanya Stephens's Civilized Man-Sharing   *208*
    CHAZELLE RHODEN

11 Power and the Construction of the Erotic   *221*
    KAREN CARPENTER

    Epilogue: "A Bunch of Righteous Freaks": Tanya, God, Christians
    and the Bible   *243*
    ANNA KASAFI PERKINS

    Appendix   *263*

    Contributors   *265*

Foreword
Dancehall Culture Upsetting Delicate Sensibilities

CAROLYN COOPER

IN HER BOLD PREFACE TO THIS DISTINCTIVE COLLECTION, *Rough Riding: Tanya Stephens and the Power of Music to Transform Society*, Tanya Stephens asserts, "Today we have to upset delicate sensibilities, because the time for being petite in our proceedings has passed. Occasionally we will have to rip some fabric." Stephens's deployment of the trope of ripped fabric appears to be a rather delicate way of alluding to Jamaican "bad" words that signify female genitalia and bloody menstrual cloths. Nice and decent people, with refined sensibilities, are not supposed to utter these profane words. They should not let rip, colloquially speaking, in polite society or even in private. Women, especially, are expected to contain themselves with decorum. Contesting stereotypes of passive femininity, Stephens decisively rejects the label "petite". With its seemingly complimentary connotations of adorable daintiness, the epithet actually diminishes women, turning them into purely decorative objects.

Stephens rips fabric as a political act, tearing down the veil of respectability that conceals the rot in society. Violence against women and girls is her primary preoccupation in the preface. But she also punches holes in the façade of propriety that barely conceals a wide range of social injustices that oppress marginalized groups in Jamaica. Stephens assumes the role of warner woman calling down damnation on the perpetrators of institutionalized brutality in a language that is far from delicate. The "fabricated" words to which Stephens alludes cannot be simply dismissed as "bad". They are often the most appropriate expression of both intense pleasure and disgust.

The upsetting of delicate sensibilities that Stephens audaciously advocates can be much more broadly extended to encompass the destabilizing politics of dancehall culture. Subversion is a quintessential feature of the disconcerting ethos of the dancehall. Conventionally deprecated as violently misogynist and homophobic, dancehall culture, nevertheless, may be read as an emancipatory practice that controverts the dehumanizing construction of working-class identity in Jamaica. The "vulgar" body/language of the dancehall articulates sustained resistance against the systemic devaluation of African-derived culture that is encoded in the fictive construction of Jamaica as a multiracial nation state. The self-aggrandizing white and brown elites disparagingly attempt to discount the black majority, relegating the dominant creators of culture to the margins of the society.

But the survivors of transatlantic human trafficking have recreated traditions of dance, music, poetry and spirituality that have sustained them for generations. The percussive sounds of dancehall music and the characteristically vigorous dances that privilege pelvic rotation originate in a philosophy of embodied spirituality with a long lineage. The divide between the sacred and the secular that is fetishized in Western epistemology is transcended in African diasporic cosmologies that conceive the sexualized body as a medium through which possession by regenerative ancestral spirits can be potently manifested. The religious rituals of Kumina, for example, provide a vocabulary for organic dancehall choreography. The frontal pelvic thrust and propulsive body contact between men and women in the "sacred" circle become acts of "daggering" in the explicit, "secular" language of the dancehall: the vaginal sheath embracing the phallic sword.

Much to the disdain of delicate sensibilities, dancehall scholarship over the last three decades has attempted to recuperate the positive elements in this much-maligned expression of Jamaican popular culture. The problematic features of dancehall culture, such as its rampant homophobia, are not disregarded. It is the broad spectrum of the culture that is now taken into full account in the substantial corpus of scholarship that has been consolidated. This volume makes an outstanding contribution to the field with its focus on the body of work of the "spunky, fresh, feminine, human" Tanya Stephens – a truly exceptional artiste whose lyrics eloquently articulate the complexity of Jamaican popular music and its revolutionary potential to rip fabric, upset delicate sensibilities and reset our world.

Preface

Be Bold for Change: On Violence against Women and Girls*

VIVIENNE (TANYA STEPHENS) STEPHENSON

BEING BOLD MEANS BEING WILLING TO TAKE A RISK, a willingness to exceed set limits, even the limits which were set by us. This boldness can be a big action, challenging us to step outside of our own personal space, and enter the space of others. One example from US history is a black woman who brazenly sat at the front of the bus in a time of racial segregation. A more recent example closer to home was demonstrated by a "spunky woman" who impulsively used a tambourine to impact an unapologetic "alleged" sex offender, giving the Tambourine Army its name.

Most of us would not even dream of being that bold! That's okay. We don't all have to be bold in the same way. Those acts are necessary catalysts in every revolution. But of equal importance is the bold action which needs to follow. For some of us being bold will mean allowing others to be bold without our interference or even simply acknowledging and appreciating the potency of our sisters' works. On that note, let me pause to acknowledge a sister who last year pioneered this spot from which I speak and has made her position very clear in this revolution. I extend my gratitude and appreciation to my sister Imani Duncan-Price. Women like her, Latoya Nugent, Nadeen Spence and Taitu Heron inspire and motivate me every day to push harder, to breach boundaries, to get up out of retirement and pick up back weapon because this is war. And, if dem

---

*Speech delivered at the Women's Empowerment for Change Ltd (WE-Change) annual #HerLegacy International Women's Day event in March 2017. The event was hosted as part of the Tambourine Army's activism in support of victims and survivors of sexual and gender-based violence.

want war, you know wi a go deal wid di case cause mi have piece a sopn weh mi keep pon mi waist! Identify your weapon and back it. This is war.

Not everyone will understand what you're doing. Neither will everyone agree with your methods or expression. Some people will just be uninterested, while some will even be offended. Don't you allow that to faze you. When you know what you are doing and you can see clearly the path leading from your actions to the solutions you seek, do not break your momentum to explain anything to anyone who isn't instrumental to the process. Some people work for applause and awards, but your perseverance depends on those who work for results. People with good intentions will advise you to aim at building a fan base. Thank them graciously and continue building your momentum. Don't waste time worrying about who and who get big up and who breaking bread. You waah break bread wid dem? I much prefer a rich, moist, gooey chocolate cake anyway. So let us allow them to break bread while we continue to break the chains that bind us. When it comes down to it, we really are not here to impress each other. We are here to effect change. The speeches we need to worry about are the ones which inadvertently reinforce a dangerous present. The speeches we need to worry about are the ones that subliminally blame and muzzle victims or survivors of violence and abuse. We need to frame our statements so that they remain aligned with our intentions.

As a survivor of gender-based violence, I do not appreciate even the slightest suggestion that improving on my resume could possibly have prevented attacks on my person. Education, independence, and safety are not interchangeable words. When we speak, people don't hear our intentions, they hear what we say. So, we must make sure to say what we have to say in the way we mean. Let us be responsible enough to know when to simply be supportive. Do not try to silence a victim; a survivor. Especially when they are identifying their attackers. People who are lucky enough to enjoy the freedom of speech purchased by the spilt blood of our ancestors should never allow themselves to get so lax, so cocky, and so arrogant, that they fail to appreciate the luxury of it.

We are going to have to operate by a higher standard than we demand from men. The truth is, we can demand more from men than we women demand of each other. But this will only undermine our credibility and return results which defeat our purpose. Hence it is time we start loving us, start being more aware of what we do to us, even unwittingly. Because continuing on the same old path is not an option. Continuing to live by the archaic superficial and demeaning models for women set by chauvinists is no longer an option. It is not conducive to the safety and well-being of women today. And, as we progress and seek more for our offspring, it will be even less acceptable for the women of the future.

Today we have to upset delicate sensibilities, because the time for being petite in our proceedings has passed. Occasionally, we will have to rip some fabric. It is not sustainable for us to stand under machine gun fire while we maintain composure and worry about [our] image. The only images we should be concerned about are the images of mutilated bodies of women and children being displayed on the nightly news, images of crimes and crime scenes being circulated all over social media, the desensitization of our population to the wholesale verbal, psychological, physical, emotional, sexual, and economic abuse of our women and girls, with fear silencing too many of us. Those are the images we need to worry about. Stop fixating on preserving the integrity of the language of our ancestors' enslavers. Understand that our speech reflects our passion and is nuanced to impact those at whom our communication is aimed. Communication is about getting your point across. And, effective communication means getting your point aligned with your intention.

Some of us have allowed ourselves to become outmoded in this new era of media and communication, presiding pompously over a dying kingdom. Mrs Bucket and all of your friends, we love you. But I have news for you! The new breed of advocates that I am proud to call my family are not about finding ways to survive in this hostile environment. We are not about maintaining the tradition of suffering in silence while we wait for the prayers to kick in. We are not about preserving the image created for us by those who offend and oppress us. We are not about the family portrait with the paedophile patriarch resting his hands triumphantly on his victims' shoulders. Dat naa hang pon fi wi wall!

We are not about treading lightly. We will not allow ourselves to be content with patiently chipping away inches of rubble while our oppressors are laying rows of brick and building new and even more intrusive walls. We do not limit ourselves to your methods and neither do we limit you to ours. We respect your immense potential and we want to combine our varied efforts. But please, stop trying to bring us "back into the fold". We prefer to be bold! The times we are living in [demand] it.

Acknowledgements

THIS VOLUME BEGAN ITS JOURNEY AS A SHARED idea among three friends. It later grew into the symposium "Rough Riding: Tanya Stephens and the Power of Music to Transform Society" and now this book. We thank the many people who walked the journey with us.

Tanya Stephens, we are thankful to you for your approving nod to the symposium on your body of work and contribution to the genres of dancehall and reggae. As one of the great lyricists in dancehall and reggae, we firmly believe that your cultural work lives up to the words of Haitian writer Edwidge Danticat, who said of her own work: "Create dangerously, for people who read dangerously. This is what I've always thought it meant to be a writer." Continue being your dangerous, rough riding, badass self!

Much love and appreciation to the presenters at the symposium for the diverse angles from which you approached Tanya's work. You are the foundation on which this publication was constructed. Thanks to the contributors of chapters who came on board after the symposium. You added important elements to the examination of the artistic phenomenon that is Tanya Stephens.

We would like to big up the various offices at the University of the West Indies for enthusiastically embracing the idea of an academic exploration of Stephens's work, namely the Institute for Gender and Development Studies Regional Coordinating Office and its Mona campus unit, the Office of the Board for Undergraduate Studies, and the Institute of Caribbean Studies. Thanks are also due to Sandrea McLean and Ingrid Nicely, who assisted with the behind-the-scenes work that made the symposium a huge success.

To Carolyn Cooper, thanks for encouraging us to make the symposium the basis for a unique publication on the organic intellectual and dancehall/reggae artiste Tanya Stephens; importantly, thanks for being a foundation traveller on this intellectual journey. Your penning the foreword to this text is a most gracious act of solidarity, and for that, we are exceedingly grateful.

We appreciate the helpful and insightful comments, suggestions and questions of the reviewers of the chapters. You all made a qualitative difference to the final product that is this book.

Special thanks to photographer Jean-Pierre Kavanaugh for working with us to produce the cover image. To Erin MacLeod, thank you for your support and guidance from the early stages of the manuscript. Many thanks to the members of the editorial team at the University of the West Indies Press, Shivaun Hearne, Irina du Quenoy and Althea Denise Gooden, whose patience, diligence and generous accommodations have given birth to *Rough Riding: Tanya Stephens and the Power of Music to Transform Society.*

Prologue

Rough Riding: Tanya Stephens and the Power of Music to Transform Society

ADWOA NTOZAKE ONUORA, ANNA KASAFI PERKINS AND
AJAMU NANGWAYA

THIS COLLECTION GREW OUT OF A COLLABORATIVE EFFORT of the three co-editors – a gender and development scholar, a theologian/quality assurance professional, and a cultural studies researcher – that resulted in an interdisciplinary symposium held at the University of the West Indies, Mona, Jamaica, in 2017. It was the first attempt at subjecting Tanya Stephens's oeuvre to sustained critical reflection among various publics, including students, scholars, activists and fans. (She had previously delivered a public lecture at the Mona campus in 2011.) The fertile intercourse among the participants was enriched by an online interaction with Stephens, who had just returned to the island. Snippets of the exchange were featured by local traditional media. The University of the West Indies' Institute of Gender and Development Studies also presented Vivienne "Tanya" Stephens, "reggae artiste extraordinaire", with a citation "for her contribution to discourses on gender, social justice and human rights for the people of Jamaica and beyond". A copy of the citation is found in the appendix. Revised versions of some of the presentations from the symposium as well as responses to a wider call for papers are combined in this collection.

This exploration of Stephens's work is guided by several objectives. First, the book provides the space for a wide-ranging scholarly examination of many of the themes or topics that are explored in her ouevre. Indeed, it is the first, and so far only, book-length exploration, academic or otherwise, of the output of this cultural worker, who has mostly made her mark in the reggae and dancehall genres. As outlined in more detail below, most of the chapters engage in theorizing concepts that animate the inquiry into Stephens's lyrical contribution. This foundational theorizing sets the philosophical and theoretical course for other researchers who might engage her body of work in the future. Both dancehall and reggae have amassed significant scholarly attention over the past thirty years, culminating in the pioneering works of reggae studies scholars such as Carolyn Cooper (1986; 1989), Donna Hope (2006) and Sonjah Stanley Niaah (2010), to name a few. However, while there has been an expansion in academic engagement with both genres as modes of social inquiry, very few researchers have engaged the output of this seminal cultural worker and organic intellectual. Yet, her lyrical contribution, range of subjects covered, social justice commentary, political analysis and delivery may well be on par with her more recognized, socially and politically conscious musical counterparts, such as Bob Marley, Peter Tosh, Mutabaruka, Burning Spear and Linton Kwesi Johnson.

Second, in critically engaging with Stephens's work, the authors attempt to demonstrate the relevance of her interventions in social, political, cultural and economic discourses at both the local and global levels. In particular, this examination of Stephens's musical output critically assesses the way that she approaches issues as varied as women's oppression and liberation; gender relations; social conformity and transgression; the status of lesbians, gay men, bisexuals and transgendered persons; religion; power and problematics of the erotic; the construction and deployment of language; the artiste as organic intellectual; and conscientizing, or political education. The wide-ranging explorations here demonstrate that Stephens shines a torchlight on the social inequities abroad in society, even in cases where the characters in her songs reinforce the dominant, oppressive beliefs and practices. Many people are unaware that much of her discography features songs that fall within the framework of protest songs wailing against social issues that unfairly impact the lives of socially dominated groups. Her protest songs, for better or for worse, ring out in a global context in which there is a dearth of the kinds of consistent social movement activism that defined the 1960s and 1970s. Yet these songs can serve the purpose of educating, reminding and/or legitimizing Stephens's fans' concerns about the sociocultural and socio-economic issues that impact their lives and those of their neighbours. Therefore, it is important to determine the degree to which the subjects that are engaged in the artiste's songs undermine or reinforce the oppressive social order.

Lastly, and perhaps most importantly, the chapters in this publication are impelled by the objective of exploring Stephens's songs to uncover their capacity for engendering critical consciousness and contributing to social transformation. Protest songs have objectives such as the politicization of listeners and directing their attention to solving social problems. As such, it is important to examine how her body of work could be presented to the public as instruments of public education, rather than simply entertaining and titillating first-person narratives of male-female sexual play, deceit and subterfuge. Rather, Stephens calls her retelling and repositioning of matters erotic, cultural, religious and socio-economic into play to engender critical consciousness.

As feminist social critic bell hooks argues, memory and confession can be useful in politicizing oppressed peoples:

> When I chart a map of feminist politicization, of how we become more politically aware, I begin with an insistence on commitment to education for critical consciousness. Much of the education does start with examining the self from a new, critical perspective. To this end, confession and memory can be used constructively to illuminate past experiences, particularly when such experience is theorized. Using confession and memory as ways of naming reality enables women and men to talk about personal experience as a part of a process of politicization which places such talk in a dialectical context. This allows us to discuss personal experience in a different way that politicizes not just the telling, but the tale. Theorizing experience as we tell personal narrative, we have a sharper, keener sense of the end that is desired by telling. (1988, 109–10)

A socially conscious artiste such as Stephens is quite aware of the role of songs in consciousness raising and deliberately sets out to educate the listeners of her music. She wants them to know that the personal, even if the experience is not specifically hers, can be political in its articulation. It is the possibility of theorizing from the stories that Stephens tells in her songs that contributes to critical consciousness and societal transformation. Social change is a long-term process and conscientizing work today, through protest songs, can enable social movement activism tomorrow, particularly when focused on youth.

WOKE AND SIGHTING UP REALITY

Anyone paying attention to youth vernacular and social media platforms today cannot help but be struck by the seemingly viral interpolation of the phrase #StayWoke into mainstream parlance. This activist catch phrase, coined by African American recording artiste Erykah Badu in her song "Master Teacher", gained traction in 2014 in the wake of the Black Lives Matter protests against the killing of racialized men and women by police in the United States; it denotes a level of awareness, a knowledge of self and social injustices (Palmer 2018), and focuses attention on the current state of political apathy and dispiritedness within the ranks of the oppressed (Bohonos et al. 2019). Affirming the term's political thrust, *New York Times* columnist David Brooks explains in his column entitled "The Problem with Wokeness" that "wokeness jams together the perceiving and the proposing [and] puts more emphasis on how you perceive a situation – how woke you are to what is wrong – than what exactly you plan to do about it. 'To be woke' is to understand the full [magnitude of] injustice" (Brooks 2018).

Often deployed as a consciousness-raising tool, the term's variants "woke" and "wokeness" encourage a wholesale rejection of the violence of structural racism: high unemployment, inadequate access to education, housing and health care, inequities in the criminal justice system, and discrimination on the basis of identity markers of difference. Thus, by summoning societal "wokeness", Badu implicitly calls for a kind of critical assessment of the social world needed to usher in transformation, in much the same way that Stephens does. It is possible, therefore, to engage with "wokeness" in treating with Stephens's work, making it accessible to a younger cross-cultural generation. In the Americas, it is standard for African descendants to sample or borrow relevant ideas from each other in our struggles for freedom. Stephens herself borrows from, and engages with the Afro-American struggle for civil rights in songs like "Do You Still Care" and "Come a Long Way" (2006), showing her broader awareness of the link between social struggles across various contexts. Her musical oeuvre shows the influences of genres like American pop music, jazz, Negro spirituals and black preaching, to name but a few.

Embedded in this important call to "wokeness" is the notion that there are large segments of society that remain in a state of induced sleep, dreaming, as opposed to actively creating the conditions necessary for advancing the emancipation of humanity. This call for the oppressed to #StayWoke is thus a revolutionary springboard akin to the Rastafari deployment of the term "sight up" in the Jamaican language, Patwa. It is a call that invites an opening up of the mind to perceive the intricacies and deception of neocolonial domination in both the historical past and the contemporary moment. Such a call ought to be followed by action to put an end to social injustices. Beyond race-centred understandings of oppression and domination, however, wokeness signals an intersectional paradigm shift, one that takes stock of the multifaceted manifestations of hetero-patriarchy, sexism, ableism and homophobia as part and parcel of the project of domination. It therefore unites disparate groups under the banner of revolutionary social change. The very act of waking up, the opening up of our eyes, is one that necessitates a critical reading of the world; a sort of conscientization, as articulated by Brazilian educator Paulo Freire, which will embolden change agents to intervene prescriptively in creating a more socially just world (Freire 2009).

While Badu's invitation to wokeness may seem new to younger generations in the social media era, it is a calling that has deep historical roots in the context of Afro-indigenous cultures. Throughout our history, African musicians have been powerful agents of social and political transformation. Take for instance Marcus Garvey's call in 1937 at Menelik Hall in Sydney, Nova Scotia, to descendants of formerly enslaved Africans to "emancipate ourselves from mental slavery" knowing that "none but ourselves can free the mind". Garvey's pan-Africanist call for the decolonization of African minds was popularized by global Rastafari and reggae icon Bob Marley, who immortalized this call to arms in the lyrics of the freedom ballad "Redemption Song". Along with Marley's extensive revolutionary discography, this highly spiritual and political song positions him as one of the chief architects of black- and African-centred consciousness raising.

SONGS OF PROTEST

Africans in the Americas, particularly in the Caribbean, have traditionally used songs to communicate the conditions of their enslavement, their post-emancipation experience and living in the neocolonial, post-independence era. Abrahams (1983) documents some of the protest songs about the servitude of enslaved Africans, as well as those that speak to sexuality and relationships. In the post-emancipation period, African-created musical genres, such as calypso, mento and reggae, were used as texts to speak about everyday experiences and structural concerns informed by racism, capitalist exploitation, colonialism and patriarchy. In both the decolonization period of the late 1950s, 1960s and 1970s and the post-independence period, Africans in the Americas maintained the tradition of using songs to represent the way that they experienced the world and their demand for self-determination. Their influence is most pronounced in the body of protest songs that foreground historical and contemporary social movements such as the abolitionist movements under enslavement, the civil rights and women's rights movements, Black Power movements, and even contemporary social movements such as Black Lives Matters. These contemporary movements push back against state-sanctioned racial apartheid. Both the recent Women's March's response to Donald Trump's right-wing extremism and the #MeToo movement's political project seek to dismantle patriarchal male privilege through the systematic outing of alleged perpetrators of sexual violence. Countless examples of artistically inspired wokeness – or sighting up – abound in traditional African American spirituals and congregational songs, such as the Freedom Singers' "We Shall Not be Moved" and "We Shall Overcome", civil rights activist Billy Halliday's "Strange Fruit", Nina Simone's "Young, Gifted and Black", Curtis Mayfield's "Choice of Colors", James Brown's "Say It Loud, I'm Black and I'm Proud", as well as Sam Cooke's "Change Gonna Come". Threads of this cultural conscientization can also be found in the music of anti-apartheid advocate Miriam Makeba and punctuate the lyrics of the late Nigerian musician Fela Kuti. The list of Caribbean artistes writing songs imbued with similar themes in calypso, rock steady and reggae is also a long one, including artistes as diverse as calypsonian the Mighty Sparrow. These musicians have undoubtedly been catapulted into the pantheon of social justice activists who have championed the fight for a more socially just world. They have used their artistic expressions to significantly alter the course of history, activating movement building and effectively boosting the morale of the historically oppressed during times of struggle. Even in death, their music continues to serve important solidarity-building functions, uniting people experiencing multiple and intersecting forms of oppression (Bohonos et al. 2019).

In their capacity as cultural workers, musicians continue to inspire shifts in the social order and the consciousness of the downtrodden in society. In calling into question dominant systems of power and privilege, their art becomes a vehicle for shoring up collective action among people whose economic, political and social rights have been violated (Palmer 2018). The contemporary popularization of the phrase #StayWoke, as evidenced by its entry into Merriam Webster's online dictionary platform in 2017, affirms the potential for artistes to become key knowledge producers who influence mainstream thought and transformative praxis (Rashid 2016; Gibson 2018).

In underscoring the vital role of indigenous culture in liberation struggles, Amilcar Cabral, Guinea-Bissau's most prominent leader in the independence struggles against Portuguese colonialism, had this to say:

> When Goebbels, the brain behind Nazi propaganda, heard culture being discussed, he brought out his revolver. That shows that the Nazis – who were and are the most tragic expression of imperialism and of its thirst for domination – even if they were all degenerates like Hitler, had a clear idea of the value of culture as a factor of resistance to foreign domination. The study of the history of national liberation struggles shows that generally these struggles are preceded by an increase in expressions of culture, consolidated progressively into a successful attempt to affirm the cultural personality of the dominated people, as a means of negating the oppressor culture. Whatever may be the conditions of a people's subjection to foreign domination, and whatever may be the influence of economic, political and social factors in practicing this domination, it is generally within the culture that we find the seed of opposition, which leads to the structuring and development of the liberation movement. (Cabral 1974, 39)

Similarly, in writing on the sociopolitical importance of music in engendering recognition of criticality among the oppressed and marginalized, Peter McLaren, one of the foremost intellectuals on critical pedagogy, reminds us that "what song and 'musicing' can do ... is to provide alternative and oppositional ontologies and epistemologies that can then serve as mediating languages for reading the word and the world dialectically" (McLaren 2011, 141). McLaren's assertion foregrounds the potential for music to provoke paradigmatic shifts among the downtrodden in society.

HISTORICIZING THE CONTEMPORARY CANONICAL WOKENESS IN THE MUSIC OF TANYA STEPHENS

Reggae and dancehall, two of Jamaica's most influential forms of popular cultural art forms, have been known for their social critique and for engaging with social justice issues, albeit in different ways (Patterson-Shabazz 1999; Attas 2019). Reggae, more so than its contemporary dancehall, is distinguished by its sociopolitical thrust as well as its activist orientation. Whereas both genres have incited revolutionary shifts in our consciousness, there has also been, over the last few years, a significant waning in their awareness-raising potential

(Patterson-Shabazz 1999). Yet, reggae still contains pockets of consciousness-raising political orientation, as evidenced in the songs of Luciano, Garnett Silk, Etana, Morgan Heritage, Sizzla, Anthony B, Alpha Blondy, Queen Ifrica, the Marley Brothers and the current artistes grouped under the reggae revival label. Nevertheless, roots reggae's educative impetus can be traced back to the pioneering works of Rastafari musicians, whose scathing critiques of Babylon's oppressive power structure (a power structure borne out of colonization, the enslavement of Africans and capitalist exploitation) inspired working-class Jamaicans to rebel against the racial and class oppression they experienced in the post-independence or neocolonial era.

As a mode of African diaspora indigenous cultural expression, reggae emerged as a symbol of African liberation (Bohonos et al. 2019, 256). Indeed, it arose out of "resistance . . . to the oppression and enslavement of black Africans and the partition of Africa under white colonial rule" (Kapp 1992, 68). Even today, the music of Rastafari artistes continues on this trajectory of validating African epistemologies and ontologies. This is especially so with the ascension of reggae revival artistes like Chronixx, Kabaka Pyramid, Hempress Sativa, Jesse Royal, Mortimer, Sevana, Lila Ike, Protoje, Jah9 and Koffee (the latter's chart-topping songs like "Toast" have garnered global attention and a Grammy award). The songs of these contemporary cultural workers address themes similar to those engaged by the pioneering reggae notables of the 1960s, 1970s and 1980s; perhaps more importantly, the way they speak to these issues has met positive reception by contemporary young people. (The preceding assessment is based, in part, on the type of reggae artistes that students at the University of the West Indies favoured on the buses during annual field trips commemorating the 2 November 1930 coronation of His Imperial Majesty Haile Selassie at the Pitfour Nyahbinghi Centre in Montego Bay, Jamaica. Overwhelmingly, the students want to listen to the reggae revival artistes as opposed to reggae artistes from the 1960s to the 1990s. This is an understandable phenomenon, given that young people are typically not into the artistes beloved by their parents and grandparents.)

TANYA STEPHENS, CRITICAL CULTURAL WORKER

Stephens (born Vivienne Stephenson in St Mary, Jamaica) is one of the most critical-thinking cultural workers and organic intellectuals to emerge from within reggae and dancehall. Lauded as one of the best lyricists in the history of both genres, which are traditionally male-dominated, Stephens has maintained her relevance in the music industry for over two decades and has used it as a platform for social commentary and political education (Perkins 2013). In her own words, "Music has the power to shape society. . . . It is not the sole responsibility of musicians to raise our children or to shape our society, but music does have the power to do this and as a result, it is important that we wield it responsibly" (Walters 2011a). It is for this reason that Stephens tackles unflinchingly issues such as women's oppression and liberation, homophobia and the human rights of the LGBTQI community, social inequality, the toxicity of hegemonic masculinity, international politics, critical reggae/dancehall erotica, and women's liberated sexuality. Indeed, she is singular in her advocacy of queer rights.

As hinted at previously, the present collection aims to broaden social justice discourse in the Caribbean in a way that challenges academics, activists and advocates to think through how we can collectively bring social justice issues back into the centre of critical discursive practices through engaging the contribution of cultural workers such as Stephens. Accordingly, all the contributors engage in critical content analysis of selected Stephens lyrics from a variety of perspectives, including critical social theory, critical pedagogy, critical literacy, theories on sexuality and the erotic, and ethical and theological approaches. This collection begins by asking (and wherever possible, answering the questions): What role does Stephens's body of work play in bringing social change and social consciousness of our transformative praxis? To what extent are her ideas related to empowerment, nonconformity to dominant values, and social transgression useful for solidarity building, organizing and transforming society at large? In exploring these questions, it is critically important for us to explore the background of Stephens as well as the forces that inform who she is as a cultural worker and the type of lyrics that she has produced for the public.

Stephens has used the platforms of dancehall and reggae to articulate the oppressive condition faced by African-descended working-class women as well as other marginalized peoples in society. The feminist, revolutionary and educator bell hooks asserts that "awareness of the need to speak, to give voice to the varied dimensions of our lives, is one way women of color begin the process of education for critical consciousness" (1988, 13). It is this critical awareness of the need for women to be heard and to use prophetic words to challenge oppressive conditions that motivates Stephens to address a broad range of social issues that impact the lives of women and girls. Stephens is a black feminist organic intellectual and cultural worker who engages in accessible theorizing and prescribing on the domination and liberation of women, especially those of African descent. Indeed, throughout this book we explore the works of several African diaspora feminists to substantiate the claim that Stephens is a black feminist thinker and advocate, notwithstanding her disavowal of the term "feminist" as a political identity.

KNOWING TANYA STEPHENS: THE PERSON AND CULTURAL WORKER

Stephens is a product of the African working people whose presence on the island came from the imperative of capitalism for a dependable, expendable and affordable pool of servile labour to produce wealth for the dominant classes in Britain. She came from a relatively large family, whose lived experiences were quite familiar to the labouring classes of rural and urban Jamaica, as evidenced in an interview with the artiste herself:

> I'm the sixth of seven children. I have three brothers and three sisters so I'm from a pretty large family. I was basically the typical Jamaican growing up in the country. I didn't have anything special or different about me than anybody else. It's poverty, but you don't know it's poverty until you grow up. When you're exposed to adults when you get a little older, adults can be cruel. They'll let you know that you're poor, but prior to that I had no idea and I had no problems with it. (Gardner 2002)

Stephens is a cultural worker who uses the dancehall and reggae musical genres to educate, interrogate, provoke, incite, excite or enlighten fans about substantive social, economic, political and cultural issues relevant to the lives of different oppressed groups. Her lyrical contribution to national culture falls within the edutainment category, because it serves as a balm to the bruises to the body and soul, lifts the spirit and feeds the body with humour and wicked riddims, while providing us with ideas about social change and transgressive social possibilities. Her music provides the stimulating context for the execution of the pleasurable act, a feat that she attributes to the music of Beres Hammond, Marvin Gaye and Smokey Robinson: "Music amplifies and adds urgency to emotions as evidenced by successful use of love songs to set the mood for a romantic escapade" (Walters 2011a). Stephens cannot be credibly accused of taking up space by producing cultural products that are socially irrelevant, frivolous, intellectually empty and a grand waste of human and material resources. In the song "Who Is Tanya?" from her *Rebelution* album, this progressive and socially conscious artist leaves no doubt about her self-conscious and purposeful mission in the music business:

> Well I am not validated by di style a mi clothes
> Fuck fashion, call me personified prose
> No care who pass mi an skin up dem coke nose
> Who dem haffi rate lata, eeh?
> Who yuh suppose??
> Di fus ting Chris see an endorse at a glance
> Or di gyal weh consistenly gi unnu substance
> Recognize, mi no do dis jus fi pay bills
> An yuh no haffi like me but yuh haffi respek mi skills

In the entertainment business (and in all sectors of society, for that matter), women artistes are expected to function as fashion slaves on and off the red carpet or social media spaces. Stephens challenges that patriarchal and capitalistic expectation when she asserts, "Well, I am not validated by di style a mi clothes / Fuck fashion, call me personified prose." This political stance is a mature development, based on her sighting up of the forces behind the expectation that women should be fashionistas. Stephens admits that in the past, "mi paycheck used to done pon clothes" (cited in Batson-Savage 2016), but she has since moved beyond the gendered sartorial decrees of patriarchy and capitalism. She tells us that she has a track record of delivering musical output with social substance that will stand the test of time. Of equal importance in trying to understand the motivating forces behind her vocation as a cultural worker is the declaration that she is not producing songs simply to pay her bills. On the one hand, she is conceding that lower order needs such as food, shelter and clothing are factors in her career choice. However, she is also compelled by higher order needs, such as liberation, autonomy and self-actualization for herself and others. After all, there is a compelling reason behind Stephens's commitment to being "di gyal weh consistently gi unnu substance".

Stephens provides both fans and the wider society with socially relevant substance in her songs. She is cognizant of the fact that she has a social responsibility to her class of origin, oppressed (working-class) women and other groups who have been exploited, neglected and/or abused by this Babylonian system, as Rastafari would have it. As a prolific songwriter, she deploys her pen in crafting songs that rock the musical nation and broader society. It is for this reason that, in introducing herself to the people in "Who Is Tanya?", this cultural worker unreservedly declares that she is the "gyal weh come fi change di whole game wid a pen". Indeed, Stephens's pen is a weapon of struggle that facilitates her intellectual production in the cultural-cum-musical arena. The microphone is the instrument that communicates and amplifies the output from Stephens's pen, which she confidently frames thus: "di mic a mi favorite utensil". It puts her in her element because when she "stan up pon di mic, [she] rock di mic (Right)". Stephens is aware of the scope of her responsibility to and in society and the potential of her influence on others. She provides examples of the capacity of music to play a role in the process of social change, highlighting her awareness of the social possibility and impact of her musical production when she states, "from the chanting of Negro spirituals by slaves as a method of keeping the dream of freedom alive and conveying hope; to Public Enemy's 1989 single Fight the Power; a call to arms in which rapper Chuck B instructed the African American community to revolt, music has been an effective means of rallying the masses and creating ideological groundswell" (Walters 2011a).

The cultural workers in the reggae and dancehall genres who do not use their cultural productions in "rallying the masses and creating ideological groundswell" will earn a deserved rebuke from Stephens as from the Old Testament prophets. In Stephens's outlook, artists must carry out their social responsibility to society and be fully aware of the fact that their work may impact peoples' behaviour, whether positively or negatively. In fact, she has observed that some artistes are quite conscious of the fact that the lyrics that they are peddling in the public square are not good for the proper social development of children and an inclusive human rights agenda. As she put it in a 2011 lecture at the University of the West Indies' Mona campus:

> I have listened with concern to female (artistes) admitting publicly that they don't allow their own children to be exposed to their own music. If you do not think that you affect others, why would you limit your own children to exposure of yourself?
>
> Even some of our artistes who claim to be humanitarians and who hide behind culture labels, promote bigotry and a variety of human rights violations. The music that once spoke to and spread messages of peace and love, now merely judges, condemns and provokes. (Walters 2011b)

It is usually people from historically marginalized groups who end up suffering the most, when they embrace the socially backward behaviour being promoted by certain musicians. Therefore, it is quite commendable when artistes question the problematic ideas or actions of others within the music industry. From the biblical days to the present, prophetic voices are not people who win popularity contests. This progressive attitude makes it clear that the subject matter that Stephens takes on might be a source of discomfort to many people within society: "No topic is taboo. As a matter of fact the more 'taboo' it supposedly is, the more compelled I feel to speak about it. I'm not afraid, neither do I pigeonhole myself. . . . I do nothing for external validation. This is who I am and this is how my music is made. Freedom, equality, evolution, that's my sound. Truth, respect, empathy, that's my sound" (Steckles 2011, 22). As taboos are sanctioned by the oppressive forces and the oppressed, Stephens's utter disregard for the former may put the sacred cows of large sections of society on the hamburger grill of social transgression. The preceding might lead some people to silence, condemn or interrogate the messenger's commitment to taboos that are the source of injustice perpetrated against marginalized members of society.

Prophetic voices such as Stephens will not win popularity contests or congeniality awards, especially among those who are oppressors of women, lesbians, gay men, bisexuals, transgendered, the poor and other socially marginalized people. In essence, she echoes the sentiments of the revolutionary intellectual and feminist Angela Davis, who wrote that "art can function as a sensitizer and catalyst, propelling people toward involvement in organized movements seeking to effect radical change. Art is special because of its ability to influence feelings as well as knowledge" (Davis 1990, 200–201). As an organic intellectual, Stephens creatively and courageously works on the affective (feelings/the emotive) and cognitive (thinking) states of people in order to simultaneously remind them of oppressive relations in society and the possibility of a better world.

OUTLINE AND STRUCTURE OF CHAPTERS

Stephens, the organic intellectual, theorizes through her music and, in so doing, creates scholarly art or scholartistry (Knowles et al. 2008). To this end, the chapters in this volume engage in theory building around music, social activism, culture and gender. To facilitate an understanding of the lyrics to the songs, many of which are written in Jamaican or Patwa (the first language of the African Jamaican working-class majority), a translation into English is offered where needed.

The book is divided into four thematic sections, named for either the title of or a phrase from one of Stephens's songs. The sections demonstrate how her work clusters around certain critical areas, such as the autobiographical (through which the artiste is revealed in her art); knowledge production and dissemination (which uses the tools accessible via her folk culture and experience to contribute new answers to shaping the world); sex and sexuality (an area fraught with passion, pain and possibility); and the religious (less often subject to critique in some circles in the local space but forthrightly chastised by Stephens). Of course, the placement of individual chapters in themed sections does not indicate that their content does not intersect with the themes of other sections of the book – such is the richness of Stephens's repertoire.

Part 1 explores Stephens the artiste, and is aptly titled "Who Is Tanya". It begins with a piece by Ajamu Nangwaya, co-editor and cultural studies scholar, which positions Stephens as an organic intellectual. This chapter, which is a revision of Nangwaya's keynote presentation at the symposium, presents his argument that Stephens has used the platforms of dancehall and reggae to articulate the oppressive conditions faced by African diaspora working-class women as well as other marginalized peoples in both Jamaican and global societies. According to Nangwaya, Stephens stands in the tradition of women of colour, who, according to bell hooks, "[recognize] the awareness of the need to speak, to give voice to the varied dimensions of our lives, [. . . as] one way women of color can begin the process of education for critical consciousness" (hooks 1988, 13). As a significant part of this tradition, Stephens has boldly, transgressively and consistently addressed a broad range of social issues that impact the lives of women and girls more than any other cultural worker in the dancehall and reggae musical genres (Perkins 2013). Nangwaya further explores the works of African diaspora feminist writers to substantiate the claim that Stephens is a black feminist thinker and advocate, notwithstanding her disavowal of the term "feminist" as a political identity. In exploring and locating Stephens's work within the revolutionary and radical traditions of black feminism, the issues of the construction of race and racial identity and the extent of her ideological development around the class struggle and capitalism are examined.

Melville Cooke's chapter 2 uses lyrics from approximately two decades of Stephens's recordings to counter any misconceptions of her music as being inherently derisive of or aggressive toward men. Tanya Stephens's "tenderness" and Vivienne Stephenson's "vulnerability" show a woman who cares deeply about males and family. This tenderness – a practical level of caring about the well-being of others – is extended to social crises, as Stephens displays vulnerability to the pain of others, debunking the hard-shelled image suggested by a cursory scan of her most popular lyrics. She also presents her personal vulnerability – emotionally and physically – to hurt. This is particularly evidenced in the title track of the 2010 album *Infallible*, where she speaks more as the mother, Vivienne Stephenson, than the rough riding deejay Tanya Stephens.

Tanya Batson-Savage closes out part 1 (chapter 3), arguing that female deejays are critical to an analysis of identity and representation in dancehall. Given Stephens's long career, which has extended beyond that of many of her peers of either gender, hers is a critical voice in this venture. Stephens's album *Gangsta Blues*, released in 2005 by VP Records, presents a microcosm of her feminist agenda, wherein the feminist, the defender of female sexuality, the voiceless and the defenceless, is defined as a gangsta. *Gangsta Blues* celebrates woman as a lover, mother and rebel. Batson-Savage demonstrates that Stephens projects a feminist or womanist agenda that redefines the gangsta as a feminist. She contends further that while the gangsta can be seen as a social predator, one who makes a living through violence and often preys on the members of the working class, an understanding of the dynamics of inner-city culture quickly highlights that such a narrow definition lacks nuance, as the gangsta can be both predator and protector.

The chapters in part 2, "'Still #1 with a #2 Pencil': Producing and Disseminating Knowledge", address a range of matters covered by Stephens in her writing. The authors break ground with some new theory on several fronts in light of Stephens's liberatory praxis of the power of the pen. Central to their work is a deepening of the epistemological questions for contemporary times. In chapter 4, co-editor Anna Kasafi Perkins, theologian and ethicist, unveils and critically examines the meaning and value of emotional tears in the particular cultural context of Jamaica, and, by extension, the Caribbean. Perkins argues that no research has been done on emotional tears from within the context of the anglophone Caribbean, much less from an ethico-cultural perspective. Her chapter, begins such an exploration, using selected items from Stephens's discography to make the meaning and value of tears more transparent. In so doing, Perkins unveils the values and attitudes embedded in emotional crying for Jamaicans, and perhaps, in the same vein, Caribbean people more generally.

In chapter 5, Ajamu Nangwaya and Adwoa Ntozake Onuora draw on the work of critical literacy theoreticians to make the case for a critical reggae/dancehall epistemology as a progressive and transformative educational approach that can spawn a reassessment and challenging of capitalism, racism and patriarchy. Critical reggae/dancehall epistemology, they contend, can serve as a corrective for the social and economic inequities that exist in the Caribbean today. To this end, they delineate a connection between critical literacy and Afro-indigenous orature. More specifically, Nangwaya and Onuora explore ways in which Caribbean learners can utilize reggae/dancehall as a sign system to facilitate a rereading of the world. A critical reggae/dancehall literacy programme of education, they contend, can become the catalyst for radical social transformation and the liberation of the African-descended working class in the Caribbean.

In chapter 6, Elsa Calliard-Burton utilizes Stephens's songs "Warn Dem", "The Other Cheek" and "What a Day" to investigate the possibility of popular opinion and inner-city realities influencing government policies in relation to unemployment, poverty and violence. Stephens's lyrical critique of the inability of the government to address these issues is examined using critical social theory. Additionally, Calliard-Burton investigates the validity of engaging the recommendations posited in those songs as solutions to the social issues Stephens discusses. In so doing, she explores the extent to which music can move beyond being a means of communication to serving as a vehicle to influence change. Calliard-Burton asks: Is dancehall an effective means of communication? How can it inspire change? To whom does it speak, and is the message received as intended?

Nicole Plummer analyses a sample of Stephens's music through the lens of cultural studies in chapter 7, particularly, Stuart Hall's work on language and representation. Using Hall's analysis, Plummer examines how Stephens weaponizes language in her music to challenge gender, class and racial hegemony in Jamaica and the world in general. In many respects, Hall's groundbreaking analysis, which sheds light on the perspectives of minority groups, mirrors Stephens's ability to represent marginalized groups' experiences or perspectives in a society that often discounts their existence and ridicules their viewpoints. The author begins with a discussion of Hall's ideas on representation and the role of language. Next, she undertakes an analysis of selected lyrics, particularly focusing on how Stephens uses language as a weapon of resistance against hegemonic structures.

In part 3, "'Put It on You': Tanya Stephens's Erotic Playbook", Alpha Obika's chapter tackles Stephens's contribution to the Jamaican music industry. Based on Stephens's versatility and power as an exemplar and leader in the industry, he is able to claim that she is a beacon of female empowerment through her music. Obika works up to his conclusion through a juxtaposition of selected works of Stephens with those of Trinidadian soca artiste Fay-Ann Lyons-Alvarez. The juxtaposition demonstrates that both artistes are pillars of female representation and opinion in a music industry that continues to control and manipulate the perspectives on and of women.

Infectious disease scientist Sara Suliman, in chapter 9, maintains that Stephens is an influential reggae artiste who has been instrumental in popularizing lyrics that challenge the perceived opposition between Rastafari and sexual equity. She also confronts what Rastafari deem taboo sexual acts, such as oral sex. The chapter highlights how Stephens's music continues to be a voice of defiance in a context that distorts the erotic, and, consequently, stifles the free expression of the deepest desires of both women and men in favour of an orthodox patriarchy. Suliman engages in taboo acts herself by queering Rastafari practices and beliefs. Queering is the act of questioning how gender and sexual identity are portrayed in literature, music and popular culture and the historical constructions that inform normativity and power dynamics in that depiction. It is a literary practice that calls into question what we consider "normal", particularly when dissecting how these constructs have historically served to assert certain power dynamics that rely on women being confined to certain gender and sexual roles. Heteronormativity refers to the assumption that heterosexuality is the acceptable norm for sexual relations in society. Thus, queering Rastafari is calling its roots in patriarchy and heteronormativity into question, especially since the movement preaches equality and liberation.

In chapter 10, postgraduate student Chazelle Rhoden seeks to unpack how Stephens constructs and deconstructs the roles of "wifey" and "matey" within the Jamaican context. Rhoden interrogates the way in which Jamaican women regard and disregard marriage, family, monogamy and polygamy. She unravels the possibilities for agency, freedom and disempowerment to simultaneously exist within these "wifey" and "matey" constructions, though this possibility is seemingly paradoxical. She situates these constructions within Jamaica's plantation legacy, our African and Amerindian indigeneity, assertions of collective and individual resistance and survival, and nation-building. In so doing, Rhoden questions the role of music as both constructor and transmitter of gender roles by asking, "What does the reception of Stephens's message around these issues indicate?"

Karen Carpenter's chapter 11 sets out to challenge the intentionality expressed in Stephens's female and male stereotypes by interrogating the female to male sexual dynamic, the female to female power dynamic, and by comparing these to earlier empirical data from Jamaica on sex role stereotypes. In this chapter, sex and relationship therapist Carpenter adopts a phenomenological perspective to explore how people make meaning of their world. In particular, she explores how their worldview helps them to achieve their relational goals and the ways in which their intentionality is directed at each other in pursuit of the erotic. In the pursuit of her objective, Carpenter treats Stephens's lyrics as social commentary on relationships in Jamaica in general.

The book closes with an epilogue, Anna Kasafi Perkins's second contribution, which offers the beginnings of a Caribbean theological reading of selected pieces from Stephens's repertoire, particularly focusing on three key theological concepts: discipleship (Christians living Christianity), God (concept/doctrine of the existence, nature and purpose) and the Bible (inspired writings for Christian faith and life). In so doing, her chapter acknowledges that in the music of the Caribbean, the cutting edge of theological reflection is evident and that Stephens, therefore, functions as an unwitting thea-logian – a theologian who takes seriously the concerns of women of African descent.

The essays in *Rough Riding: Tanya Stephens and the Power of Music to Transform Society* are born out of critical reflections on Jamaica's current socioeconomic reality, a colonial history replete with violence and a future that seems even more uncertain for members of its unwashed masses. These critical reflections arise out of a deep desire for a shift in our consciousness and our collective yearning to inculcate awareness that gives rise to a transformative pedagogy by and for the working class. Toward this end, the essays foreground the life and work of a significant African Jamaican woman from the working class who has made her mark in two male-dominated musical genres. This book answers the call to this state of wokeness and sighting up – for music that seeks to advance a social justice agenda. It is our hope that it will incite, excite, provoke, illuminate, motivate and educate its readers.

REFERENCES

Abrahams, Roger D. 1983. *After Africa: Extracts from British Travel Accounts and Journals of the Seventeenth, Eighteenth, and Nineteenth Centuries Concerning the Slaves, Their Manners, and Customs in the British West Indies.* Yale University Press.

Attas, Robin. 2019. "Music Theory as Social Justice: Pedagogical Applications of Kendrick Lamar's *To Pimp a Butterfly*". *Music Theory Online* 25 (1). https://mtosmt.org/issues/mto.19.25.1/mto.19.25.1.attas.html.

Bohonos, Jeremy W., Kimberly D. Otchere and Yoon Pak. 2019. "Using Artistic Expression as a Teaching Strategy for Social Justice: Examining Music from the Civil Rights and Black Lives Matter Movements". *Advances in Developing Human Resources* 21 (2): 250–66. doi:10.1177/1523422319827942.

Brooks, David. 2018. "The Problem with Wokeness". *New York Times*, 7 June. https://www.nytimes.com/2018/06/07/opinion/wokeness-racism-progressivism-social-justice.html.

Cabral, Amilcar. 1974. *Return to the Source: Selected Speeches of Amilcar Cabral.* New York: Monthly Review Press. ("National Liberation and Culture" essay is available at https://www.blackpast.org/major_speeches/1970-amilcar-cabral-national-liberation-and-culture/.)

Cooper, Carolyn. 1986. "Chanting Down Babylon: Bob Marley's Song as Literary Text". *Jamaica Journal* 19 (4): 2–8.

———. 1989. "Slackness Hiding from Culture: Erotic Play in the Dancehall". *Jamaica Journal* 22 (4): 12–31.

Davis, Angela. 1990. *Women, Culture and Politics.* New York: Vintage Books

Freire, Paulo. 2009. *Pedagogy of the Oppressed.* New York: Continuum.

Gardner, Laura. 2002. "Reasoning with Tanya Stephens". *Jah Works*, 1 July. https://jahworks.org/admin/reasoning-with-tanya-stephens/.

Gibson, Casarae L. 2018. "Social Media: A Vital Tool in Teaching Contemporary Black American Protest". *Midwest Quarterly* 59 (4): 386–409.

hooks, bell. 1988. *Talking Back: Thinking Feminist, Thinking Black.* Toronto: Between the Lines.

Hope, Donna. 2006. *Inna di Dancehall: Popular Culture and the Politics of Identity in Jamaica.* Kingston: University of the West Indies Press.

Kapp, David. 1992. "Reggae against Racism, but What About Sexism". *Agenda: Empowering Women for Gender Equity* 8 (14): 68–70.

Knowles, J.G., S. Promislow and A.L. Cole, eds. 2008. *Creating Scholartistry: Imagining the Arts-informed Thesis or Dissertation.* Halifax, NS: Backalong Books.

McLaren, Peter. 2011. "Radical Negativity: Music Education for Social Justice". *Action, Criticism and Theory for Music Education* 10 (1): 137–47.

Palmer, Elizabeth S. 2018. "Literature Review of Social Justice in Music Education: Acknowledging Oppression and Privilege". *Update: Applications of Research in Music Education* 36 (2): 22–31.

Patterson-Shabazz, Rodney. 1999. "The Rise, Downpression and Accession of Roots-Reggae". Order No. 9966002, Temple University.

Perkins, Anna Kasafi. 2013. "Love the Long Ding Dong: Tanya Transgresses Christian Sensibilities?" In *International Reggae: Current and Future Trends in Jamaican Popular Music*, edited by Donna P. Hope, 94–123. Kingston: Pelican.

Rashid, Kamau. 2016. "Start the Revolution: Hip Hop Music and Social Justice Education". *Africology: Journal of Pan African Studies* 9 (4): 34–63.

Stanley Niaah, Sonjah. 2010. *Dancehall: From Slave Ship to Ghetto*. Ottawa: University of Ottawa Press.

Steckles, Garry. 2011. "Nothing's Taboo for Tanya Stephens". *Caribbean Beat*, no. 108 (March/April). https://www.caribbean-beat.com/issue-108/nothings-taboo-tanya#axzz5PhbG5SyY.

Walters, Basil. 2011a. "Music Has the Power to Shape Society – Tanya Stephens". *Jamaica Observer*, 3 April . http://www.jamaicaobserver.com/entertainment/Music-has-the-power-to-shape-society-Tanya-Stephens_8618191.

Walters, Basil. 2011 b. Tanya Stephens talks female responsibility. *Observer All Woman*, 11 April. http://www.jamaicaobserver.com/magazines/allwoman/Tanya-Stephens-talks-female-responsibility_8641212.

PART 1
WHO IS TANYA?

CHAPTER 1

Tanya Stephens as a Black Feminist Organic Intellectual of Dancehall and Reggae

AJAMU NANGWAYA

MANY DANCEHALL AND REGGAE FANS ARE CONSCIOUS of the fact that Tanya Stephens occupies the role of an intellectual in society – someone who engages in the discussion, critique and advocacy of ideas and practices in her songs and public pronouncements. As an educator, I have had the opportunity to both hear and read student evaluations of Stephens's contribution to ideational discourse. My women students generally laud her for expressing ideas that advance women's empowerment and self-determination, especially in the context of female/male relations and female erotic/sexual autonomy. In the wider society outside the classroom, I have heard reggae and dancehall fans extol her ability to raise ideas about various oppressed groups and bring a frank and unapologetic tone to speaking truth to both the powerful and the powerless. The academy is not the exclusive home of intellectuals: indeed, many of them do not need the stamp of approval from the bourgeois university to be so designated.

Linking Stephens with the category "intellectual" might inspire some people to ask the question, "Who exactly is an intellectual?" The Tanzanian intellectual Issa Shivji (2018) provides us with two generic and universally applicable functions of the intellectual:

> Intellectuals are producers and purveyors of ideas. They produce all kinds of ideas, many ideas: ideas to rationalize and legitimize, ideas to explain and deceive; ideas to mystify and mesmerize; ideas to decorate and demonize; ideas to inform and entertain – all kinds of ideas. They may produce ideas gratuitously or for a price – these days, more often than not, for a price. Thus ideas become a commodity, an artificial commodity.

At the same time, the above proposition does not robustly speak to the fact that intellectuals are not neutral actors in the white supremacist, patriarchal and capitalist social order. An intellectual serves either the cause of the oppressed or that of the oppressor, and it is for that reason that I am inclined to use Antonio Gramsci's category "organic intellectual" and apply it to Stephens's role in society.

TANYA STEPHENS AS ORGANIC INTELLECTUAL OF THE OPPRESSED

The Italian Marxist theorist and political leader Antonio Gramsci asserts that "All men are intellectuals, one could therefore say: but not all men have in society the function of intellectuals" (Gramsci 1971). Here, Gramsci declares that while we all produce and disseminate knowledge, we do not all necessarily effect or fulfil that role as our major, daily preoccupation. However, Stephens clearly creates and circulates ideas as part of her regular vocation, which is directed at a mass public with the aim of influencing people's thoughts and actions. Consequently, I believe most, if not all, of us can see Stephens in Edward Said's (1996, 69) characterization of the intellectual:

> The fact is that the intellectual ought neither to be so uncontroversial and safe a figure as to be just a friendly technician nor should the intellectual try to be a full-time Cassandra, who was not only righteously unpleasant, but also unheard. Every human being is held in by a society, no matter how free and open the society, no matter how bohemian the individual. In any case, the intellectual is supposed to be heard from, and in practice ought to be stirring up debate and if possible controversy. But the alternative is not total quiescence or total rebelliousness.

I choose to read Said's admonishment against "total rebelliousness" as advice to the intellectual to neither become a rebel without a cause nor stand opposed to everything in society just for the sake of playing devil's advocate. An intellectual from the ranks of the labouring classes or other oppressed groups must be rebellious in the stance against the forces of Babylon, or social domination. Being an "uncontroversial and safe figure" (Walters 2011) is definitely not the path that Stephens has taken as a cultural worker, one who pays significant attention to the relationship between women and men and eroticism. Indeed, an artist who critically and interrogatively speaks to the social inequities that undergird sexual relations within the heterosexual relationship and the oppressive and overbearing presence of patriarchy in regulating that area of social life will court the male backlash of the religious and social forces invested in perpetuating the status quo.

The dominant society is very much aware of the power of ideas in maintaining its influence and interest. Therefore, it is quite cognizant of the disruptive role and effect of individuals or groups that offer countervailing, anti-systemic ideas aimed at the oppressed masses. It is in this context that the intellectual is a potential threat to the ruling class in all societies. Even more specifically, it is the organic intellectual who has committed herself to the cause of the socially dominated who is the certified gravedigger of the racist, patriarchal and capitalist social order. Conversely, she is also the midwife at the birth of the good and just society. Per Gramsci, the organic intellectual provides her or his organizing knowledge, skills and attitudes to either the forces of oppression or the members of the exploited in society. The organic intellectual is central to organizing the masses because she is actively located at the centre of the creation and/or circulation of ideas. Gramsci has a very expansive take on the people who fall within the category of the organic intellectual, which might be surprising to many people whose notion of the intellectual is someone who is associated with an institution of higher learning or a bookish or highly cerebral person who lives in the world of ideas. In his view, organic intellectuals who serve the ruling class include "the industrial technician, the specialist in political economy, the organisers of a new culture, of a new legal system" who are tasked with the responsibility of creating the conditions for the success of business as well as "organising the general system of relationships external to the business itself" (Gramsci 1971). In this current period, organic intellectuals would also cover functionaries such as "broadcasters, academic professionals, computer analysts, sports and media lawyers, management consultants, policy experts, government advisers, authors of specialized market reports, and indeed the whole field of modern mass journalism" (Said 1996, 8–9).

As each class or social group has its own organic intellectuals to articulate and advance its fundamental interests, the labouring classes also have their own, such as Stephens, who function as "organisers of a new culture" by presenting and promoting ideas to the socially marginalized to encourage them to develop a consciousness of their own interests and to work at making themselves the hegemonic force in society. Stephens is a product of the labouring classes in Richmond, St Mary, and this objective reality makes her an organic intellectual formed by her class of origin. She is a member of the petite bourgeoisie who has committed what Amilcar Cabral has labelled "class suicide" and become one with "the deepest aspirations of the people" (Cabral 1969, 110). She has sided with the suffering masses, in their diversity, despite the opportunity to cast her lot with the bourgeois class to which she belongs by virtue of her material accomplishment. This cultural worker, Stephens, fulfils the role of Gramsci's organic intellectual as "permanent persuader" and not just a simple orator. She largely (re)presents a "humanistic conception of history" (Gramsci 1971), which makes the case for the capacity of people to creatively take measures to challenge oppressive conditions and work for their liberation. In the song "Welcome to the Rebelution" (from her critically acclaimed album *Rebelution*), Stephens constructs the progressive cultural worker or artist as an organic intellectual-cum-persuader who attempts to inspire the masses toward unity and revolution:

> Stay grounded and not get caught up with this illusion
> Cuz that the problem and right now I'm only into solutions
> So I say to you now, the Rebelution is urgent
> Stand before you not as queen, but as your humble servant
> Fake leaders claim thrones without building kingdoms
> Same as the music business in Kingston
> We need to fight for the future, for our daughters and so
> Instead you're trippin your brothers, fightin for crumbs
> But we will not be deterred by knives or guns
> Go tell it on the mountain, the rebelution has come
> Well You can fight it or hide it
> Or seize the moment and ride it
> Instead of fallin divided
> Why don't we stand up united
> Differences put aside it would be easier had if we tried it
> But even if we dont
> Change must come
> Change must come

The dominant ideological illusions of the capitalist, patriarchal and white supremacist ruling class must be challenged by radical or revolutionary artists in their capacity as organic intellectuals. When Stephens calls on the labouring classes and other oppressed groups to stop "fightin for crumbs", she is demanding that the socially dominated struggle for control and ownership of the "bakery" in order to ensure an emancipated future for their children. The emancipatory themes present in Stephens's body of work come from her lived experience as a member of the working class and a woman as well as her observation of people located in socially dominated categories, such as LGBTQ individuals.

In "Welcome to the Rebelution", Stephens locates the organic intellectual as an organizer of the people and takes a humanistic and oppositional stance toward a top-down relationship with them. She sings, "So I say to you now, the Rebelution is urgent / Stand before you not as queen, but as your humble servant / Fake leaders claim thrones without building kingdoms." The cultural worker-cum-organic intellectual claims leadership by virtue of her practical work among the oppressed through the development of alternative institutions, programmes and projects. It is not done through the outdated and socially backward idea of the divine rights of queens or kings. The organic intellectual is "your humble servant" and not one of the "fake leaders" who populate many social movements. Stephens's recognition of the need for practical action and not simply functioning as an orator at the microphone or on stage is a critically important one. It is necessary for progressive, radical or revolutionary cultural workers to become members of social movement organizations with practical connections to the masses. It is through this type of organic ties to the people that Stephens's pronouncement that the people "will not be deterred by knives or guns" becomes possible as a real force and not empty sloganeering or overheated rhetoric.

Since walking the talk is the way of the socially engaged organic intellectual of the oppressed, and the best articulation of ideas of liberation is its representation in concrete actions, it is a positive development to see Stephens's association with the Tambourine Army. This protest formation was recently created in Jamaica to challenge and destroy the culture of sexual violence against women and girls. Stephens has placed her moral authority and status as a public figure behind the goals of the Tambourine Army by publicly sharing her experience of being sexually assaulted (Grizzle 2016). She wrote about her experience of being raped and circulated it on social media, after which it was picked up by traditional broadcast media and online publications. In her attempt to inspire a new culture, Stephens might find it prudent to become a member of social movements or social movement organizations. It is through these structures, with their material and human resources, that people are mobilized or organized for social change. In the absence of involvement in movements that are doing the thankless, risky but necessary organizing around challenging the structures of oppression, the cultural worker-cum-organic intellectual is likely to become frustrated by the unchanging and oppressive nature of society.

It is only through organizing with others in existing structures that an organic intellectual such as Stephens will prepare the people to engage in revolutionary struggles and dedicate themselves to achieve the good, just and self-managed society. In the song "Welcome to the Rebelution", Stephens poses the following question to the assembled masses: "Are you ready for a Rebelution?" If the organic intellectual were already organizing with the people in their class-based, feminist, racial justice and/or queer liberation organizations and social movements, the question would be a redundant one. "Rebelution" is a very purposive category, exhorting the people toward rebellious, revolutionary engagement. The question "Are you ready for a Rebelution?" is not a rhetorical one and it indicates that Stephens is not sure that the people are ideologically, politically and organizationally ready for revolution. It would indeed be redundant to ask the question, if the people were already carrying out the tasks of the revolution through alternative, self-managed institutions, programmes and projects as well as making the state ungovernable. It is the lack of or limited presence of popular revolutionary organizations that led Stephens to produce these lines in the song "Turn the Other Cheek" on the album *Gangsta Blues*:

> The people dem seh dem a talk
> And nobody nah listen all along
> So dem want me to put it
> In the form of a song

People do not join mass organizations and other types of formations with the intent of appealing to the ruling class to listen to them. Instead, they organize and impose their demands on the exploiters based on the strength of their organizing. When the people operate as a collection of individuals, they are dependent on cultural workers and others to articulate their needs to the people in power. Progressive artists will need to avoid the seductive and glamorous appeal of the mobilizing approach of protests because it is episodic and elite-led; indeed, the rank-and-file members function as mere props at demonstrations, marches, rallies or occupations (Nangwaya 2014). When Gramsci (1971) characterizes the organic intellectual as a political actor whose reason for existence "can no longer consist in eloquence, which is an exterior and momentary mover of feelings and passions, but in active participation in practical life, as constructor, organiser, 'permanent persuader' and not just a simple orator", he is privileging the organizing approach to revolution and emancipation. Such an approach calls for building the capacity of the people to do the work of liberation and establishing initiatives and structures through which they may attempt to address their concrete needs as well as prosecute the struggle (Nangwaya 2014). While the majority of people in the dancehall or the wider society do not see Stephens as an intellectual, they would definitely view her as a cultural worker who is an advocate for the liberation of women from the structures of patriarchal society. Or they might simply define her as a person who is in favour of the equality of women. It is, then, social conditioning and prejudiced notions of who is or is not an intellectual that may be preventing the masses from understanding that an artiste such as Stephens falls into this category.

TANYA STEPHENS'S STANCE TOWARD THE FEMINIST LABEL

As we reflect on Stephens's stance toward the term feminist as a marker of political identity, the common saying "if it walks like a duck and clucks like a duck, then it must be a duck" comes to mind. Despite the perception of Stephens as a feminist or advocate of feminism (one writer describes her as a cultural worker who "has brought sex-positive feminism to the world of dancehall slackness [eroticism]" [Taylor 2012]), she firmly denies that political identity or label: "Many people called me feminist. I am not. I stand up for myself, I happened to be female" (Walters 2011). In doing so, this socially progressive artiste is being consistent in avoiding political markers of identity that could constrict her ability to access social opportunities. She has similarly rejected the female artiste label. Stephens is correct in asserting that the qualifier "female" before the word "artiste" is informed by lower expectations and a gendered conformity to what is expected of women who happen to be cultural workers in the dancehall and reggae genres (Batson-Savage 2016). In qualifying the term "artiste" by placing "female" before it, one implicitly declares that such women are misbegotten versions of the category "artiste", which is intrinsically associated with being a human male or a man. In this interpretation, it would be preposterous or repetitive to utter "male artiste", because an artist is a man.

Neither "feminist" nor "feminism" are terms of endearment in patriarchal and/or homophobic societies; indeed, they are wrongly linked to the hatred of men by the agents of patriarchy, both women and men, and even by some politically sophisticated activists. It is possible for a woman to advocate for the essential demands of feminism but reject the political marker of identity by declaring that "I am NOT a feminist. I don't hate men." For example, Ranking Ann, a reggae/dancehall artiste based in Britain and noted for songs that advocate for women's autonomy, made it clear in the song "Feminine Gender" (cited in Sabelli 2011, 145) that she is not a feminist:

> Let me tell you something, weh happened to me
> Seh one Friday night, me inna party
> Seh here come a dread
> Him a walk up to me
> "Hear Ranking Ann, tell me dis: is it true what them say, that you are feminist?"
> Me seh no Rasta
> Me are individualist
> Seh open your eyes and you must realize
> You can't come and try fe categorize
> When you call me "feminist", me know where you mean
> The thing that you want do is a different kind of sin
> Seh god create woman
> And god create man
> And inna this time they have their function
> So I don't put them down
> So don't get me wrong
> It's just feminine, a feminine, seh feminine gender-genda
> Mi seh we no go surrender-renda

In the lines "When you call me 'feminist', me know where [what?] you mean / The thing that you want do is a different kind of sin", Ranking Ann seems to imply that the Rasta man is insinuating that she is a lesbian or woman who has sex with women. Ranking quickly follows this up with the lines "Seh god create woman / And god create man / And inna this time they have their function" to assure the Rasta man and her fans that she is a devotee of compulsory heterosexuality and the seemingly natural social roles of women and men. Yet, the conservative message in "Feminine Gender" is in tension with these lines from another song by Ranking Ann, "Liberated Woman" (1982):

> Mi a liberated woman
> Mi a liberated woman
> Mi seh dem really want fi change up mi life
> Mi seh, some of dem people want fi control me life
> Some of dem people really want fi control mi life
> Come Ranking Ann, yuh haffi change yuh life
> Come Ranking Ann, yuh haffi be a housewife
> But mi a liberated woman
> Yuh can't control mi life

The song "Liberated Women" ought to be seen as a feminist anthem within the genres of dancehall and reggae because of its critique of patriarchal domination and women's assertion of autonomy and self-determination. Elsewhere, Ranking Ann reflects on the way in which she expressed herself in the early stage of her career and how her gender politics came to be negatively labelled:

> Within all of that, it was a way of educating people about important issues happening around them of which they may have had no knowledge. Today those same principles apply. The difference today is maybe I'm a little more lyrically diplomatic. Well in your teens and 20s, no PC constraints, whatever came into your head, you said it without necessarily thinking it would be misconstrued and taken out of context or labeled with some kind of "ist" or "ism". So admittedly when I write now, I tend to edit language that may come across as being particularly harsh or "subversive". But then and now it's always been about expression – not just "style n fashion". (NiceUp 2019)

The "ist" and "ism" to which Ranking Ann refers to here are more than likely the dreaded politically loaded terms "feminist" and "feminism". The fear of the distraction of being labelled a manhater and/or lesbian is the likely source of both Ranking Ann's and Stephens's avoidance of the political identifier "feminist" (Female Science Professor 2013; Scharff 2019).

The capitalist patriarchy has seen to it, through its control over the means of communication and the instruments of public and formal education, that the terms feminism and feminist are seen as stigmatizing badges that sensible women and men would avoid like the plague. As a result, many women will avoid openly embracing an ideology that could otherwise be used as a weapon by them against patriarchy, white supremacy, homophobia and capitalism. It is my belief that Stephens, much like other women (and men) in Jamaica/the Caribbean, is responding to the negative label associated with these terms. As a politico who is an advocate of anarchist communism, I know the pressure to not openly and unreservedly identify with a political identity marker that might lead people to shut down, tune me out or become outright antagonistic toward anarchism. In this case, most people are largely ignorant of the political ideology behind women's emancipation. Therefore, the feminist organizer is presented with teachable moments when she overtly claims a feminist ideological commitment or identity.

Stephens's reluctance in embracing the term "feminist" is not just a Jamaican state of affairs but a universal outcome of the negative response of patriarchy to the possibilities represented by the emancipatory claims of the radical or revolutionary ideological streams of feminism (Brancaccio et al. 2018; Scharff 2019). It would be a pity if women and men of good conscience continue to avoid this ideological outlook that can serve as the basis for liberating society from the structural oppression of sexism and patriarchy. The African American revolutionary feminist, humanist and educator bell hooks offers a way to deal with the apprehension that Stephens and many others have expressed about being connected with feminism and the feminist movement:

> To emphasize that engagement with feminist struggle as political commitment we could avoid using the phrase "I am a feminist" (a linguistic structure designed to refer to some personal aspect of identity and self-definition) and could state "I advocate feminism." Because there has been undue emphasis placed on feminism as an identity or lifestyle, people usually resort to stereotyped perspectives on feminism. Deflecting attention away from stereotypes is necessary if we are to revise our strategy and direction. I have found that saying "I am a feminist" usually means I am plugged into preconceived notions of identity, role, or behavior. When I say "I advocate feminism" the response is usually "what is feminism?" A phrase like "I advocate" does not imply the kind of absolutism that is suggested by "I am." It does not engage us in the either/or dualistic thinking that is the central ideological component of all systems of domination in Western society. It implies that a choice has been made, that commitment to feminism is an act of will. It does not suggest that by committing oneself to feminism, the possibility of supporting other political movements is negated. (hooks 1984, 29)

If we find ways to get around framing the commitment to feminism as a personal identity, those of us who are racialized and based in the Caribbean might be accused of embracing a white, Western ideology that is not culturally relevant and applicable to the concrete realities of the region. However, we can point to a revolutionary from the Caribbean, Claudia Jones, who pioneered the concept of intersectionality (before it had a name) through her integrated analysis of race, class and gender in explaining the condition of African working-class women in the United States (Nangwaya 2016a). African diaspora women (and some men) are not "Abenas-come-lately" to the world of theorizing on feminism or the liberation of women. Women such as Amy Ashwood Garvey, Amy Jacques Garvey, Anna Julia Cooper, Una Marson (Nangwaya 2014; Tomlinson 2014) and others have made contributions to the question of women's emancipation and pan-Africanism (Nangwaya 2016b). For her part, as a cultural worker, Stephens is not afraid to identify with the global struggle to free women from patriarchal social domination. On her album *Gangsta Blues*, she recorded a remake of Helen Reddy's feminist anthem "I Am Woman". She has even done covers of iconic songs of self-determination, such as "Respect" by Aretha Franklin and "I Will Survive" by Gloria Gaynor; clearly, Stephens is not apprehensive about making internationalist solidarity with ideas and struggles outside of Jamaica. It is the stigma or character assassination that comes from identifying with the categories "feminist" and "feminism" that likely explains her stance toward these terms. But Stephens's internationalist sensibilities anchor her in both the black radical tradition (Hudson 2014) and the Caribbean radical tradition (Reddock 2014), so her gender ideology cannot avoid being located in the African diaspora's ideational and political struggles in the Americas as well as ideologies of emancipation present on our terrain of struggle.

BLACK FEMINISM AND EXPERIENCE AS A WAY OF KNOWING AND THEORIZING

Black feminism is a body of thought and action committed to raising the consciousness of African women about the interlocking nature of the systems of oppression in their lives and offering practical interventions to advance their emancipation. In *Black Feminist Thought: Knowledge, Consciousness and the Politics of Empowerment*, Patricia Collins states that black feminism is a "process of self-conscious struggle that empowers women and men to actualize a humanist vision of society" (1991, 39). African American anthropologist Irma McClaurin offers a more expansive definition of black feminism: "An embodied, positioned, ideological standpoint perspective that holds Black women's experience of simultaneous and multiple oppressions as the epistemological and theoretical basis of a 'pragmatic activism' directed at combatting those social and personal, individual and structural, and local and global forces that pose harm to black (in the widest geopolitical sense) women's well-being" (cited in Hall 2016, 90).

Both Collins's and McClaurin's definitions of black feminism are sensitive to the global character of the fight of African women to eliminate patriarchal and other forms of oppression. Too often black feminism is seen as a United States-based phenomenon despite the tendency of the various movements for African emancipation to generously sample processes, ideas, strategies, tactics and rhetoric from the African American freedom struggle. The struggle of Africans in the United States is often the target of the highest degree of comradely borrowing or sampling – a notable practice found in hip hop and dancehall. I believe this is the case because they (African Americans) live in the centre of world imperialism. Their thoughts and actions are amplified and made more accessible to outsiders as a result of both proximity to the means of communication in the centre of the world's major imperialist power and the level of development of their struggle for racial justice.

Black feminism is rooted in the struggle for freedom of African women in the Americas from white supremacy, patriarchy, capitalism and other forms of structural oppression. Within the context of fighting global white supremacy, pan-Africanist feminists "practised the art of navigating a variety of complex positions around race, gender, class, national origin and culture within the larger goal of the liberation of African peoples internationally. These political positions place them easily within current understandings of transnational black feminism" (Boyce Davies 2014, 78). Transnational black feminism is inextricably linked to the internationalist nature of the struggle for African liberation and its struggle against capitalism and imperialism, while centring the fight for women's liberation (Boyce Davies 2014). Transnational black feminism asserts that "black feminism as a movement could never be framed solely as a national movement when the very structures [for example, white supremacy, patriarchy and capitalism] that black women were resisting were not confined to the nation-state" (Blain 2017). Kia Hall (2016) offers four fundamental principles of transnational black feminism that resonate and exemplify the way in which Stephens lives her gender politics through her artistic productions in the reggae and dancehall genres as well as in the rest of her life: intersectionality (which examines lives of peoples at the intersection of multiple groupings such as sexuality, gender, race and (dis)ability); scholar-activism (which draws on feminist and humanistic emancipatory concepts and supports global human rights issues); demonstration of solidarity with those experiencing oppression; and the willingness to put forward issues and engage in advocacy that transcends social and physical borders and boundaries erected by the status quo. As an organic intellectual, Stephens's emancipatory consciousness-raising work is largely articulated through the lyrics in her songs and the public commentaries that she makes by way of social media and interviews.

In the song "Do You Still Care" (2006), Stephens brings the intersectionality analytical framework to bear on how race, sexual orientation, gender and class ideologies inform our identity formation and experience of the world. In the second verse of the song, she demonstrates how multiple categories are at work in understanding privilege and oppression:

> Where Bigga grew up boys were supposed to be tough
> Girls were trophies every man always kept a few of
> When he was hurt and the tears would sting in his eyes, his mother said "stop the noise yuh a girl' real boys don't cry"
> He learn in order to be a man he had to know how to fight
> And had some very definitive rules about what's wrong or right
> He never had the luxury of being able to choose
> So to him for being different there was no excuse
> Bigga was hustling on the corner, making some cash
> When he bumped into some beef that he had from the past
> He watched the guns raised and the bullets fly
> In disbelief as his friends all jumped in their rides
> Left him in the gutter didn't care if he died
> He was rescued by a car with a plates that said gay pride
> It would have been fatal that shot in your head,
> They saved your life tho you always said chi chi fi dead.

Bigga is a working-class, African diaspora man raised in a homophobic, queer-hating context in which women are possessions and the model of the negation of rationality (prejudiced against undue emotional display). Thrown into the underground drug economy to survive (a reflection of his subordinated race and class status), he nonetheless operates at privileged locations within the dominant discourse of patriarchy and heteronormativity. He is a straight or heterosexual man, which allows him to share these points of privilege despite the unevenness of his enjoyment of them given his class and racial alienation in society. The scene painted by Stephens about Bigga could have happened on the streets of Kingston, Jamaica; Jane and Finch in Toronto; or Flatbush in New York. One of the points in this song is the importance of an intersectional and diasporic framework in understanding and explaining our multiple social locations and their relevance in theorizing on oppression and privilege.

In another song, "Come a Long Way" (on the *Rebelution* album), Stephens puts on display her internationalist, solidarity-building and border-crossing sensibilities on the question of African freedom:

> So we've come a long way from picking cotton, many never thought they'd live to see the day when Bush pick Rice
> But if all you've become is another house nigga baby tell me was it worth all the sacrifice
> Get outta my way while I climb to the top now but be sure to catch me if i fall from grace
> Cause heaven forbid
> If what I chase should reject me
> You know I'm gonna need a warm black embrace
> We used to stack guns, prepare for revolution
> Was the only way of getting wrong put right
> Now we think all our problems
> Can be solved with shooting
> And we've forgot why we started to fight

Here, Stephens is referencing the struggle of African Americans in the United States, in a clear demonstration of her pan-Africanist political commitments. Most fans might not identify her as a pan-Africanist in the way that they would other organic intellectuals, such as Linton Kwesi Johnson, Rita Marley and Mutabaruka. When she dismisses former US president George Bush's appointment of the African American conservative woman Condoleezza Rice as national security advisor in 2005, Stephens is clearly critiquing liberal or bourgeois feminism. Rice is an African woman, but she is a privileged woman whose aspiration and interest are at variance with those of poor or working-class women. The artiste is correct in depicting Rice as a "house nigga" or race traitor. However, Rice was being loyal to her role as an organic intellectual of the political and economic elite and promoting her class interests as a member of the petite bourgeoisie. Stephens's referencing of icons of pan-Africanism in the lines below expresses her fidelity to the approach of transnational black feminism or black feminism:

> Tell me now Malcom, do we hurt you pride?
> Can you hear me now Rosa,
> Was it worth the ride?
> Can you see me now Marcus
> We're still not unified, no we're not
> So tell me now Martin, is this why you died?

Rosa Parks, Malcolm X, Martin Luther King and Marcus Garvey are icons of African liberation and the impact of their work went beyond national boundaries. In the same spirit, transnational black feminism is committed to transcending borders in building networks of resistance and the sharing of ideas and material resources from the diasporic struggle for liberation. This political commitment by Stephens is inclusive of women, children and men, even while she accentuates the oppressive condition of women. The best tradition of black feminism tends to take a broad approach to human rights. For example, the Combahee River Collective's political stance on this question was quite clear and progressive:

> Although we are feminists and Lesbians, we feel solidarity with progressive Black men and do not advocate the fractionalization that white women who are separatists demand. Our situation as Black people necessitates that we have solidarity around the fact of race, which white women of course do not need to have with white men, unless it is their negative solidarity as racial oppressors. We struggle together with Black men against racism, while we also struggle with Black men about sexism. (Combahee River Collective 1982, 16)

Black feminism is committed to ending sexist oppression, which unevenly provides benefits to working-class men as opposed to ruling-class men, while exploiting the former in their capacity as workers and/or racialized men. Men can also be feminists, as seen from Collins's universal and inclusive definition of black feminism. It simply centres the concerns of women but not to the exclusion of others with whom coalitions and alliances would be formed to work on areas of mutual or common interests. Working-class men are not the enemies of working-class women, despite the former's participation in oppressive practices against women from their own social class. When middle-class or bourgeois feminists take such a politically misguided line, they tend to find that working-class women are hostile toward them as class-privileged women who normally do not work in the interest of women from the labouring classes (see hooks 1984, 67–81).

Stephens draws on her experience as an African woman from the labouring classes and that of similarly situated women to articulate themes of women's suffering, self-determination, autonomy, liberation, sexual autonomy and agency, and economic marginalization and resistance. In this, she follows the tradition of generations of African women for whom experience has been a source of knowledge, understanding and call to arms. Experience has taught them that their oppression is not solely racial or exclusively gendered. From the period of chattel slavery, they knew that their gender or status as women opened them up to sexualized violence that was largely not a part of the lives of their enslaved African male counterparts. Within black feminist thought, the intersection of race-, gender- and class-based forms of oppression might orient African women toward a "distinctive group consciousness, but it in no way guarantees that such a consciousness will develop among all women or that it will be articulated as such by the group" (hooks 1984, 25). If one is not exposed to concepts that describe and analyse the issues that impact one's life, it is difficult to develop the critical awareness of why and what can be done about them. In the Combahee River Collective's statement on black feminism, these African American feminists explain the problematic of experience, consciousness and group behaviour:

> Black feminists often talk about their feelings of craziness before becoming conscious of the concepts of sexual politics, patriarchal rule, and most importantly, feminism, the political analysis and practice that we women used to struggle against our oppression. The fact that racial politics and indeed racism are pervasive factors in our lives did not allow us, and still does not allow most Black women, to look more deeply into our own experiences and, from that sharing and growing consciousness, to build a politics that will change our lives and inevitably end our oppression. (Combahee River Collective 1982, 15)

Through their work in the cultural and political spheres, feminists and organic intellectuals such as Stephens may contribute significantly to raising mass consciousness about the fact that gender norms are not natural. Stephens's work as an organic intellectual involves the communication of ideas or concepts around sexist oppression and women's liberation. She provides the language and space to assist women "to look more deeply into [their] own experiences" on the lack of personal fulfilment in their gendered roles in society, sexual dissatisfaction in the erotic area of their lives, or being confronted with sexual or physical violence from the men in their lives. For example, in the song "Weather Change",

Stephens draws on experiential knowledge, whether personally gained or from observation of what other women go through, to interrogate and condemn physical violence by men in domestic relationships. She informs women that the ample supply of men in society should create a zero tolerance approach toward beatings and bruising from these patriarchal tyrants.

> A tell you there's so many men
> It impossible to done dem all
> So tell me how one a dem
> Coulda mek mi spend mi whole life a bawl
> If mi nuh bawl say di weather change
> Tell me why mi woulda bawl say di bredda change
> Every few days the sheet and the spread a change
> Occasionally all the fellow inna di bed a change
>
> Mek mi tell you dis
> You can call him any old thing
> Except victim as a man turn a mistake
> So mek a break tim
> Even the batton weh beat mi so sweet
> Mi still a bruise it
> So if a hand rise against me him a go loose it
> You know me . . . eeh?
> Mi nuh have no problem with the cheating
> But can you picture me a tek beating
> No star, yuh mad, a nuh dat a my style
> No blurt nort tears nuh deh back a my style
> Cause mi real out a road
> Make-up nuh conceal how mi feel out a road
> Nah breach no road code
> How you fi say you love har and you fisting the girl
> There should've been one less fist in the world

In the above-mentioned song, this radical cultural worker gives the impression that a battered woman can simply leave a violent relationship because "there are plenty of fish in the sea". In the song "After You", the divorced wife celebrates the fact that she has acquired a significant proportion of the assets generated during the marriage. But she points to a reason that could keep some women in relationships that are dangerous to their physical and mental well-being:

> After you
> Yuh see wah you a cause, you know seh me nuh stay so
> But wah you expect me fi do
> All a this a fi yuh fault
> Cah yuh nuh leff me no choice
> A woman my age wid four kids
> Which man a go pick me up?!
> I don't have a certificate I don't even have a marketable skill
> And when me tell you say me wah work pon a career
> Yuh say not a rahtid
> Yuh wife nah fi work
> And boops yuh breed me again
> Thirty-six months me spend a carry yuh pickney dem inna my gut
> Dat a thirty-six month outta my life way me couldn't look dung and see me toe

The woman character in "After You" is theorizing from experience about being saddled with multiple children and the lack of "a marketable skill" as reasons that may make her less appealing to prospective partners. These factors would conspire to keep women in relationships that have passed their "best-before" date. The character in the song is fortunate that the divorce law in her jurisdiction allows her to keep 50 per cent of the assets accumulated in the marriage so her life will not be governed by the notion that a heterosexual woman is just a divorce away from poverty. In "Weather Change", Stephens excoriates batterers who use children to manipulate women into staying in physically violent relationships:

> Hold me hostage by mi womb
> Dem ting deh mi nuh inna
> Some a dem a use yuh yute fi control yuh mind
> But mi nuh join no pickney production line
> As that nuh seems like the world in need a dem
> Mi cut mi eye pass the serial breeder dem
>
> (Hold me hostage by my womb
> Those things I am not into
> Some of them using your children to control your mind
> But I do not join the baby production line
> As that do not seem like the world is in need of them
> I look at the serial breeders with disapproval)

Stephens appears to be unsympathetic toward "the serial breeder dem" who might not actually have control over their reproductive lives in terms of having the autonomy to use contraceptives or demand that the men use condoms or undergo a vasectomy. The "serial breeders" might not live in jurisdictions in which abortion is legal, and in such situations financial barriers are likely to prevent working-class women from accessing safe abortions from medical practitioners willing to break the law (Cooper 2019). The victim of violence must also deal within the cultural environment that works against many women fleeing violent domestic situations. According to bell hooks (1988, 89),

> Within patriarchal society, women who are victimized by male violence have had to pay a price for breaking the silence and naming the problem. They have had to be seen as fallen women, who have failed in their "feminine" role to sensitize and civilize the beast in the man. A category "battered woman" risks reinforcing this notion that the hurt woman, not only the rape victim, becomes a social pariah, set apart, marked forever by this experience.

Personal, cultural and structural forces are at work constraining acts of self-determination of many women victimized by violence. Nonetheless, Stephens draws on personal and group experiences of women (and other socially dominated groups) to facilitate a collective consciousness of oppression and liberation possibilities. In doing so, she hearkens back to black feminist thought, especially transnational black feminism, which centres, affirms and frames the experience of African women's oppression in African liberation, feminist, anti-imperialist and anti-capitalist frameworks. An example of such an approach is Stephens's African Jamaican forebear Cathryn McKenzie, who railed against patriarchal exclusion by declaring that "just why woman has been denied all the rights which are accorded to man is one of the unexplained relations of life, except that it is man alone who has made the laws denying such rights" (Ford-Smith 1991, 73).

ACTIVIST ORIENTATION OF BLACK FEMINISM

Activism is a critical element of both black feminism and transnational feminism, and Stephens's behaviour through her work as an artiste is the epitome of merging thought and action as a positive contribution to the struggle for liberation. Additionally, Stephens's role as an organic intellectual intersects with the social engagement orientation of black feminism. Within black feminist thought there is an organic connection between idea and action. According to Collins, "This interdependence of thought and action suggests that changes in thinking may be accompanied by changed actions and that altered experiences may in turn stimulate a changed consciousness" (1991, 28). As an organic intellectual and cultural worker, Stephens carries out the work of public education when she is on the concert stage, creates songs, engages in dialogue on social media or shares her thoughts as a public speaker. Teaching about oppressive conditions and articulating the terrain of freedom and justice in her songs and other forms of public engagement are ways of acting in the world and fall within the rubric of activism. Her message of women's emancipation resonates with constituencies who have the lived experience of the characters in her songs as well as with people who stand in solidarity with those oppressed.

Based on the general and positive response of the women students in my courses to Stephens's songs and her public pronouncements, it would not be implausible to declare that she is engaged in a critical pedagogy that appeals to the lived reality of oppression by working-class and petite bourgeois African women in Jamaica and elsewhere. Angela Davis (1990) attests to the ability of the arts to affect feelings and knowledge and this is certainly an outcome of the work of this organic intellectual. In the essay "Revolutionary Black Women", bell hooks (1992, 56) speaks to the importance of the type of critical pedagogy that informs Stephens's body of work and her (re)presentation of her life and thought in the public realm:

> Critical pedagogy, the sharing of information and knowledge by black women with black women, is crucial for the development of radical black female subjectivity (not because black women can only learn from one another, but because the circumstance of racism, sexism and class exploitation ensure that other groups will not necessarily seek to further our self-determination). This process requires of us a greater honesty of how we live. Black female (especially students) who are searching for answers about the social formation of identities want to know how radical black women think but they also want to know about our habit of being. Willingness to share openly one's personal experience ensures that one will not be made into a deified icon.... Sharing the contradictions in our lives, we help each other learn to grapple with contradictions as a part of the process of becoming a critical thinker, a radical subject.

Stephens has confirmed an autobiographical element in her body of work as well as the channelling of observations of other people's experience: "The experiences [in my music] are not all mine but all of my lyrics are me because it's either my experience or my take on somebody else's experiences. So, it's all stuff I can back up. It's stuff that I would stand by and be able to defend even if everybody disagreed with it, because it's what I actually think" (Gardner 2004). The events in her life and that of other members or groups in society are the raw materials that are used in the production of ideas of oppressive conditions and liberatory possibilities. As a black feminist organic intellectual, Stephens seeks to describe the realities reflected in the lives of women and then brings an analysis as to the causes behind the concrete manifestation of social, economic and political phenomena in their lives. Through all means that she uses to describe and analyse the events, she also offers prescriptions or solutions. Her activism within her music is also indicative of a theorizing about the existential state of women's lives under the racist, capitalist patriarchy. In a sense, she is affirming W.E.B. Du Bois's take on the social realism purpose or activist-oriented nature of art, which he believed should be directed at engendering critical consciousness and human liberation: "All art is propaganda. . . . I do not care a damn, for any art that is not used for propaganda" (Rampersad 1976, 184). In the song "The Other Cheek" from the *Gangsta Blues* album, Stephens indicates that the poor will respond in kind to the structural violence of capitalism, racism and patriarchy that delivers poverty, unemployment, low-income, unsafe neighbourhoods and inadequate essential services and physical infrastructure:

> Providing no jobs and
> Telling us stop the crime
> Is like beating a child
> And telling him not to cry
> With all the highways you a build
> And go through
> You never build a little avenue
> Fi di youths dem earn a buck
> Things a run a muck
> Tell me what the fuk
> You really think a go happen
> If dem nuh earn a buck, gun a buss

There is a Jamaican proverb that says, "Every day the bucket goes to the well, one day the bottom is going to drop out." Stephens's message to the wealthy mirrors the essence of this proverb when she declares:

> Even the richest man haffi go
> Learn fi tek a stance when
> Them realize seh dem no safe
> Inna dem mansion
> Is a tough way fi learn seh yuh
> No really secure
> When the problems of the poor
> Come kick dung yuh door.

Essentially, Stephens is saying that there is a limit to the patience of the poor, who will one day rise up to end the structural violence of the systems of oppression. Indeed, Stephens clearly understands that the failure of the capitalist state and class to provide for the basic needs of the economically marginalized is an act of structural violence, as can be seen in the song's chorus:

> Do you expect me to turn
> The other cheek
> Taste my tears and admit defeat

The message is quite clear: the masses will engage in collective action to force change from below and extract economic and social concessions from the haughty and uncaring economic and political elite. As an organic intellectual operating in the arena of knowledge production and circulation, Stephens is legitimizing the people's use of liberatory violence against the structural violence of the social order. The people will not turn "the other cheek" and continue to suffer the indignities of poverty and other forms of suffering. The artiste has insightfully sight up that social change is normally the result of the protest action of the oppressed, as demonstrated during slavery and the labour rebellions of the 1930s in the Caribbean.

In "The Other Cheek", Stephens should have made the effort to be crystal clear that she is not encouraging the predatory violence of the criminalized lumpen elements that are present in many working-class or poor communities. Instead, she is privileging the liberatory violence that has been used in national liberation struggles or social revolutions. The latter form of violence would serve as a corrective or solution to the daily structural violence of the economic and political elite. It is Stephens's belief that the thoughts of artists have the capacity to influence behaviour and it is for this reason she asserts that cultural workers in general and singers in particular should be very mindful about the content of their cultural production. They should be intentional about raising questions that may educate, motivate or incite women to interrogate the taboos or received wisdom that have been inherited in the anti-African, patriarchal and capitalist world. The realm of the erotic is one at which Stephens has directed her lyrical bullets to indicate to women (and men) that the erotic can be a space of power for women.

CONCLUDING THOUGHTS

As an organic intellectual and a cultural worker in the reggae and dancehall genres, Stephens has used these musical forms to articulate the interests of women, the poor, queers and African people. She uses her knowledge, skills and attitude as one would expect from an organic intellectual serving the oppressed – placed at the disposal of the dispossessed – to encourage, motivate, admonish and incite them toward becoming more aware of their otherness or oppression and to take purposive action to "burn down everything and start clean". Cleansing the world of oppressive conditions calls for an intersectional understanding of oppression as multisystemic, which demands that one recognizes the many ways in which people are oppressed and bring an analysis to the fore that speaks to class, gender, race and gender identities/heterosexism. It is this broad understanding of the multiple factors of oppression that impose themselves on the lives of women, and Stephens's self-conscious embrace of it in her body of work, that places her in the black feminist tradition of the Combahee River Collective. However, an area in which her black feminist radicalism could be better articulated is in her representation of capitalism. She does not name this economic system as one of oppression despite the fact that its class character and relations and accompanying liberal capitalist democracy are critiqued in her work for their inability to engender self-determination and justice. This shortcoming could be the result of Stephens's political development coming about during the neoliberal capitalist turn that was ushered in during the Reaganomics and Thatcherism period of the early 1980s. She did not have the progressive and revolutionary political and ideological environment of the 1960s and 1970s as a context for overtly interrogating capitalism as a system of oppression.

Stephens's interrogation of the repressive sexuality code for women is indeed a liberating one because it centres women enjoying erotic pleasure and fulfilment. Additionally, her work gives licence to women to determine how and with whom they decide to share intimate moments. To openly trample on the monogamy code for women in her songs is an act of transgression against the patriarchy, because, unofficially, only men may have their cake and eat it. At times, it would appear that Stephens is merely inverting the existing behaviour of men by simply having women on top. It could be the case of her not being a systematic thinker making it possible for there to be serious contradictions between articulated positions in her body of work. Nonetheless, if we see that the struggle of oppressed people is not about changing masters but about creating human emancipatory social relations that are not about exploiting, using or abusing people, we would have to agree that the thrust of Stephens's work tends toward emancipating women and realizing the full humanity of all.

REFERENCES

Batson-Savage, Tanya. 2016. "Tanya Stephens Talks Sex, Reggae and How Hatred Shaped Her". *Susumba*, 31 March. http://www.susumba.com/music/interviews/tanya-stephens-talks-sex-reggae-and-how-hatred-shaped-her.

Blain, Keisha N. 2017. "On Transnational Black Feminism". *Black Perspective*, 14 April. https://www.aaihs.org/on-transnational-black-feminism/.

Boyce Davies, Carol. 2014. "Pan-Africanism, Transnational Black Feminism and the Limits of Culturalist Analyses in African Gender Discourses". *Feminist Africa* 19:78–93.

Brancaccio, David, Jonaki Mehta and Sarah Menendez. 2018. "Most Millennials Believe in Gender Equity, but Avoid the 'Feminist' Label". *Marketplace*, 27 August. https://www.marketplace.org/2018/08/27/most-millennials-believe-gender-equity-avoid-feminist-label/.

Cabral, Amilcar. 1969. *Revolution in Guinea: Selected Texts*. New York: Monthly Review Press.

Collins, Patricia. 1991. *Black Feminist Thought: Knowledge, Consciousness and the Politics of Empowerment*. New York: Routledge.

Combahee River Collective. 1982. "Combahee River Collective Statement: A Black Feminist Statement". In *All the Women Are White, All the Blacks Are Men, But Some of Us Are Brave: Black Women's Studies*, edited by Gloria T. Hull, Patricia Bell Scott and Barbara Smith, 13–22. New York: Feminist Press.

Cooper, Carolyn. 2019. "Women Dying for Abortion Rights". *Gleaner*, 10 March. http://jamaica-gleaner.com/article/commentary/20190310/carolyn-cooper-women-dying-abortion-rights.

Davis, Angela. 1990. *Women, Culture and Politics*. New York: Vintage Books.
Female Science Professor. 2013. "Fear of Feminism". *Chronicle of Higher Education*, 22 April. https://www.chronicle.com/article/Fear-of-Feminism/138631.
Ford-Smith, Honor. 1991. "Women and the Garvey Movement in Jamaica". In *Garvey: His Work and Impact*, edited by Rupert Lewis and Patrick Bryan, 73–83. Trenton, NJ: Africa World Press.
Gardner, Laura. 2004. "Reasoning with Tanya Stephens". *Jah Works*, 1 July. http://jahworks.org/admin/reasoning-with-tanya-stephens/#.W4m2_vZFxlY.
Gramsci, Antonio. 1971. *Selections from the Prison Notebooks*. Translated and edited by Q. Hoare and G.N. Smith. New York: International Publishers. http://marxism.halkcephesi.net/Antonio%20Gramsci/prison_notebooks/problems/intellectuals.htm.
Grizzle, Shereeta. 2016. "'I Was Raped Twice' – Tanya Stephens Talks about Ordeal". *Jamaica Star*, 3 December. http://jamaica-star.com/article/entertainment/ 20161203/i-was-raped-twice-tanya-stephens-talks-about-ordeal.
Hall, Kia M. Q. 2016. "A Transnational Black Feminist Framework: Rooting in Feminist Scholarship, Framing Contemporary Black Activism". *Meridian* 15 (1): 86–104.
hooks, bell. 1984. *Feminist Theory: From Margin to Center*. Boston: South Bend Press.
———. 1988. *Talking Back: Thinking Feminist, Thinking Black*. Toronto: Between the Lines.
———. 1992. *Black Look: Race and Representation*. Toronto: Between the Lines.
———. 1993. *Sisters of the Yam: Black Women and Self-recovery*. Toronto: Between the Lines.
Hudson, Adam. 2014. "Any National 'Conversation about Race' Must Include Black Radical Tradition". *Truthout*, 16 February. http://www.truth-out.org/news/item/21859-any-national-conversation-about-race-must-include-black-radical-tradition.
Nangwaya, Ajamu. 2014. "'Organization Is the Weapon of the Oppressed': Ferguson, Mobilization and Organizing the Resistance". *Dissident Voice*, 20 August. http://dissidentvoice.org/2014/08/organization-is-the-weapon-of-the-oppressed/.
———. 2016a. "Claudia Jones: The Unknown Pan-Africanist, Feminist and Communist". *Telesur*, 10 February. http://www.telesurtv.net/english/opinion/Claudia-Jones-Unknown-Pan-Africanist-Feminist-and-Communist--20160210-0020.html.
———. 2016b. "Pan-Africanism, Feminism and Finding the Missing Women". *Telesur*, 24 May. http://www.telesurtv.net/english/opinion/Pan-Africanism-Feminism-and-Finding-the-Missing-Women-20160524-0054.html.
Nice Up. 2019. "Ranking Ann Interview and Jealous Man / War in the City 12 Review". *NiceUp*, 23 January. http://niceup.org.nz/ranking-ann-interview-jealous-man-war-in-the-city-12-review/.
Rampersad, Arnold. 1976. *The Art and Imagination of W.E.B. Du Bois*. Cambridge: Harvard University Press.

Reddock, Rhoda. 2014. "Radical Caribbean Social Thought: Race, Class Identity and the Postcolonial Nation". *Current Sociology* 62 (4): 493–511.
Sabelli, Sonia. 2011. "'Dubbing di Diaspora': Gender and Reggae Music inna Babylon". *Social Identities* 17 (1): 137–52.
Said, Edward W. 1996. *Representations of the Intellectual*. New York: Vintage.
Scharff, Christina. 2019. "Why So Many Young Women Don't Call Themselves Feminist". *BBC News*, 6 February. https://www.bbc.com/news/uk-politics-47006912.
Shivji, Issa. 2018. "Revolutionary Intellectuals". *Africa Is a Country*, 23 May. https://africasacountry.com/2018/05/revolutionary-intellectuals.
Taylor, Angus. 2012. "She's Royal: Strong Female Voices in Reggae". *United Reggae*, 18 August. http://unitedreggae.com/articles/n1072/081812/she--s-royal-strong-female.
Tomlinson, Lisa. 2014. "Una Marson: An Anti-Colonial, Feminist, Anti-Racist, Pan-Africanist Champion of Good Causes". *Feminist Wire*, 19 March. http://www.thefeministwire.com/2014/03/una-marson-anti-colonial-feminist-anti-racist-pan-africanist-champion-good-causes/.
Walters, Basil. 2011. "Music Has the Power to Shape Society – Tanya Stephens". *Jamaica Observer*, 3 April. http://www.jamaicaobserver.com/entertainment/Music-has-the-power-to-shape-society-Tanya-Stephens_8618191.

DISCOGRAPHY

Ann, Ranking, vocalist. 1982. "Liberated Woman". Track B2 on *A Slice of English Toast*. Ariwa.
Stephens, Tanya, vocalist. 2004. "After You". Track 11 on various artists, *Drop Leaf Riddim*. Don Corleon Productions/The Streetz Records.
———. 2004. "I Am Woman". Track 9 on *Gangsta Blues*. VP Records.
———. 2004. "The Other Cheek". Track 15 on *Gangsta Blues*. VP Records.
———. 2006. "Come a Long Way". Track 14 on *Rebelution*. VP Records.
———. 2006. "Do You Still Care?". Track 15 on *Rebelution*. VP Records.
———. 2006. "Welcome to the Rebelution". Track 1 on *Rebelution*. VP Records.
———. 2012. "Weather Change". Track 6 on various artists, *Penthouse Showcase Vol. 9*. Penthouse Records.

CHAPTER 2

The Tenderness of Tanya, the Vulnerability of Vivienne
Reassessing Dancehall's Ruff Rider

MELVILLE COOKE

THIS CHAPTER USES LYRICS FROM APPROXIMATELY TWO DECADES of vocalist, songwriter and Tarantula Records co-owner Tanya Stephens's recordings to counter any misconceptions about her music being inherently derisive of or aggressive towards men. These notions may have resulted from the content of some of her earlier popular songs, notably "Yuh No Ready fi Dis Yet" (released on the *Joy Ride* compilation album in 1996), "Handle the Ride" and "Draw fi Mi Finger", both on the 1998 *Ruff Rider* album. The latter album's cover art, like its name, parodied the packaging of the still popular Rough Rider condoms. However, an examination of Stephens's lyrics beyond the limited number of her songs made popular by radio, television and sound systems shows a woman who cares deeply about men and family structure. This tenderness – a practical level of caring about the well-being of others – is extended to social crises, as Stephens displays vulnerability to the pain of others, debunking the hard-shelled image which a cursory scan of her lyrics may create. She also presents her personal vulnerability, emotionally and physically, to hurt. This is particularly evidenced in the title track of the 2010 album *Infallible*, where she speaks more as the mother Vivienne Stephenson than the deejay Tanya Stephens.

CHECK IT! FEMALE-MALE EQUATIONS

Stephens's "Yuh No Ready fi Dis Yet" – on the Joy Ride riddim, produced by Dave Kelly on his Mad House Label and released on the *Joy Ride* compilation album in 1996 – offers a fascinating confluence of meanings. For where else would a woman express her deep dissatisfaction with the quality, intensity and duration of a man's "bedroom jockey" efforts but on a riddim (rhythm) named for the celebration of riding and being ridden, as well as evoking a jolly, but purposeless and forgettable, journey? How could Stephens offer us something serious – seriously entertaining – and memorable in this confluence of names, at about the time when the most popular nightclub on the New Kingston strip was literally a musical mad house – the Asylum?

I did not encounter "Yuh No Ready fi Dis Yet", or other Stephens songs which seemed to challenge the Jamaican male's God-given joyriding proficiency, at the New Kingston dancehall Asylum. Fortunately, I was a bit past the stage of consuming Jamaican popular music mainly at fetes at the University of the West Indies' Mona campus. Instead, I listened to her 1998 *Ruff Rider* album as a body of work, having been exposed previously only to the popular songs. Two tracks on that set had me hooked on Stephens. In "Boom Wuk" from the renowned *Gangsta Blues* album, she sings, "mi jus' a cut an go tru, fling de kitty pon yuh, an if de claw dem hol you good luck star" (I am just doing what I want, throwing the pussy [vagina] on you, and if you're hooked, then that is your problem). The feline under consideration has not been tossed at, upon or around me for my joyriding efforts and her assessment. However, Stephens's lyrics did kiss my brain (as she requests on the exquisite album *Infallible*) and the lobes above the earlobes of many others – female and male – for over two decades.

Listening to *Ruff Rider* in its entirety allowed me to hear songs that would have had limited, if any, dancehall rotation. One was the very short, a cappella "Man ah Fraction", in which she sings:

> If yu see me a flex wid tree different man
> One a dem a half an two a quarter
> So dem add up to one
> Yu might tink seh me flex like a skettel bomb
> But de tree a dem a fraction an dem add up to one
> Check it!

> (If you see me hanging out with three different men
> One is half a man and the others are a quarter each
> So, they add up to one man
> You may think I am behaving like a sexually immoral woman
> But the three of them are fractions and add up to one
> Check it!)

The double meaning or instruction in the invitation to "check it" – in standard English "to add up with her and see that the sum of male parts is right", but even more so, in Jamaican, "to assess her reasoning" – was irresistible. I did so, and added a third meaning of check, putting a "tickie" designating a stamp of approval beside the track. My mental application of a schoolteacher's mark indicating a correct answer was not only mathematical but also reflected an appreciation of Stephens's argument that if one man falls short of her needs in a heterosexual relationship, then her right to emotional and sexual fulfilment guarantees her freedom from the societal dictates of female monogamy – moral standards which are often inequitably imposed upon women.

At that time, I was checking (also a Jamaican term for courting) the lady to whom I am now married and visiting her at the Postgraduate Flats on the Mona campus of the University of the West Indies. This was the closest I thought I would ever get to a higher degree. I was generally aware of the term feminist (enough to know that it was not synonymous with man-hater) and knew nothing about the concept of organic intellectual. Many years later, Gramsci's term for that "strata of intellectuals which give it homogeneity and an awareness of its own function, not only in the economic but also in the social and political fields (1971, 5)" became part of my engagement with the university's cultural studies programme. For this reassessment of dancehall's "Ruff Rider", I use the term organic intellectual in light of Adamson's (1980, 143) understanding that Gramsci "was referring generally to anyone whose social function is to serve as a transmitter of ideas within civil society and between government and civil society".

Although I did not then know a formal term for Stephens's dissemination of concepts of equality in the give and take of female and male intimate relationships, I did understand that a general reading of Stephens as a "man-hater" at worst, or a ridiculer of men at best, was wrong. She was not expressing disrespect of men or dismissing us; rather, she was stating a dissatisfaction with what some of us, within the context of hegemonic masculinity, were bringing to the plate. And, there is no pun intended there, as she says in "Good Ride" from the *Gangsta Blues* album: "man to the way you move skill wid yu fingers / yu no haffi indulge inna no cunnilingus" (man, you are so skilled with your fingers / you do not have to perform cunnilingus). Stephens consistently claims her sexual power and proficiency and, naturally, sets a matching standard for her male partner.

I submit that contrary to popular perception, Stephens is in fact very tender towards men. The conceptualization of male and female relationships that she generates and transmits in her capacity as an organic intellectual is gentle towards my gender within the context of a society in which I believe simultaneous dual (or multiple) intimate relationships are more the norm than the exception. Numerically, at least, men and women in the Jamaican society continue to hover around an equal balance; the "seven women to one man" ratio in Jamaica is, and has always been, a myth. This particular untruth may be grounded in the Bible, as Isaiah 4:1 states: "And in that day seven women shall take hold of one man, saying, we will eat our own bread, and wear our own apparel: only let us be called by thy name, to take away our reproach."

In presenting the relevant statistics from the 2011 population and housing census, Ken Chaplin (2012) advises Jamaican men to "hold [their] excitement. The population ratio between men and women is not one man to seven women, as many Jamaican men believe. That's a myth, says Dr Valerie Nam, director of Censuses, Demographics and Statistics, at the Statistical Institute of Jamaica." That census showed that there were 1,363,450 women and 1,334,533 men in a population of 2,697,983. The trend of slightly more women than men is maintained up to the end of 2017, when the Statistical Institute of Jamaica reported that there were 1,377,472 women and 1,351,392 men in a Jamaican population of 2,728,864 (STATIN n.d.). Therefore, even with all the adjustments for unavailability and undesirability made, it is impossible in Jamaican society for so many men to truthfully boast about having "nuff gal inna bungle" (many women), as deejay Beenie Man says in his song "Nuff Gal", without quite a few women having more than one, if not nuff, man. Evidence of men who have found out they are wearing a jacket when they finally see the child's birth certificate and the results of paternity tests done as part of the emigration process to the United States helps to support this assessment of the situation. A 2009 diplomatic cable from the US embassy in Kingston to its Washington headquarters stated that "approximately 10 per cent of all cases where DNA is done result in no biological relationship. This percentage does not include those applicants that choose to abandon their case rather than undergo DNA testing" (Alleyne 2011). So, when I say Stephens is tender, it is within the context of the reality of these types of sexual relationship arrangements in Jamaica.

Stephens spoke about male music performers putting down female performers when she stated, "it bun [hurts] me. It has been bunning [hurting] me for 20 years. . . . The least talented male artiste will stand in front of me and say 'you are talented for a girl'." However, Stephens makes a clear distinction between exercising femininity in her personal life and her approach to a career, saying that "in my personal life, I am very female. I love to have the chair pulled and the door opened. But in my professional life, I will pull the door and slam it in a bway [boy] face." This insistence on professional equality extends to declining to participate in all-female shows or be a part of all-female crews; in her view, by participating in such groupings, "we are going to attract sympathy, not respect" (Cooke 2016). Additionally, in "Welcome to the Rebelution" which opens the 2006 *Rebelution* album, she dismisses the manufacturing of female stars by privileging sensuality over intellect, a process in which the women are complicit and men are in control:

> Came to pass in the days of glorifying everything wrong
> That the standard for girls became a bra and a thong
> Wholesome values like curling up with a good book and a bong
> Went out the window along with making a good song
> Everybody's got a new image, new management team
> New lawyers negotiating new dreams
> Even if they came true I still wouldn't wanna be ya
> Got everything new except a new idea
> Why do I get the feeling I heard all this before?
> I guess it's because I heard it before
> And I'm sure I'm gonna hear it some more
> Cause everyone thinks he's the one who invented being a whore

Although her reaction is cynical, it shows that Stephens, despite being secure in her creativity, is affected by the calculated misdirection of other female performers. Despite her strong individualism, Stephens is affected by issues that impact groups which she is a part of by virtue of her humanity. Also on *Ruff Rider* is "2000 Years", a slower song showing the vulnerability of Vivienne towards human folly beyond her control yet which she wishes she could change:

> We've been your cooks your gardener and nannies to your little monsters
> For every job that's demeaning my people are the natural answers
> You've been putting us down, pushing us round for too long now
> But as God is my witness something's gonna blow

And there is also personal vulnerability, but first let us examine the tenderness.

TENDERNESS, FALSEHOODS AND MATERNAL INSTINCT

In one of her more commercially celebrated songs, "Little White Lie" (2004), Stephens details the jacket, or paternity fraud process from a woman's perspective. We can argue at length about the use of the word "white" to denote a category of untruth that is not the most morally reprehensible. However, there is no mistaking her concern for the man to whom she has falsely attributed paternity of her child:

> The emotions on his face when he's looking at you
> I couldn't tell him he aint your Papa if I wanted to
> He's got your picture tattooed on his arm
> Now he's bragging to his friends about his first born
> And I love him, really, I do
> If he ever found out it would kill me too
> Now I'm caught between a rock and a really hard place
> I'll give anything to keep that smile on his face
> So I lied

Of course, he may just literally kill her before his demise and her figurative death from guilt. Thus, Stephens's little white lie could also be self-protection. But she also makes the mother's choice of the best man to raise her child, as Stephens says to the baby, "I hope you understand / the man who thinks he's your father is a much better man." This choice runs counter to patterns of patriarchy in which the selection of a child-bearing partner is often the privilege of men who have financial resources which women wish to access, but who may not be the best father for their child.

It is the same mother's tenderness in "It's a Pity", also on *Gangsta Blues*, where Stephens considers the future of the child she could have had with the man she loves, even as she is involved with another man. The desire for a child in "It's a Pity" and the decision to not disabuse a man of his assumption of paternity in "Little White Lie" reflect different stages of the reproductive process. Even so, the issue is the same. A woman's agency in selecting her ideal person to be a father for her child is an agency which, in a patriarchal society, must sometimes be exercised by subterfuge. So, while in "Little White Lie" Stephens feels forced into maintaining silence after the child is born, in "It's a Pity" she expresses the frustrated desire for maternity in a mature and responsible manner. She is considering the long-term consequences for the child, who should not have to be oblivious of their biological father, when she says, "I wudda cut out di smoking an di party an di rum / an buss a extra wine an mek wi seal up a son" (I would stop the smoking, partying and rum drinking / and make an extra gyration and let us create a son). The gender of the desired child changes further in the song, but the care is revealed:

> I tink di two a wi can mek a beautiful daawta
> But it wud be selfish to an innocent likkle yute
> To bring har come an cannot tell har di truth
>
> (I think both of us can make a beautiful daughter
> But it would be selfish to an innocent child
> To bring her into the world and be unable to tell her the truth)

And the tenderness towards the object of her desire is expressed in a determination to not disrupt his family's equilibrium:

> Fi buck yu up inna public an cyaa even touch
> It really fuck me up because me check fi yu so much
> Di respeck whe mi have fi yu woman fi yu kids
> Believe mi rude bwoy mi criss a no matey dis
> Who knows, maybe one day the world will be evolved enough
> We'll share you in a civilized manner between the two of us
> But until then I would a love fi see you again
> We know we have to play it by the stupid rules of men
>
> (To happen upon you in public
> And not be able to touch you
> It really fucks me up
> Because I like you so much
> The respect I have for your woman and your children
> Believe me down-to-earth man I am fine, this is not the typical other woman)

The tenderness also shows up in unusual circumstances. In "Gangsta Gal" on *Gangsta Blues*, a track which showcases her as the main performer and features deejay Spragga Benz, Stephens deals with the chronic (marijuana) until her fingers are stuck with the gum and then wipes down the bullets while her man cleans the gun. Stephens promises to go on the witness stand and do what is necessary to secure her man's freedom. As she is the one with the combination or password to the safe, she reassures her lover by declaring, "Don't worry honey, I will be there with the bail money." Throughout the song, Stephens does not show any signs of being coerced or fear of her outlaw lover. She willingly partners with him, knowing that he has other women, but is reassured of her sexual and use of firearms superiority when Spragga Benz says "you being replaced is not an issue". Stephens's tenderness persists even in the face of an almost certain demise. She is fatalistic as she pledges,

> Don't know if we're blessed or cursed
> but I'm prepared for the best or the worst
> I'll be there til we ride in a hearse."

In "Gangsta Gal", Stephens is the key to her male partner's temporary physical liberation from lockup; she is also the saviour of men entangled in unhealthy relationships in "To the Rescue". There, she expresses her empathy by saying:

> So tell di man dem we a work fi protec' dem interest
> Cause some gal out deh have man unda pure stress
> So we rescue di one dem whe wi check fi de bes'
> Di man willing fi spen any amount a cash
> Fi get a quieta mout an a tighta punash
> Fi get a respectful gal whe no search man phone
> Dem woulda give up all house an home . . .
> Dis is a rescue
> Run whe di gal dem whe a stress you
> Wi come fi perform a save roun' here
> Cause some gal nah behave roun here
>
> (So tell all the men we are working to protect their interests
> Because some girls have them under pure stress
> So we are rescuing the ones we like most
> The men are willing to spend any amount of money
> To get a woman who talks less and has a tighter vagina
> To get a respectful girl who does not search her man's phone
> They are willing to give up house and home
> This is a rescue
> Dismiss the girls who are stressing you
> We have come to perform a rescue mission around here
> Because some girls are not behaving around here)

However, Stephens's criticism of the stressful women referred to in the song is based on their failure to generously provide sexual satisfaction for their men and adequately perform domestic chores, as she advises them to "remember you a di one weh did chase weh yu spouse / wi put on di gas mask tek him out a di dirty house" (remember you are the one who chased away your spouse / we put on the gas mask and took him out of the dirty house). Stephens also recognizes a man's desire for a woman who observes his privacy boundaries. Although not stated outright, the implication is that she will perform to the required standards of the rescued man, being more of an obedient, acquiescent partner than the woman she replaces. However, Stephens injects a home wrecker disclaimer, again showing her regard for domestic boundaries as she says, "wi no search, wi jus rescue" (we don't go searching, we only rescue).

I believe the most striking expression of her tenderness towards men is "Still Alive", on the *Infallible* album. Stephens tells the story of HIV transmission between husband and wife from the husband's perspective; the song then evolves into a tale of the man's resilience. In the introduction, she says:

> Johnny was a good man
> He had two kids and a beautiful wife
> He loved her very much
> She was the pride of his life
> He would never do anything to cause her pain
> Unfortunately for him though
> She never saw it quite the same
> Johnny was busy giving her everything he had to give
> And in return she gave him a test that came back positive
> The news spread like wildfire and pretty soon
> Johnny would walk in through the door and he would empty the room
> His boss said to him Johnny
> I wanna keep you but my hands are tied
> God knows I've tried
> But nobody wants to work by your side
> And you've been a good asset to us Johnny
> I'm indebted to you
> Tell me, what would you have me do?

After a verse in which Johnny questions the lack of empathy – stating "how could you watch me live in pain if your love could heal me? / touch me every day, how can you not feel me?" – and is stunned by being abruptly abandoned, as he says in the lines, "after everything I gave / I can't believe you are all digging my grave while I'm still alive"), the chorus of "Still Alive" rings out homage to his fortitude:

> Every day I live I'm alive
> With every breath I give I'm alive
> Oh take it from me
> I'm still writing pages of testimony
> I'm alive no matter what they say
> I'm alive and this is how I'll stay
> I'm alive and I'm not ready to go
> I want everybody to know that I'm still alive

VULNERABILITY AND PERSONAL TRAUMA

In her status as the other woman or being cast aside, Stephens is not emotionally impregnable. She shows her emotional vulnerability to being jilted with these lines from "Can't Breathe" on *Gangsta Blues*:

> You want me to take it like a man but I'm a girl who cries
> So if I puncture your tires don't be too surprised
> And while I'm at it hell, may as well key up your car
> Cause what you did to my heart was an act of war

And she does wish that her ex-partner's new lover "is cheating, juggling nuts like a squirrel / better yet, I hope she leaves you for a girl". She is also the jilted lover seeing the man she loves going to the altar with another woman in "Damn You" from *Rebelution*. After going to the wedding without an invitation, she sings:

> I wanted to scream your name
> Let everybody see my pain
> When you said I do I died

Since this is Stephens, the vulnerability is blended with realistic relationships. She pleads with her inattentive partner to "Try Me" on the *Infallible* album, to stick some money into her waist band and pretend to buy her. She assures him that her bedroom skills are now much improved, as Joe Grind (her other lover) has taught her to ride. In "These Streets" on *Rebelution*, Stephens tells her man, who has changed with new-found wealth, "I wish you woulda treat mi like yuh Glock / I woulda love it if yuh keep mi pon cock." By this she means she is ready to engage in the sex act at a moment's notice. Stephens's physical yearning is further emphasized as she says,

> I wish yuh woulda treat mi like yuh yacht
> Keep mi wet while de waves dem a rock
> Why yuh cyaa stay pon mi like de corna
> an' keep yuh lips pon mi like yuh marijuana?
> I woulda love it if yuh treat mi like yuh club
> Stay up inna mi whole night jus' a bump an' grin' an rub.

Yet when it all crashes, and he is facing the judge and possible imprisonment, she is still in his corner even when "mi nuh see nuh hot gal, mi nuh si none a yuh kruu" (I don't see any hot girls, I don't see any of your crew members).

I tend to think of Tanya Stephens as Vivienne Stephenson in her more publicly vulnerable moments. Contributing to this perception is her tendency towards a conversational tone, intensifying her treatment of topics and issues which are, unfortunately, not part of Jamaican popular music's accustomed lexicon. At these times, I feel a more personal engagement with someone I feel I know on a first-name basis, Vivienne, rather than admiring the skill and fortitude of the outstanding writer Stephens on a stage. Among those moments are "Spilt Milk" on *Rebelution*, which is a send-off for a lover who "would have gone sour anyway", and "Cherry Brandy" (also on *Rebelution*), the drowning of sorrows in liquor, even to the point where she goes to a building's top floor and cannot find the courage to jump. But alcohol also makes her vulnerable physically, as when in "Saturday Morning" Vivienne wakes up with a strange, ominously self-satisfied man named Bigga Blacks – who she can't recall seeing before – after a night of drinking. And my all-time favourite is "Infallible", the title track of *Infallible*, where she is the mother Vivienne speaking to her daughter, Kelly, confessing that "I am not infallible, I am only human / I used to give your grandma trouble too, that much is true man". She exposes her own vulnerabilities to the next generation, singing "you have never been as low as I have been". Vivienne asks her daughter to stick around, singing, "I will have your back and you will have my shoulder." Additionally, Stephens begs, "Please allow me to share the little I do know."

Also on the album *Infallible* is "No Means No", which is about a man raping a woman. In this song, the rapist presents his best face in court and the victim becomes the villain. It struck me upon listening but took on added meaning when Vivienne spoke about her personal experience of rape. The Asylum nightclub was a part of the story, as it was there she cried as she heard a song about a woman being gang-raped or, in Jamaican terminology, "batteried". I did not include her experience of being raped in Cooke (2016), but she subsequently spoke about it at greater length on social media. However, being vulnerable to this extreme manifestation of hegemonic masculinity has not broken her, as is clear from her body of work and willingness to publicly speak about it. For while she affirms that "Man fi Rule" on *Ruff Rider*, Stephens is adamant that "no fool cyaa rule Tanya" (no fool can rule Tanya). Vivienne is vulnerable, but not a perpetual victim.

Having the same tone as "2000 Years" is a song which I believe to be more widely known, "The Other Cheek" on *Gangsta Blues*. In this song, the artiste again pins herself to the vicissitudes of life in a country where "things must really get wicked / when you pay cheque is less than you speeding ticket" (the situation must be extremely bad / when your salary is less than your speeding ticket). Still there is resistance, as Stephens concludes when she asks, "Do you expect me to turn the other cheek / taste my tears and accept defeat?"

Not accepting defeat while acknowledging vulnerability is the essence of Stephens's delightfully defiant approach. At forty-six years old, she has released "Fuck Boy", which pushes back against society's attitude of downplaying – or even denying – women's sexuality as they get older. In the spoken introduction, Stephens says,

> everybody acts like as soon as a woman start get a little bit older
> she supposed to automatically get corny
> well my body take a break for a while and come back extra bloodclaat horny
>
> (everybody acts as if when a woman gets a little older
> she automatically becomes less of a woman
> well my body paused for a while and has returned more horny than ever).

The desire for sex is expounded on before Stephens specifies a minimum age for the job opening, saying "a one ting mi have pon mi mind, anything over twenty-nine can apply / I have a vacancy fi a fuck boy inna mi life" (there's one thing I have on my mind, anything over twenty-nine can apply / I have a vacancy for a fuck boy in my life). She therefore acknowledges her vulnerability to ageism, compounded by gender bias. However, Stephens not only rabidly resists but reverses the older man–younger woman syndrome. She does not call herself Vivienne in the song but instead uses a term which is laden with notions of propriety, naming her daughter as she says:

> A one somebody matter y'nuh
> Kelly seh Mummy everyting is aaright
> Jus mek yusself happy tonight
>
> (Only one person matters you know
> Kelly says Mommy everything is alright
> Just make yourself happy tonight)

Stephens demands, "how dem a move so, like as wi get a little bit older wi too old fi do adult stuff? Weh oonu seh, wi fi leave it to di children dem? Set a bloodclaat eediats. Wi cyaa wear shorts? Wi cyaa show cleavage? Wi definitely cyaa ride a dick? Stop wi nuh" (Why are they behaving like that, as if as we age we get too old to do adult stuff? What are the saying, that we should leave it to the children? Set of bloodclaat idiots. We cannot wear shorts? We cannot show cleavage? We definitely cannot ride a dick? Try to stop us then). She is caustic, comical and correct.

FINAL FRACTION

This is a little bit – a fraction – of what I consider to be Tanya Stephens's tenderness and Vivienne Stephenson's vulnerability. It would take a much longer time, graphics, audio and in-depth analysis of a body of work over twenty years to do her justice on this aspect of herself. But as we consider Stephens as an organic intellectual and feminist, we should not construe her as a man-hater, a charge too often lobbied at feminists. She has literally made her positions clear, such as in "Siddung Pon It" from *Infallible* and "I Am Woman" on *Gangsta Blues*, that the same feet that fit so comfortably on a man's shoulders will be the same ones to stand her ground. As an organic intellectual she is a gleefully independent thinker. In "Do You Still Care?" on *Infallible*, her tenderness extends to a man intolerant of homosexuality who is shot while hustling in the streets.

A final thought on *Ruff Rider*. The album is subtitled "Studded for Pleasure", while the condom packet is branded "studded for more pleasure". Brand infringement considerations aside, could leaving out the word "more" from the album's title mean that the stud (the man, and not the raised surfaces on the Rough Rider condom) is needed for any pleasure at all, and the finger that can be drawn for is simply not an option on its own? The level of nuance is certainly not beyond Stephens and, even if not deliberately done to convey that interpretation, it is intriguing that an album with several songs asking more of men in sexual relationships could state in its title how indispensable men are in the heterosexual sexual act. It is certainly a position Stephens holds to in her lyrics. And I cannot help replacing s-t-u-d-d-e-d with s-t-u-d-i-e-d as we do so and find lasting substance and pleasure in Stephens's work. The connection between the carnal and the intellectual contributes to making an engagement with Stephens's lyrics a fascinating foray into a world where syncretism is normal and the sexual and cerebral are not opposing choices but inseparable components of the search for balance within the feminine self and between genders.

REFERENCES

Adamson, Walter L. 1980. *Hegemony and Revolution: A Study of Antonio Gramsci's Political and Cultural Theory*. Berkeley: University of California Press.

Alleyne, Mervyn. 2011. "Jackets: Made in Jamaica". *Gleaner*, 25 May. http://jamaica-gleaner.com/gleaner/20110525/lead/lead31.html.

Chaplin, Ken. 2012. "Don't Get Too Excited Men: It's Not Seven Woman to One Man". *Jamaica Observer*, 23 October. http://www.jamaicaobserver.com/columns/don-t-get-excited--gentlemen--it-s-not-seven-women-to-one-man_12819340.

Cooke, Melville. 2016. "Female Fury". *Gleaner*, 3 April. http://www.jamaica-gleaner.com/article/entertainment/20160403/female-fury.

Gramsci, Antonio, Quintin Hoare, and Geoffrey Nowell-Smith. 1971. *Selections from the Prison Notebooks of Antonio Gramsci*. New York: International Publishers.

Statistical Institute of Jamaica (STATIN). n.d. "Population Statistics 2011–2017". http://statinja.gov.jm/Demo_SocialStats/PopulationStats.aspx.

DISCOGRAPHY

Beenie Man, vocalist. 1996. "Nuff Gal". MP3 audio. Track 2 on *Maestro*. VP Records.

Stephens, Tanya, vocalist. 1998. "Draw fi Mi Finger". MP3 audio. Track 1 on *Ruff Rider*. VP Records.

———. 1996. "Yuh No Ready fi Dis Yet". MP3 audio. Track 8 on *Joy Ride*. VP Records.

———. 1998. "Draw fi Mi Finger". MP3 audio. Track 1 on *Ruff Rider*. VP Records.

———. 1998. "Handle the Ride". MP3 audio. Track 2 on *Ruff Rider*. VP Records.
———. 1998. "Man ah Fraction". MP3 audio. Track 4 on *Ruff Rider*. VP Records.
———. 1998. "Man fi Rule". MP3 audio. Track 14 on *Ruff Rider*. VP Records.
———. 1998. "2000 Years". MP3 audio. Track 12 on *Ruff Rider*. VP Records.
———. 2004. "Boom Wuk". MP3 audio. Track 3 on *Gangsta Blues*. VP Records.
———. 2004. "Can't Breathe". MP3 audio. Track 13 on *Gangsta Blues*. VP Records.
———. 2004. "Gangsta Gal". MP3 audio. Track 11 on *Gangsta Blues*. VP Records.
———. 2004. "Good Ride". MP3 audio. Track 5 on *Gangsta Blues*. VP Records.
———. 2004. "I Am Woman". MP3 audio. Track 9 on *Gangsta Blues*. VP Records.
———. 2004. "It's a Pity". MP3 audio. Track 7 on *Gangsta Blues*. VP Records.
———. 2004. "Little White Lie". MP3 audio. Track 6 on *Gangsta* Blues. VP Records.
———. 2004. "The Other Cheek". MP3 audio. Track 15 on *Gangsta Blues*. VP Records.
———. 2006. "Cherry Brandy". MP3 audio. Track 11 on *Rebelution*. VP Records.
———. 2006. "Do You Still Care?" MP3 audio. Track 15 on *Rebelution*. VP Records.
———. 2006. "Damn You". MP3 audio. Track 7 on *Rebelution*. VP Records.
———. 2006. "Saturday Morning". MP3 audio. Track 10 on *Rebelution*. VP Records.
———. 2006. "Spilt Milk". MP3 audio. Track 9 on *Rebelution*. VP Records.
———. 2006. "These Streets". MP3 audio. Track 18 on *Rebelution*. VP Records.
———. 2006. "To the Rescue". MP3 audio. Track 6 on *Rebelution*. VP Records.
———. 2006. "Welcome to the Rebelution". MP3 audio. Track 1 on *Rebelution*. VP Records.
———. 2010. "Infallible". MP3 audio. Track 13 on *Infallible*. Tarantula Records.
———. 2012. "No Means No". MP3 audio. Track 11 on *Infallible*. Tarantula Records.
———. 2012. "Siddung Pon It". MP3 audio. Track 6 on *Infallible*. Tarantula Records.
———. 2012. "Still Alive". MP3 audio. Track 10 on *Infallible*. Tarantula Records.
———. 2012. "Try Me". MP3 audio. Track 16 on *Infallible*. Tarantula Records.
———. 2018. "Tanya Stephens Fuck Boy (Raw)". Accessed on YouTube, 24 August 2018. https://www.youtube.com/watch?v=hGuP6aX.

CHAPTER 3

The Gangsta as Feminist in the Lyrics of Tanya Stephens*

TANYA BATSON-SAVAGE

> One must assume the feminine role deliberately, which means already to convert a form of subordination into an affirmation and thus begin to thwart it.
> (Irigaray et al. 1985)

> And what is a woman's head but dispensable?
> A dutty wining machine, a hypnotist's string,
> a windmill.
> (Shirley 2014)

DANCEHALL REVELS IN THE PERFORMANCE OF GUN TOTING, gyrating hyper-heterosexual masculinity. The image of the deejay as gangsta replete with a "lyrical gun" (Cooper 2004, 145–78) firing metaphorical bullets of verbal sound power from throbbing speaker boxes is the embodiment of this performance. On the one hand, dancehall music appears unapologetically patriarchal and is often vilified as violent and misogynistic. Whether in the gyrations "bubbling" on the dance floor or the lyrics that often explore all the crevices of a woman's body, the music, the culture and the space that houses them have been defined as the enemy of woman, thriving on her objectification as she is reduced to breasts, bottom and pum pum (vagina). On the other hand, defenders of the genre have argued that, rather than degrade, dancehall celebrates woman as a full sexual being, and therefore many deejays often maligned as misogynists may in fact be interpreted as projecting feminist viewpoints. Indeed, in *Caribbean*

---

*A version of this chapter was previously published as "Gangsta Poetics: Femininity in Tanya Stephens's *Gansta Blues*", *Jamaica Journal* 29, nos. 1–2 (2005): 6–11.

Currents: Caribbean Music from Rumba to Reggae, Peter Manuel explores the paradoxical position of women in dancehall, raising the intriguing argument that the simultaneous degradation and celebration of women represents gender negotiations taking place in a traditionally patriarchal society that also celebrates female strength (Manuel et al. 2006, 206–8).

It is undeniable that identities are often being negotiated, contested and created in both the geographical space of the dancehall as well as the metaphorical topographies charted by the deejays' lyrics, which in addition to spending much time celebrating dancing, sex and violence are dedicated to prescribing correct social behaviour. Even so, unpacking the question of woman's position in dancehall is complicated by the fact that, while there are currently far more female deejays than ever before, men continue to dominate the roles as deejays and (perhaps even more importantly) as producers. Where women often dominate is on the dance floor. Even in that space, however, there have been frequent shifts in dominance over time. Admittedly, we would be remiss to view the dancer as merely a writhing, silent vessel for the deejay. Sonjah Stanley Niaah underlines the importance of dancers to dancehall in *Dancehall: From Slaveship to Ghetto*, writing that "the freedom to move in the dance, to create and maintain spaces of production and consumption simultaneously, constitutes an effective move beyond history, to transform the local present while making an impact on the global" (2010, 148). Even so, there is no doubt that the deejay – the one controlling the microphone – is also the one in control of the dance. As many a 1980s deejay declared, it is the deejay who has the responsibility to "ram dancehall and cork party". The space behind the microphone remains dominated by men, and whether they glorify or condemn woman – while often discussing and dissecting her body – the female half of the story has rarely been told. This relative silence (because the deejay depends heavily on her screams, so she is not actually quiet) problematizes the issue of representation, of which voice is such a pivotal aspect.

Female deejays are therefore critical to an analysis of identity and representation in dancehall. Tanya Stephens has had a long career that has extended beyond many of her peers of either gender. Her album *Gangsta Blues* (2004)[1] presents a microcosm of Stephens's feminist agenda, wherein the feminist, the defender of female sexuality, the voiceless and the defenseless, is defined as a gangsta. *Gangsta Blues* celebrates woman as a lover, mother and rebel. Alicia Suskin Ostriker in *Stealing the Language: The Emergence of Women's Poetry in America* cites Audre Lorde's statement, "If we do not define ourselves we are nothing. If the world defines you it will define you to your disadvantage" (Ostriker 1986, 59). The female deejay thus allows women to define themselves in the dancehall space.

Through *Gangsta Blues*, Stephens projects an agenda that redefines the gangsta as a feminist. In it she subverts the opposition between masculine and feminine. Indeed, the feminine can be read as a combination of the revolutionary and the subversive with the sensitive and sensual. Stephens makes it clear that the woman's space is both in the bedroom and the war office, as she moves easily from domestic issues to political ones.

While the gangsta can be seen as a social predator, one who makes a living through violence, often preying on members of the working class, an understanding of the dynamics of inner city culture quickly highlights that such a narrow definition lacks nuance. In this chapter, I argue that the gangsta can be both predator and protector. Within this context, the gangsta is the inheritor of the mantle of the revolutionary and rudie, and several of the personas in *Gangsta Blues* embody this trait.

The *Dictionary of Caribbean English Usage* gives a lengthy definition of "rude", which includes "making a display of rough, disorderly or sexy behaviour" (Allsopp 2003, 479). It also includes the history of resistance in its definition of the term: "In Jamaican, the word 'rude' often refers to anyone openly defiant of constituted authority" (Allsopp 2003, 479). By interrogating sex, sexuality and the broader society, Stephens displays both sides of the "rude gyal" persona.

It is important to note that Stephens's embrace of the role of gangsta is not an assumption of masculinity. Instead, she redefines the feminine to assume traits that are traditionally ascribed to both genders. Stephens's gangsta therefore also embraces the traits of the "Cunny Jamma Oman", as described in Carolyn Cooper's *Noises in the Blood: Orality, Gender and the 'Vulgar' Body of Jamaican Popular Culture*. According to Cooper (1995, 47–67), who uncovers this female sensibility in Louise Bennett's poetry, Bennett uses Anansi-like cunning and often engages in "self-protective verbal abuse" through the art of tracing. Stephens's lyrics reveal continuations of this "Cunny Jamma Oman", as her words become both defensive and offensive weapons.

Interestingly, while the act of "tracing" (or hurling insults) is often viewed as the female's terrain, the deejay is steeped in the verbal arts so that he can defend himself in a sound clash where his lyrical virility is contested. The "Intro" to *Gangsta Blues* acts as a challenge to other deejays and the establishment, in which Stephens details her position both as a talented lyricist who has paid her dues and as woman. Simultaneously, she declares a sense of individuality and refuses Otherness that would come from being defined solely by her position as female. An integral part of this is the struggle for recognition that the female deejay faces. Where female writers may be getting a room of their own, the average female deejay still struggles for a studio, having to battle hard to gain and retain command of the phallocentric microphone. Thus, in the "Intro", Stephens scoffs that she has worked ten times harder than a man, yet all she gets is "half-hearted regard". This stance is again taken up in "We A Lead", where she strikes a riposte and lays down a challenge with her pen as she calls:

> Pass di paypa, gi mi a pen
> an mek mi slap some lyrics inna some fool face again
> Run di riddim, Andrew gimme di track
> An when mi spit dis, mi wan' see dem fin' a come back
>
> (Pass the paper, give me a pen
> and allow me to slap some lyrics in some fool's face again
> Run the rhythm, Andrew give me the track
> And when I spit this, I want to see them find a comeback/adequate response)

With these introductory lines reminiscent of Louise Bennett's cantankerous persona, Stephens exudes the traditional bravado of the deejay in a landscape where self-praise is the ultimate recommendation. She declares herself as unstoppable once she has pen and paper in hand, and dares anyone to contest her claim.

Sexuality is also an important part of Stephens's definition of femininity and she is able to let loose with the best of them, embracing her sexuality as an important part of her identity. In this regard, Lady Saw is very much Stephens's forerunner. The two diverge, however, with Stephens's insistence that sex is about her pleasure. In Isaac Julien's 1994 documentary *The Darker Side of Black*, Lady Saw admits that much of her talk about sex is aimed at making men feel good about themselves. There is no such hint from Stephens, as the woman's pleasure is constantly foregrounded. Indeed, this is where Stephens also diverges from much of mainstream "slackness" in dancehall. The dancehall space acknowledges and even celebrates woman as a sexual being, yet it is a pyrrhic recognition. Her sexual prowess or power is not usually about her pleasure. Often it is a commodity in the sexual economy, as epitomized in Shabba Ranks's "Gone Up".

It is important to note that, despite Shabba's lyrics, girls are generally raised to protect their virtue, while men are encouraged to be sexually prolific. In *Learning to Be a Man: Culture, Socialization and Gender Identity in Five Caribbean Communities*, Barry Chevannes points to the differences between how men and women are shaped according to proscribed sexuality. Chevannes (2001, 217) argues that African Caribbean men are encouraged to have casual or promiscuous relationships with women (as in multiple relationships simultaneously): "A woman has no such licence. Beyond casual relationships, she is stigmatized: whore, prostitute, jammette, mattress, loose." Chevannes also points out that a man is not identified as a "real man" unless he is heterosexually active. As such, the vagina becomes the space used to prove male hyper-heterosexuality, making the woman's pleasure secondary to his manhood. Additionally, the violent imagery evoked by a sexual term such as "stabbing" or "digging" erodes the sense that giving pleasure is the man's goal.

With Stephens, however, the woman's sexual pleasure is always paramount in a sexual encounter. It is a part of her definition of self and insistence on the validity of woman as a sexual being. Additionally, much of the discourse that argues against slackness purports that it makes woman a sex object. With Stephens, she is always the subject. In "Boom Wuk", the most explicit of the songs on *Gangsta Blues*, she declares:

> It's not the way you walk
> And it's not the way you talk
> It's not your beat up car
> You definitely ain't no movie star
> And it's not the clothes you wear
> And it ain't your nappy hair
> It ain't your gangsta flex
> Baby it's all about the sex
> Mi jus love off yuh boom wuk
> (I just love off your boom work)

While one can argue that one woman's "boom wuk" is another woman's "digging", the words themselves make a difference. While "boom" (bomb) suggests an act that is explosive, it has none of the pain potentially found in "digging" or "stabbing"; rather, it connotes waves of pleasure. "Boom Wuk" turns the sexual value system on its head, as Stephens dismisses many of the reasons to value a man in dancehall culture, negating his looks, his position as a gangsta and his money. She tells us that she is simply in the relationship for the pleasure he provides her. She chants, "Mi nuh even understand a why yuh wife a bruk war / yuh mighta love me but to me you's just a wuk star." Furthermore, the man in question is not simply celebrated for having a big penis. His value lies in his ability to use it, not to shake up her "strukcha" (structure or body), as male deejays traditionally boast, but to please her.

In turn, "Damn You" presents an unequivocal refusal to submit sexual pleasure to intellectualism. The mock-narrative poem details an almost successful date. The date in question is able to satisfy her mind and treats her opinions with respect while showing gallantry. Unfortunately, his performance falls well below par and he is unable to satisfy her sexually. Therefore, he is discarded as unsatisfactory. The track highlights the fact that mental stimulation and sexual pleasure are equally important. It discards the sentimental notion of a man who only respects her mind. Her body also needs attention. Her demands keep her from ever being a sexual object, as her selfhood is never displaced. She claims her rights to pleasure in and out of the bed.

Stephens also embraces the persona that Clarissa Pinkola Estés calls the obscene or dirty goddess. Pinkola Estés celebrates a woman's "heat" as well as provides rude jokes that only women get and that allow them to deal with the trials of life. She argues, "A woman's heat is not a state of sexual arousal, but a state of intense sensory awareness that includes but is not limited to, her sexuality" (Pinkola Estés 1992, 383). Stephens embodies this "heat", which blazes from her lyrics. Furthermore, Stephens subverts the notion that a woman who celebrates her sexuality cannot also be a strong woman. This is particularly distinctive in the re-versioning of "I Am Woman", which is one of the most poignant pieces on the album. The blues effect of the a cappella song helps to firmly seat Stephens in the tradition of strong women who celebrate womanhood and mourn the trials of the sex.

Stephens juxtaposes strength and sexuality, highlighting that she can be both sexual and strong at the same time when she chants, "The feet that fit so comfortably on your shoulders / are the same ones that's gonna stand my ground". Interestingly, it is with this line that Stephens departs from the original song, declaring her brand of femininity while adding her voice to the feminist tradition with this re-versioning. In much the same way, Stephens correlates the man's physical strength with his strength of character by declaring, "with all the muscle that yuh building / Yuh must be strong enough to lift your standards make me wanna hang around." In this piece, Stephens declares that her aim is simply to gain respect and not be judged by her sexuality. "I don't wanna be no guy / Just wanna be respected by the I", she sings. In so doing, her lyrics subvert stereotypical descriptions of femininity, as she asserts that a disconnect between sexy/sexual and serious (particularly the notion that a woman wearing a short skirt should not be taken seriously) is neither a marker of nor diminishes her potential. "Thong-thong-thong, don't mean a lack of common sense", she declares.

Stephens's lyrics also unearth new ground from which to interrogate issues concerning women that are most often told from the male perspective in dancehall. One of these is the story of the other woman – the matey – in "Tek Him Back". In most dancehall lore, the matey is an often vilified and satirized figure, maligned as a thief who is unable to gain a man of her own and bask in the achievement of being the "wife". Interestingly, while these songs by no means suggest that the man's seeking multiple partners is wrong, the woman who has to settle for part-time affections is described as lacking. While there are songs such as Mad Cobra's "Tek Him", which advises "a gyal man a run yuh dung gyal a nuh fi yuh fault / tek him, tek him gyal a nuh fi yuh fault", most of the songs in the genre decry the matey. As in "Matie" by Beenie Man, the matey figure is often seen as a blight upon society, as she lacks the qualities that would make her a good "wife". Stephens flips this portrait of the "matey" as scorned woman. "Tek Him Back" is delivered from the perspective of the "matey" who refuses to put up with the shortcomings of her lover and instead attempts to return him to the "wife". She gives up the man, not because of society's conventions about the other woman or any sense of morality, but because he does not live up to her expectations of what a good man should be.

Stephens proves equally disruptive to the patriarchal social order. Carolyn Cooper's *Sound Clash* also illustrates the revolutionary nature of dancehall if it is read through the right lens, or at least with the blinders and prejudices removed. In the chapter "'More Fire': Chanting Down Babylon from Bob Marley to Capleton" (Cooper 2004, 179–206), the author explores the line of fire that connects Capleton and other fire-brandishing deejays to Bob Marley. Noting that their fire is often mistakenly treated literally, Cooper explores the idea that deejays like Sizzla, Capleton and Anthony B are simply continuing to interrogate the sociopolitical structure as they chant against the ills of society, becoming Marley's ideological heirs. She argues:

> But, surely, without detracting from the distinctiveness of Bob Marley's sensibility and the profundity of his contribution to Jamaican and world culture, it must be appropriate to acknowledge the social, political, economic, and other conditions in Jamaica that combined to create his not-so-unique circumstances, against which he rebelled with such passion. These dehumanizing conditions remain potent social forces shaping the consciousness of a new generation of artists and constitute for them sources of inspiration, creativity, as well as despair. (Cooper 2004, 181–82)

Though Stephens is not among those known for brandishing fire, she is clearly among those who have inherited Marley's ideology in continuing to chant down Babylon. Songs such as "What a Day", "Sound of My Tears" and "The Other Cheek" securely place her in this category. Indeed, Stephens is more than linked in spirit, as in "What a Day" she calls on the cleansing power of fire hoping for that day after one has "bun down everyting" so that the society can "start clean".

Stephens's social commentary is often haunting and goes well beyond pointing fingers across the class divide. In "What a Day", which echoes Marley's "One Love", "Redemption Song" and John Lennon's "Imagine", she looks at the ills of society on all levels. The song rests social decay at the feet of corrupt politicians, religious "freaks", corrupt preachers as well as the "baby mother" and "baby father" phenomenon that has replaced real parenting. "What a Day" is easily the most poetic piece on the album, containing intense metaphoric language wrapped tightly around the rhythm. The deejay lists the numerous things of which she is tired, and she is particularly dismissive of the church as she laments:

> Tired a leavin church feelin like a just been robbed
> Two hours of ramblin' not much mention of God
> The richest man's the only one who does not have a job
> A bunch of righteous freaks extorting worse than a mob

She then promotes the vision of the world she would like to see, one where spirituality, as opposed to religious fanaticism, can flourish:

> I got a vision of a whole other plane
> Where the spiritual can flourish again
> I'm just waiting for the fire to rain
> Bun dung everyting an start clean

Even so, she is cognizant that this utopian ideal may never become a reality. The song therefore ends with the notion that this long visualized peace may be nothing more than wishful dreaming:

> Maybe hoping for a change is a dream
> Maybe life ain't as bad as it seems
> But if dreaming is the best I can do
> Then I'll be dreaming my whole life through

Though this may be a dream, it is pointed in labelling society's problems. Additionally, economics is subject to scrutiny in the line "when life is finally worth its cost". The statement plays with the idea of cost of living. It underscores the role that the cost of life itself and poverty plays in violence among the have nots. Like the revolutionary Rasta man, she sees herself as a voice of the people. The intro to "The Other Cheek" states:

> The people say dem a talk
> and nobady naa listen dem all along
> so dem want mi to put it in the form of a song
> Cause is like seh oonu betray wi trus'
> so here's to all of you from all of us

> (The people say they are talking
> and no one's been listening to them all along
> so they want me to put it in the form of a song
> 'Cause it's like you all betrayed our trust
> so here's to all of you from all of us)

Once again, she uses explicit lyrics to break loose, but this time for another kind of rebellion. The line "what the fuck you really thing a go happen" in "The Other Cheek" is deliberately disturbing, especially in a song containing no other obscenities. The name of the song itself calls on the power of the religious sensibilities that inform so much of the culture. Here Stephens overturns these as she suggests that simply turning the other cheek is unacceptable and implausible in Jamaica's socio-economic climate. Her statement

> Wid all di highway you a build an go t'rough
> You neva build a likkle avenue
> fi di yute dem earn a buck

sheds harsh light on the difference in opportunities between the rich and the poor while simultaneously casting doubt on projects such as "Highway 2000" as representative of progress.

In her chapter "'Lyrical Gun': Metaphor and Role-Play in Dancehall Culture" Cooper (2004, 145–78) ascribes a revolutionary impetus to the violent lyrics found in deejays who chuck badness, as they continue in the tradition of the rudie. Rather than merely being a gun-toting criminal, being a "gansta" also implies ideas of rebellion carried from the tradition of the rude bwoi, who is opposed to law and order because he finds it impossible to survive inside the bowels of law and order. It is this identity that allows Bounty Killer to simultaneously sing about bloody brutality while declaring himself "The Poor People Governor". In dancehall culture, great "badness" comes with great responsibility, which seems to reflect the real-life situation wherein area dons double as area caretakers.

Stephens's lyrics also grant her kinship with these deejays. This aspect can be found throughout *Gangsta Blues*. Whether she sings of being broken-hearted or being in love, there is often a line declaring her role as warrior or "gangsta", for example, as she threatens to "pop off" (shoot) or step in the neck of any who dares to challenge her. She is most clearly seated in this tradition through "Gangsta Gyal", a duet with Spragga Benz on that album. It is especially in this song that the complexity of the gansta definition comes fully to bear.

Throughout most of the album, Stephens's use of gangsta aligns with the definition of gangsta as revolutionary, as rudie, as protector of the people. The gangsta gyal not only defends her man inside and outside of the courtroom but also carries his weapon – a subterfuge necessary to evade the police – and will use it if she has to. To the urgings of Spragga Benz, Stephens sings:

> Mi a bag up di chronic
> Till mi finga dem stuck togedda wid all a di gum
> Mi a wipe down di clip an a load di bullet
> While you a gwine ile up di gun
>
> (I'm bagging up the chronic
> Until my fingers are stuck together with all the gum
> I'm wiping down the clip and loading the bullet
> While you are oiling up the gun)

The two are working in unison with their roles. Spragga Benz's segment, in which the deejay is equivocal about his commitment, highlighting that while his gangsta gyal is special, he has other women, though with this woman "if it come down to it / she wi buss di tek (gun)". True, he does not illustrate what he means by "it may come down to", whether it is a battle between his gangsta gyal and other women or a shoot-out with the police. "Gangsta Gyal" therefore outlines that this definition is not all positive. But then no definition of the gangsta or rudie as revolutionary figure ever was. Gangstas and rude bwois are not merely maligned as criminals, they in fact engage in criminality. Therefore, as revolutionary as gangsta poetics may be, they contain an underlying destructive element.

Though gangsta references are found throughout the album, suggesting that the gangsta nature is pivotal to Stephens's definition of femininity, there is no attempt to eradicate sensitivity. Several songs reveal vulnerable moments, crying and being heart broken. In "Can't Breathe" Stephens displays the classic bitterness attributed to the woman scorned. This song makes it clear that being a gangsta does not mean she cannot cry, as she admits that she wants to hurt her ex-lover and make him "suffer" and "cry like [she] did". Indeed, Stephens defines this "badness" as part of what makes her a desirable woman. When comparing herself to the new woman, she deejays:

> She cyaa cook like me
> Cyaa jook like me
> No, nuh know yuh in and out like a book like me
> She nuh full a style like mi
> Cyan mek yuh smile like mi
> An she cyan never give yuh a beautiful chile like mi
> She nuh tight like mi
> Cyan fling it up right like mi
> An if mi buck ar one a way, she cyan fight like mi
>
> (She can't cook like me
> Can't even have sex like me
> No, doesn't know you in and out like a book like me
> She's not filled with style like me
> Can't make you smile like me
> And she can't ever give you a beautiful child like me
> She's not tight like me

Can't even fling it up right like me
And if I corner her, she can't fight like me)

Thus, she promotes the idea that the desirable woman has traditional domestic skills and so can "cook" and "jook" and is also sensitive and fertile. The crowning moment comes however in the final line, when the gangsta in her "pops off" and she threatens violence. The two – domesticity and violence – are not seen as contradictory but, rather, complimentary. Through *Gangsta Blues*, we realize that Stephens has brought a feminist (or even womanist) definition to the gangsta. Many of the ideas she espoused in this groundbreaking album are repeated throughout her repertoire. What she presents is a revolutionary take on the feminine; a blending of the unsettling violence of the gangsta in a refusal to simply accept any hand she is dealt; a willingness to cry; and the duty to speak for those she finds voiceless. Stephens presents the idea that women are not merely voiceless beings victimized by patriarchal dancehall. Her lyrics declare her a gangsta and a lover, and unmistakably a woman able to wine and rhyme with the best of them.

NOTE

1. All songs by Stephens discussed here are on the album *Gangsta Blues*.

REFERENCES

Allsopp, Richard, and Jeannette Allsopp. 1996. *Dictionary of Caribbean English Usage*. Oxford: Oxford University Press.
Chevannes, Barry. 2001. *Learning to Be a Man: Culture, Socialization, and Gender Identity in Five Caribbean Communities*. Barbados: University of the West Indies Press.
Cooper, Carolyn. 1995. *Noises in the Blood: Orality, Gender and the "Vulgar" Body of Jamaican Popular Culture*. London: Macmillan.
———. 2004. *Sound Clash: Jamaican Dancehall Culture at Large*. New York: Palgrave Macmillan.
Irigaray, Luce, and Carolyn Burke. 1985. *This Sex Which Is Not One*. Ithaca: Cornell University Press.
Manuel, Peter, Kenneth M. Bilby and Michael D. Largey. 2006. *Caribbean Currents: Caribbean Music from Rumba to Reggae*. Philadelphia, PA: Temple University Press.
Ostriker, Alicia Suskin. 1986. *Stealing the Language: The Emergence of Women's Poetry in America*. Boston: Beacon Press.

Pinkola Estés, Clarissa. 1992. *Women Who Run with the Wolves: Myths and Stories of the Wild Woman Archetype*. New York: Ballantine Books.

Shirley, Tanya. 2014. *The Merchant of Feathers*. Leeds: Peepal Tree Press.

Stanley Niaah, Sonjah. 2010. *Dancehall: From Slaveship to Ghetto*. Ottawa: University of Ottawa Press.

DISCOGRAPHY

Beenie Man, vocalist. 1999. "Matie". Track 1 on *Ruff 'n' Tuff*. Fuel 2000.

Mad Cobra, vocalist. 1991. "Tek Him". Digital-B label, DBT. 9, vinyl 12-inch. www.discogs.com.

Shabba Ranks, vocalist. 1991. "Gone Up". Track 5 on *As Raw as Ever*. Sony Records.

Stephens, Tanya, vocalist. 2004. *Gangsta Blues*. Compact disc. VP Records.

PART 2

"STILL #1 WITH A #2 PENCIL" PRODUCING AND DISSEMINATING KNOWLEDGE

CHAPTER 4

"The Sound of My Tears"
Tanya Stephens and the Meanings of Crying

ANNA KASAFI PERKINS

> Tears represent a metaphor for human feeling. There is not a person alive who has not wondered about the meaning of tears and what they say about who we are. Thousands of songs have been composed about them; almost every movie worth remembering is one that stimulates the flow of tears. Yet despite the fascination with this subject, very few people understand their own tears, much less those of others they are close to.
>
> (Kottler 1996)

> [*Gangsta Blues*] is more likely to remain an underground hit, reaching fans who already cherish Ms. Stephens' pinched but expressive voice and earthy obsessions: one spoken-word piece describes a 10-second sexual encounter that ends in snores (his) and tears (hers).
>
> (Sanneh 2004)

ONLY HUMAN BEINGS CRY TEARS (AI/YAI WAATA[1] [eye water], as Jamaicans refer to them) in response to emotional events. Yet one of the puzzles surrounding human emotions is the meaning of our emotional tears, and there is a particular lack of research into adult tears (Vingerhoets and Bylsma 2016). Importantly, the reasons human beings cry reveal much about human nature and our moral values or our sense of morality (Vingerhoets and Bylsma 2016; Kottler 1996). Without desire, there are no tears; for both gaining and losing what we desire brings tears (Lutz 1999). Lutz (1999) claims that our best understandings of tears come not from the medical sciences but rather from poetry, art,[2] fiction, drama, and cinema. Myth, religion, and music also contribute important meanings to and about shedding tears. Metaphors, images, catchphrases and arguments abound as part of our culture and a culture of tears. In this regard, various approaches are deployed in the study of emotional tears, and Vingerhoets and Bylsma (2016) recommend a multidisciplinary approach to such research. One important approach to the puzzle of tears that is lacking is perhaps best described as ethico-cultural.[3] Such an approach would unveil and critically examine the meaning and value of emotional tears in a particular cultural context, such as Jamaica, and, by extension, the Caribbean.

PURPOSE OF THE CHAPTER

To the best of my knowledge, no research has been done on emotional tears within the context of the anglophone Caribbean, much less from an ethico-cultural perspective, which takes the question of morality and culture seriously. This chapter, therefore, begins such an exploration in order to make the contextual meaning and value of tears more transparent. In so doing, it contributes to the burgeoning theoretical perspectives on emotional tears in the Caribbean context. It deploys selected items from Tanya Stephens's discography as windows into the ethico-culture of tears, unveiling the values and attitudes embedded in emotional crying for Jamaicans, and perhaps, by extension, Caribbean people.

In 2004 and 2006, Stephens released two hard-hitting parental advisory-labelled albums – *Gangsta Blues* (2004) and *Rebelution* (2006). The former album, it can be argued, was awash with tears, literal crying ("sounz a tiers" [sounds of tears]) as well as descriptions of situations that elicited tears from adults. One track on *Gangsta Blues* – "Sound of My Tears" – gives its name to this chapter. The album *Rebelution*, while less overtly tear-filled, picks up and carries forward similar themes in a fashion that can help to fill out a Jamaican taxonomy of emotional tears. Interestingly, the release of these two albums occurred in the midst of a "reboot" of a thrust then being made by the government of Jamaica to impact the values and attitudes of society through a national values and attitudes campaign (Grey 2008). At that time, there were concerns with corruption in high places and tears fell copiously, as the next section illustrates. (Other Stephens albums, including *Infallible* [2012] and *Guilty* [2013] also contain tear-jerking tracks, but *Gangsta Blues* and *Rebelution* more explicitly treat with tears and crying, as is discussed below.)

TEARFUL CRYING

Vingerhoets and Bylsma (2016. 207) point out that, during the human lifespan, crying undergoes important changes while maintaining several important characteristics. Emotional crying, as they refer to crying, is "the shedding of tears from the lacrimal apparatus, in the absence of any irritation in the eyes". Crying is often accompanied by temporary changes in the facial muscles, vocalizations and sobbings. Loud vocalizations are often referred to by Jamaicans as "baalin" (bawling) or "kow baalin" (cow bawling), and some kinds of baalin come from the depth of our beli batam (depths of our being).

Tears are believed to replace the acoustical crying of infants, which is geared at forming an acoustical umbilical cord with caregivers and soliciting care and assistance. While adult tears replace this acoustical crying, they continue to be targeted at significant others. Later, as children develop and display feelings of guilt and remorse, their empathetic skills sharpen. They may then cry because they can sympathize with the suffering of others, especially suffering they themselves cause. However, as children get older, there is usually a decrease in the crying arising from physical pain or discomfort. Physical pain, therefore, does not play as significant a role in tears for adults and the elderly. Tears can be cathartic, and, at least in some measure, can help us feel better. They can be a source of deliverance even as they express despair. Crying can turn us away from the source of our hurt and allow us to turn inwards (Lutz 1999). We turn away from the world and concentrate on our bodily sensations, coming to know more about ourselves and what we desire.

Older adults tend to cry increasingly for positive reasons; experiences that give their lives depth and meaning – usually associated with feelings of joy, elation, pride and gratitude – serve to draa yai waata (bring tears). "Tears thus may actually reflect feelings that cannot be expressed or consummated in other behaviors" (Vingerhoets and Bylsma 2016, 207). Indeed, crying is part of "an embellished language system that augments spoken words". Kottler (1996) describes crying as a dialect of a larger family of languages of emotional expression like smiling, gesturing and shouting: "Crying exists primarily to communicate that which cannot be said with strictly verbal language". Tom Lutz (1999, 24) highlights several ways that tears are deployed: "Tears are a kind of language, a primary, and often primal, form of communication. The language of crying can accomplish many different ends, expressing not just our distress but our demands, not just our desire to be understood but our desire to evade detection. Our crocodile tears can be used to ensnare, to confuse, to extort, to deceive."

Clearly, the potential of events to give life meaning makes them important in eliciting adult tears. These kinds of tears indicate important societal values and virtues. They can also be shown to indicate a trajectory of human moral development, with growth from crying mainly for egocentric reasons later broadening to more societal and humanistic reasons (sentimental and moral).[4] It is worth recognizing that tears are aimed at an audience and demand a reaction (Lutz 1999). Even tears shed in private have an imagined audience (as several of Stephens's tracks demonstrate). Invariably, crying elicits a response, even if it is a studied indifference, a pretence of no response.

The power of overwhelming emotions to elicit tears appears to vary, depending on gender, age, personality, culture. In a cross-cultural study of thirty-seven countries, including Jamaica, van Hermert et al. (2011) conclude that cross-cultural differences in crying should be seen as the result of differing tolerance for self-disclosure and less strict rules around displaying emotions. Countries with higher levels of extraverted personality types reported more crying. People tended to cry more frequently when they live in wealthier, more democratic, more individualistic countries with more demanding climates or countries with higher levels of extraversion. Several cultural and personal factors impact emotional crying and indicate moral values.

MORAL VALUES

The late renowned sociologist Carl Stone maintained that human behaviour is significantly shaped by norms and values. Values define for a society the things for which people strive and attach great meaning and significance (Stone 1992). Norms set rules of behaviour designed to express a commitment to the society's underlying values. Stone identifies dominant values in culture as those that relate to major areas of social space, such as family life, education, work and occupational activity, gender relations, class and ethnic or race relations, religion, mass communication, artistic and creative expression, sports, recreation, and politics. He argues that what is usually perceived as a breakdown or absence of norms and values in a particular social space may actually be a misunderstanding of changes in norms and values and consequent changes in behaviour traits and patterns (Stone 1992).

NORMS AND VALUES

Sociology is not the usual domain for the discussion of values and norms. Ethicists speak more precisely of moral values and attempt to say why human beings are so concerned about them. Catholic ethicist Daniel Maguire defines ethics as "the art-science which seeks to bring sensitivity and method to discovering moral value" (Maguire 1989, 533). Indeed, our human consciousness brings with it the task of having to sort through and pick from among competing values to determine what options are moral or not. Thus, to be concerned about values and attitudes is to be ethically driven, and is, clearly, not to be seen as the exclusive purview of ethicists or sociologists but rather should be embraced by all of humanity. Moral values are those things which are essential to proper human living and being. Moral values include such virtues as honesty, justice, charity, fortitude and temperance. Values are not a matter of doing just deeds or courageous acts, however, but rather of being just and courageous (McBrien 1994). They are things which we must possess in order to be fully human. Thus, one need not be physically attractive to be fully human, but one must be loving. One need not be a fast runner to be fully human, but one must be respectful of human life. Where such values are not upheld or norms are violated, the resulting hurt, anger or discomfort may lead to tears, as Stephens so forcefully demonstrates.

BAWLING BEFORE BEATING

A telling Jamaican case sets the stage for discussing Stephens and tears. In 2007, shortly after the breaking of the so-called Cuban light-bulb scandal, there was an editorial cartoon in the *Gleaner*. It shows "Mama P" (the then leader of the opposition, Portia Simpson Miller) asleep in a bed, while then energy minister Phillip Paulwell, depicted as a baby, is seen hiding under it. Then junior energy minister Kern Spencer, in nappies and all, is sitting on the floor in a pool of liquid. (It is unclear what the nature of the liquid is – tears from crying, or urine because he has wet himself out of fear? Under the circumstances, it may well have been both.) Anyway, Kern is just washing the place away with tears. And Paulwell says to him, perhaps in utter amazement, "Yuh ah cry an yuh nuh get beaten yet!" (You are crying and you have not been spanked yet!) Many Jamaicans may have wondered at the meaning of Kern's tears (Jones 2007):[5] "A we im a baal fa?" (What is he crying for/about?) In point of fact, the cartoon lampoons Spencer, who cried in Parliament as allegations of corruption were exposed by members of the ruling party.

Spencer later claimed that he was crying out of frustration caused by his inability to answer his critics on the floor of Parliament (Luton 2007). What is clear is that the cartoonist was making fun of Kern's tears while playing on the fact that, in countries like Jamaica where corporal punishment is de jure, children cry out of fear in anticipation of an imminent flogging, perhaps with the hope of reducing the punishment through an appeal to the sympathy of the disciplinarian. Sadly, anecdotal evidence suggests that the response to such anticipatory weeping is, invariably, a harsher beating accompanied by such commentary as "Yu wa mi gi yu supn fi baal fa?" (Do you want me to give you a real reason to cry")

TANYA STEPHENS AND TEARS

Stephens presents tears, crying, or bawling in two broad contexts on her albums *Gangsta Blues* and *Rebelution*: intrapersonal/personal/interpersonal and interpersonal/social/societal. In this regard, she exploits the fact that crying has become "the stuff of a million metaphors" (Lutz 1999, 25), and so her descriptions and commentaries are colourful and meaningful, as will be demonstrated. A rough taxonomy of the thirty-seven tracks across the two albums gives an indication of the weighting of tears for Stephens. *Gangsta Blues* is made up of seventeen tracks. Of these, seven (41 per cent) fall into the first category and four (24 per cent), the second. *Rebelution*, which has less direct referencing of crying, has four (20 per cent) that fall into the first grouping, and one (5 per cent) falling into the second. The remaining songs, unsurprisingly, detail events and activities that may elicit emotional tears, even if Stephens does not explicitly reference this through actual sounds or word images. Of course, some of the tracks are a mixture of more than one crying type, pointing to the interpenetration of the intrapersonal/personal and the sociopolitical. Her tracks seem to confirm the ethico-cultural prominence given to crying tears in the Jamaican society.

WAASTID WAATA

In "It's a Pity", Stephens laments, "It mek mi sad if hafi wies so much [yai] waata . . . I tink di too a wi cud mek a biyootiful daata" (It makes me sad to have to waste so much [eye] water . . . I think the two of us could have a beautiful daughter). The antecedent for this statement is her regret that both herself and the man she is interested in (or is secretly having an affair with) are in other committed relationships where "the stupid rules of men" have enforced expectations of monogamy and faithfulness. She regrets the circumstances that have caused her to waste so many tears. She clues us in to the Jamaican belief in the possibility of wasting our tears. Tears embody such an invaluable, powerful and dangerous substance (Lutz 1999) that many a child is cautioned not to cry needlessly as there may come a day – such as at the death of a loved one – when the commodity is required and will not be forthcoming. Crying should only be over things "that matter". And so, tears should not be wasted as a salve to the consequences of men and women fearing being caught in a dance of dishonesty coming out of a wrestle with unnecessary (and unnatural) monogamy. At the same time, telling someone "yu av yai waata fi wies" (you have tears to waste) dismisses that which is causing them pain and sorrow as not being worth the tears being shed. This points to contending values in a given context.

Similarly, Jamaicans reject simulation – "crocodile tears" – like the dishonest displays in court of a "gangsta gal", who is prepared to do anything to defend her man (I wuda lai pon di stan / wuda even krai pon di stan / tel dem mi gyai is innocent" (I would lie on the [witness] stand / would even cry on the stand / tell them my guy is innocent). The importance of honesty is reinforced in the fairy tale "Little White Lie", in which a woman is crying because "it is killing her inside" to lie about the paternity of her child. In Jamaican terms, she has given her partner "a jacket" and she lives in fear of being caught, not to mention the potential emotional and psychological harm that could be wrought on her child as a result: "maybe one day you'll end up on Ricki Lake / but, baby, that's a chance your mama's willing to take". The mother justifies her choice because she believes "the man who thinks he's [the child's] father is a much better man". "Better" often includes the notion of being better off and more stable. The female voice in "It's a Pity", however, rejects the possibility of bringing into the world "an innocent likl youth and cannot tell her di truth (about her paternity)".

SPILT MILK

Of course, concerns with waastin yai waata (wasting tears) are to be distinguished from concerns with behaviour deemed "jrai-yai" (dry-eye[d]). Such behaviour is barefaced and unrepentant and can elicit myriad tears. Many of the interpersonal relationships described by Stephens lead to much crying because of the jrai-yai behaviour of either a male or a female protagonist. Several of these are the wife-matey stories, where the matey berates the wife for poor performance leading to the matey needing to fill the breach, for example, in songs such as "Still a Go Lose", "Put It on You" and "To the Rescue". There is even what appears to be a real expletive-filled message left on Stephens's answering machine by an irate wife berating Stephens for her own barefaced capture of an errant spouse in the performance piece, "The Message". This apparently personal experience and the brashness in making it public elevates above "fake news" the fictional and fictionalized accounts presented in *Gangsta Blues* and *Rebelution*.

Among the "million metaphors" and popular sayings that Stephens exploits to demonstrate such jrai-yai male behaviour are "no use crying over spilt milk" in songs such as "Spilt Milk", "cry me a river" in "Damn You" and "big girls don't cry" in "Can't Breathe". In "Spilt Milk", the female voice roundly rejects an ex, who comes crawling back after unceremoniously dumping her. She calls upon the universe and Jah to punish him who left her "when she needed him the most", declaring,

> Now you sitting here crying
> Mi naa krai fi yu
> Naa baal fi yu.

Ironically, it is the male who is crying from remorse and asking for forgiveness. This male weeping is highly unusual, because Jamaican men have less of a tendency to cry than Jamaican women (Hemert, Van de Vijver and Vingerhoets 2011). Indeed, Jamaicans mock people who are judged to cry too much or too easily by calling them "krai krai biebi" (cry cry baby). This mockery is enshrined in a childhood ditty flung at many a child on the playground:

> Krai krai biebi
> muun shain, daalin
> tek aaf yu shuuz an go tu yu bed
> Wen yu go tu Sonde skuul
> yu tiicha kaal yu a big dopi fuul
>
> (Cry, cry baby, moonshine darling,
> Take off your shoes and go to bed

When you go to Sunday School
[Even] the teacher will call you a big silly fool [for crying so much])

To be sure, one of the taunts hurled at Kern Spencer from across the floor in the Lower House was "krai krai biebi". Kern was ridiculed incessantly for the ease with which he cried, the worse so for being a man who cried in public. Many dismissed his performance as rather unmasculine, and him as "soft".

Furthermore, according to Stephens's chronicling, there are two types of unrepentant male behaviour that have women dissolving into tears: selfish sexual (under)performance and betrayal. Betrayal of the worst kind is recounted in "Damn You", where a woman turns up at the wedding of the lover who had been with her the night before. She had mistakenly thought she "was a[n important] part of [his] life but now [the pastor] pronounced [them] man and wife". In her distress, she felt that "the wind pounding in [her] ears seemed to be laughing at [her] river of tears". She flees in shame lest she "flood the church with the tears [she had] cried", for she had seen "the emotions in [his] eyes" for his bride. He [the "little Judas"] had told her "believable lies". So, she declares she will waste no tears on such a man – "no baalin or krain" as he is not worth it, clearly. Yet at the same time, given the power of tears, it is best that she not "baal fi him", because it is a serious threat not to be taken lightly when a Jamaican woman tells you that she "wil baal yai waata fi yu" (she will cry tears for you). This is similar to when a mother pleads to a child not to let her tears fall to the ground. Such tears can lead to the miscreant's undoing or total destruction. At the same time, such kow baalin can be deemed necessary and healthy. For grief can "swell the heart", causing it to burst, if it does not gain expression through yai waata. Jamaicans believe that tears serve as a transport stream for waste caused by the grief and need to be released for total well-being (Sobo 1996).

The literal sound of such kow baalin accompanies Stephens's spoken word account (skit) of a "ten seconds flat" sexual encounter which had started as a fantastically promising one-night stand, but ends prematurely (for her) with the underwhelming lover curled up in a snore-filled, self-satisfied sleep, selfishly oblivious to her, supine and lonely but for her voluminous tears trying in vain to wash away the disappointment of unfulfilled desires ("Damn You").[6] In "What's Your Story", Stephens gives the female side/response to Beres Hammond's hit song, "Double Trouble", which is about the wayward husband who disregarded all his spouse's preparations for their anniversary celebrations. After all her efforts to find him prove futile, her anger dissolves into fear, causing her to "staat baal pon di fluor" (curl up on the floor crying). Ironically, he turns up with his mouth filled with lines culled from the very same Beres song, unimaginative and forgetful that she herself had bought him the album. The autobiographical "Intro" on *Gangsta Blues* gets very personal in referring to incidents that have taught Stephens wisdom and caused her "to shed a few tears". This crying could be an indication of hard work and stick-to-it-iveness, as expressed in having given "blood, sweat and tears" that she had to put into her success. She is also referring to the painful experiences with her "so-called friends" who quickly desert her when the going gets tough. Despite this, Stephens proclaims that she was now back even stronger. She picks this theme up again in the pugnacious, yet revealing, "Who Is Tanya" track.

CHEEKY TEARS

In her foray into sociopolitical critique, Stephens "turns the other cheek" by asking "Do you expect me to turn the other cheek?" In "The Other Cheek", she asks a poignant question, perhaps rhetorically, on behalf of people living in inner-city, volatile communities, like Rema, Jungle and [Dun]kirk:

> Do you expect me to
> turn the other cheek?
> Taste my tears and admit defeat?
> Do you expect me to listen
> when you speak?
> You never ever practise what you preach.

Besides alluding to the Gospel according to Matthew 5:39, Stephens paints a picture of tears running down the faces of the poor and dispossessed in inner-city Kingston. These persons cry not from personal loss or hurt but out of anger and frustration with a system that makes them into non-persons, thus devaluing their humanity. They experience social exclusion, which Horace Levy (2007) describes as the sense of having been abandoned by society – a painful experience. As the victims of social exclusion, these people not only feel abandoned and beaten down, but ignored and voiceless. So, Stephens asks on their behalf, what is expected of them? Are they simply to not retaliate against the direct harm that is being done to them by the wider society? Should they swallow their tears of frustration and give in? Au contraire. There is defiance at the heart of this song. The people for whom Stephens speaks will not give up; they will not admit defeat – not even in the face of a system that is actively working against them. Sadly, their striving may involve some unpleasant consequences, not only for the powerful in the society but also for themselves and for others like them. Stephens voices the warning that possessing social, economic and political power cannot protect us from those who feel excluded and devoid of power. "Warn Dem" delivers the message of doom that poverty is everybody's problem. Bourne (2011) would caution care in any too-easy-link between poverty and violent crime in Jamaica, however. His research leads him to conclude that people in society engage in criminal activities as a way of escaping frustration born out of inequitable social structures. Bourne urges Jamaicans to recognize that we cannot stem the crime issue without simultaneously dealing with the issue of economic marginalization and social exclusion. The society needs transformation in all dimensions – social, political and economic – so Jamaica can be a place for all Jamaicans, not just the powerful.

Similarly, the actual "sound of tears" is suggested in the piece by the same name on *Gangsta Blues*, which evokes an image that Jamaicans see so often on the news, of a woman holding her belly and bawling. In "Do You Still Care", Stephens makes women cringe as she tells the tale of how "Bigga" was brought up:

> Boys were supposed to be tough
> Girls were trophies every man always kept a few of
> When he was hurt and the tears would sting in his eyes
> His mother said "Stop di noise, yuh a girl? Real boys don't cry!"
> He learned in order to be a man he had to know how to fight
> And had some very definitive rules bout what's wrong or right
> He never had the luxury of being able to choose
> So, to him for being different, there was no excuse.

She critiques elegantly the socialization of boys and men that divorces them from their feelings, especially the ability to cry. The key proponents of such (un)manly behaviour are the mothers. Such ways of being male damage the male psyche, alienating them from their emotions and, in turn, contributing to their objectification of women ("trophies"). These are the same cultural values that made the parliamentarian Kern Spencer the butt of much criticism and ridicule, for his tears rendered him "(not) a real boy/man".

TEAR-FILLED ENDING

Song lyrics express a facet of our culture of tears and, in turn, affect our understanding of and experience of crying (Lutz 1999). Stephens, through her album *Gangsta Blues*, which by its title suggests sadness and probably tears ("the blues"), is saturated with tear-filled renditions surrounding the human condition and the myriad feelings that elicit yai waata. According to Vingerhoets and Bylsma, "Feelings of loss and powerlessness seem to remain important for crying throughout the lifespan" (2016, 208). These include losses, romantic breakups, weddings and the like, as the various protagonists in Stephens's music demonstrate. Conflicts, personal failures, criticism, social abandonment and rejection are also important for eliciting adult tears (and as she warns, much more than tears). Tears also do express complex, contradictory desires or contending values, and so yai waata can be deemed to be wasted on some things that lack value.

It is evident that Jamaicans view yai waata as deeply meaningful, powerful and potent, but conforming to the law of conservation of matter: not unlimited. Through yai waata, Jamaicans express our feelings of sadness, anger, frustration, powerlessness and resolve. Through our tears, we are connected to the larger human family, as crying is a universal and typical human expression of emotion. To point out that tears give expression to pain and sorrow is not to ignore the fact that our tears also express feelings that are of a more positive kind: joy, relief, pride, ecstasy. All in all, our tears speak and speak loudly about what it is we value, who or what we consider worthwhile, to the extent that their loss (or gain) brings us to tears. Tears and values go hand in hand, for crying out loud.

ACKNOWLEDGEMENTS

An earlier version of this paper, entitled "Tasting Tears and (Not) Admitting Defeat: Promoting Values and Attitudes through the Music of Tanya Stephens?", was originally delivered as the inaugural lecture of the Centre for Social Ethics, St Michael's Theological College, Jamaica, 12 January 2008.

NOTES

1. Jamaican Language Unit/Cassidy spelling will be used for words rendered in Patwa/Jamaican.
2. Tears were primarily a religious subject in early modern and Renaissance painting

(Lutz 1999, 24). Lutz also notes that tears are considered sacred and redemptive (19).
3. This term is not found in the literature but is rather crafted by the author to capture the intersection between ethical meanings as expressed through human culture.
4. This trajectory is very much in line with Lawrence Kohlberg's classic theory of human ethical development.
5. Jones refers to other famous Jamaican politicians, like the late Roger Clarke, member of Parliament for the People's National Party, who cried at the National Arena after he lost the vice-presidential elections.
6. Stephens treats with this particular trope of the self-praising sexually poor performing males in several of her albums. Among her more trenchant deliveries are "Draw fi Mi finger", "Handle the Ride" and "You Nuh Ready fi Dis Yet".

REFERENCES

Bourne, Paul A. 2011. "Re-Visiting the Crime-and-Poverty Paradigm: An Empirical Assessment with Alternative Perspectives". *Current Research Journal of Economic Theory* 3 (4): 99–117.

Grey, Sandra Melissa Nicola. 2008. "Social Capital Formation: A Case Study of the Jamaican Values and Attitudes Campaign". *Social and Economic Studies* 57 (2):149–70.

Jones, Ken. 2007. "Playing 'Bawl' in the House". *Gleaner*, 25 November. http://old.jamaica-gleaner.com/gleaner/20071125/news/news3.html.

Kottler, Jeffrey A. 1996. *The Language of Tears*. San Francisco: Jossey-Bass.

Levy, Horace. 2007. "The Ethics of Social Exclusion". In *Ethical Perspectives in Caribbean Business*, edited by Noel Cowell, Gavin Chen and Stanford Moore, 84–94. Kingston: Arawak.

Luton, Daraine. 2007. "Kern Wept: Former State Minister Jolted by Cuban Bulb Saga". *Gleaner*, 7 November. http://old.jamaica gleaner.com/gleaner/20071107/lead/lead1.html.

Lutz, Tom. 1999. *Crying: The Natural and Cultural History of Tears*. New York: Norton.

Maguire, Daniel. 1989. "Ethics: How to Do It". In *Introduction to Christian Ethics: A Reader*, edited by Ronald P. Hamel and Kenneth R. Himes, OFS, 533–50. New York: Paulist Press.

McBrien, Richard. 1994. *Catholicism: New Edition*. New York: HarperCollins.

Sanneh, Kelefa. 2004. "Music: Playlist; Reggae's Riddims and Crews. *New York Times*, 23 May. https://www.nytimes.com/2004/05/23/arts/music-playlist-reggae-s-riddims-and-crews.html.

Sobo, Elisa J. 1996. "The Jamaican Body's Role in Emotional Experience and Sense

Perception: Feelings, Hearts, Minds, Nerves". *Culture, Medicine, Psychiatry: An International Journal of Comparative Cross-Cultural Research* 20 (3): 313–42.

Stone, Carl. 1992. "Values, Norms and Personality Development in Jamaica". 23 March. http://gtuwi.tripod.com/stonearticle.htm.

Van Hemert, Dianne A., Fons J.R. Van de Vijver and Ad. J.J.M Vingerhoets. 2011. "Culture and Crying: Prevalences and Gender Differences". *Cross Cultural Research* 45 (4): 399–431.

Vingerhoets, Ad J.J., and Lauren M. Bylsma. 2016. "The Riddle of Human Emotional Crying: A Challenge for Emotion Researchers". *Emotion Review* 8 (3): 207–17.

DISCOGRAPHY

Hammond, Beres, vocalist. 1993. "Double Trouble". MP3 audio. Track 2 on *Sweetness*. VP Records.

Stephens, Tanya, vocalist. 1997. "Yuh Nuh Ready fi Dis Yet". MP3 audio. Track 1 on *Too Hype*. VP Records.

———. 1998. "Draw fi Mi Finger". MP3 audio. Track 1 on *Ruff Rider*. VP Records.

———. 1998. "Handle the Ride". MP3 audio. Track 2 on *Ruff Rider*. VP Records.

———. 2004. "Can't Breathe". MP3 audio. Track 13 on *Gangsta Blues*. VP Records.

———. 2004. "Intro". MP3 audio. Track 1 on *Gangsta Blues*. VP Records.

———. 2004. "It's a Pity". MP3 audio. Track 7 on *Gangsta Blues*. VP Records.

———. 2004. "Little White Lie". MP3 audio. Track 6 on *Gangsta Blues*. VP Records.

———. 2004. "The Other Cheek". MP3 audio. Track 15 on *Gangsta Blues*. VP Records.

———. 2004. "What's Your Story". MP3 audio. Track 12 on *Gangsta Blues*. VP Records.

———. 2006. "Damn You". MP3 audio. Track 7 on *Rebelution*. VP Records.

———. 2006. "Do You Still Care". MP3 audio. Track 15 on *Rebelution*. VP Records.

———. 2006. "Put It on You". MP3 audio. Track 3 on *Rebelution*. VP Records.

———. 2006. "Sounds of My Tears". MP3 audio. Track 14 on *Gangsta Blues*. VP Records.

———. 2006. "Spilt Milk". MP3 audio. Track 9 on *Rebelution*. VP Records.

———. 2006. "Still a Go Lose". MP3 audio. Track 5 on *Rebelution*. VP Records.

———. 2006. "To the Rescue". MP3 audio. Track 6 on *Rebelution*. VP Records.

———. 2006. "Warn Dem". MP3 audio. Track 16 on *Rebelution*. VP Records.

———. 2006. "Who Is Tanya". MP3 audio. Track 1 on *Rebelution*. VP Records.

CHAPTER 5

Tanya Stephens as Apostle of Critical Literacy

ADWOA NTOZAKE ONUORA AND **AJAMU NANGWAYA**

> Education either functions as an instrument which is used to facilitate integration of the younger generation into the logic of the present system and bring about conformity or it becomes the practice of freedom, the means by which men and women deal critically and creatively with reality and discover how to participate in the transformation of their world.
>
> (Freire 2009, 34)

IN HIS 1979 SONG "BABYLON SYSTEM", BOB MARLEY expresses similar sentiments as those captured in the quote above. Commenting on Babylon's system of mis-head-decaytion (to use Rastafari speak), Marley concludes:

> You can't educate I
> For no equal opportunity
> Talkin' 'bout my freedom
> People freedom (freedom) and liberty! (Bob Marley and the Wailers, 1979)

Like Freire, Marley decries the current system of education bequeathed to us by our former enslavers and maintained by the neocolonial native bourgeoisie during the current period of flag independence. This critique is continued in the song "Crazy Baldhead", when he sings:

> Build your penitentiary, we build your schools
> Brainwash education to make us the fools
> Hate is your reward for our love
> Telling us of your God above

Here, Marley also underscores the fact that the colonial educational project was not designed to free us from mental enslavement. Rather, instead of facilitating the type of critical consciousness raising needed to bring about a more socially just world, education has, for the most part, been about funnelling the African working class into a cult of normativity; one that has as its barometer of success approximation to the ruling class ethos, values and beliefs. Both Freire and Marley view the mainstream system of knowledge production as a tool for sustaining economic injustice, power inequities and social oppression. Their critiques, however, miss an important point: that members of the African working class are not simply passive recipients of colonial education. They are, by and large, implicated in perpetuating this colonial project of domination. They and other working class peoples in general have appropriated the "master's tools" (Lorde 1984, 112) through their unconscious investment in neoliberal educational paradigms.[1] Their uncritical absorption of texts that support an exploitative social, economic and political order has resulted in a situation where a majority of African educators fail to inspire learners to become agents of revolutionary social change. These educators are "graduating" learners who are incapable of imagining social alternatives outside of the politically and ideologically conservative paradigms that enchain humanity today.

There is a certain educational apartheid born out of the capitalist economic order that relies on a ready pool of exploitable labour. Ira Shor (borrowing from Galbraith) affirms this when he states that "education is situated in . . . larger conditions, where the economy is the 'decisive' factor influencing school policy and [educational] outcomes" (Shor 1999, 6). Consistent with the assertion above, he contends further that "if education were indeed neutral, boys and girls of all colours and classes would have . . . equal access as well as equal monies invested in their development" (5). This is, however, not the reality for members of the working class. For them, the structural barriers to educational access are many, and the inequitable outcomes of the current systems of knowledge production are glaring. The African working class and other racialized working-class groups are being primed by educational institutions to serve as the backbone of an exploitative economic system that relies on the continuation of class divisions for its survival. Those who operate within neoliberal educational paradigms tend to push back against any interrogative mindset or critical self-reflection within learning communities, because any critical questioning of the current social order may enable a climate that facilitates capitalism's ultimate demise.

When learners are equipped with the insight to read text in a way that identifies and exposes the ways in which social institutions perpetuate economic and social inequities, they are better prepared to challenge oppressive systems that perpetuate their suffering.

As agents of educational and social equity, we are concerned with finding pockets of resistance – both inside and outside the current learning systems in the Caribbean – that embolden learners from socially oppressed groups to become agents of transformation. In the absence of critical, radical and oppositional thought in dominant spaces of learning today, we question the extent to which educational processes in the Caribbean can be reshaped and used in the service of politicization, transformation and consciousness raising. How might reggae and dancehall be used to foster an understanding of intersectionality[2] as an analytical framework for advancing learner awareness of the material consequences of oppression? To what degree can reggae and dancehall serve as epistemological tools that can help learners hone critical thinking and organizing skills needed for revolutionary social change?

Drawing on the work of critical literacy theoreticians, we make a case for critical reggae and dancehall epistemology as a progressive and transformative educational approach that can spawn a reassessment and ultimate challenging of capitalism, racism, sexism and patriarchy. Critical reggae and dancehall epistemology, we contend, can serve as a corrective for the social and economic inequities that exist in the Caribbean today. To this end, we delineate a connection between critical literacy, Afro-indigenous orature, reggae and dancehall (Freire and Macedo 1987). More specifically, we explore the ways in which Caribbean learners can utilize reggae and dancehall as an Afro-indigenous sign system (Gee 1990) to facilitate social justice. A critical reggae/dancehall literacy programme of education could become the catalyst for radical social transformation and the liberation of the working class in the Caribbean.

CRITICAL LITERACY: A POLITICAL PEDAGOGY FOR THE "SOFARAZ"[3]

The term literacy refers to the reading and writing of texts as well as learning the mechanics of coding and encoding texts. Critical literacy, however, goes beyond this mechanistic approach where learners have a passive relationship with texts to which they are exposed (Onuora 2013). It is reading that encourages awareness of how the self has been historically and socially constituted in relation to and through systems of power (Shor 1999). Critical literacy is about developing readers' capacity to critically analyse and transform dominant paradigms that underlie modes of communication (Luke 2000).

According to Luke (2000, 6), "critical literacy has as its goal ideology critique and cultural analysis". Beyond this, however, it is concerned with problematizing issues that affect people's material realities. As a theoretical framework, critical literacy proffers a critique of dominant economic arrangements, as well as political and social institutions. To be critically literate, Morrell (2002, 73) writes, is to "understand the socially constructed meanings embedded in texts as well as the political and economic contexts in which texts are embedded". Critical literacy equips learners with the necessary analytical skills to identify hegemonic myths as well as uncover ways in which language can be used to reproduce and challenge prevailing social norms. It helps them to understand how texts are socially constructed and can therefore be reconstituted to create alternative ways of knowing (Luke 2000). Consequently, critical literacy facilitates the type of reflexive thinking that can engender in learners a more emancipated view of the world.

Critical literacy as a conceptual framework emerged out of the work of Brazilian educator and social justice advocate Paulo Freire. Born out of the context of marginalization experienced by sofaraz with whom Freire lived and worked in Latin America and Africa, the theory subsequently gained traction with leading scholars in the area, such as Ira Shor, Peter McLaren, Henry Giroux and sociologist R.W. Connel. In its ideological orientation, critical literacy is politicized literacy. Critical literacy helps learners to unmask abuses of power by various social actors. Its ultimate goal is to embolden learners to transform inequitable relations of power. In this regard, it is a theory and a practice that fulfils equity and social justice ends.

The rising inequalities and declining economic security of the working class in our midst (Johnson 2015) sets the stage for the politicization of literacy education in Jamaica and the wider Caribbean. In keeping with the social justice and progressive educational agenda of critical literacy, our position is that reggae and dancehall have the potential to advance knowledge about social issues facing the most disadvantaged in our society. As an Afro-indigenous sign system that emerged out of disenfranchised working-class communities, it can usher in the critical oppositional consciousness necessary to change inequitable arrangements that affect their social, economic and political status. Reggae and dancehall serve as key sources of ideas about justice, freedom, equity, dignity, respect and African liberation. They are expressed in idiomatic ways that resonate with the labouring classes. These musical genres can be useful in contributing to the formation of what John Foran (1997, 120) calls "political cultures of resistance". Cultures of opposition speak to the multiple sources of transgressive ideas that are essential in preparing the people for revolutionary social change. The cultural revolution with its inculcation of oppositional ethos, values, beliefs and sensibilities precedes the political revolution. Similarly, reggae and dancehall are valuable, enabling cultural resources in this respect.

"BEHOLD THE CHRONICLES OF TANYA": ADVANCING CURRICULA JUSTICE THROUGH REGGAE AND DANCEHALL

This section begins the task of exploring reggae and dancehall as sites from which to engage learners in the practice of critical literacy for social change. The body of work of Jamaican reggae and dancehall artiste Tanya Stephens will be used to demonstrate the relevance of both genres to social justice as well as the broadening of rights for specific sections of Jamaica's society, the Caribbean region and beyond. Though there are numerous artists who fall within this category, and whose songs can be used as learning tools that enact a progressive pedagogy, Stephens is one of the most potent female artistes in Jamaica. Her music can be used to "enable learners to acquire forms of critical practice that . . . interrogate, destabilize and disorganize dominant strategies of power" (McLaren 1992, 8). Stephens's body of work is consistently interrogative across a wide range of topics. Thus, it positions her as an ideal candidate for an exploration into the role of reggae and dancehall in engendering critical literacy.

The song "Do You Still Care" for instance, hones in on a number of human rights issues, facilitating greater awareness and understanding of systems of oppression and the resultant suffering, exclusion and division that social hierarchies have created among humans. It begins:

> Where Bubba grew up, kept his tobacco chewed up
> And when they use to hang ropes, they always kept two up
> Had crosses burning all night, like the Church blew up
> And if you didn't look like them, they would fuck you up
> Time passed and Bubba turned forty-years-old
> And all them Jack Daniels started taking a toll

> Seem like Bubba was about to make a final bow, none of his friends from the Klan couldn't help him now
> Family gathered at his bed side ready to sing the blues, when a doctor rushed in and said I got some news
> The good news is Bubba I've found you a liver
> Only bad news is it belongs to a nigga

In the above lines, fate is putting on a full display of its ironically morbid sense of humour by presenting Bubba with a literally existential, life and death decision. Bubba needs a liver in order to live, but it will come from a group who he and his Ku Klux Klan confederates have targeted with death and destruction. Indeed, his path to a new lease on life comes from the generosity of a despised and revolting "nigger". Here, the artiste brings into focus issues of white racism and its deadly consequences and encourages acceptance of difference.

Stephens is also critical of hegemonic masculinity and its collaborator heterosexism or heteronormativity. She highlights the ways in which these systems of domination have informed how men are supposed to operate in the world and relate to sexualities that violate the codes of compulsory heterosexuality:

> Where Bigga grew up boys were supposed to be tough
> Girls were trophies every man always kept a few of
> When he was hurt and the tears would sting in his eyes, his mother said "stop the noise yuh a girl? real boys don't cry"
> He learned in order to be a man he had to know how to fight
> And had some very definitive rules about what's wrong or right
> He never had the luxury of being able to choose
> So to him for being different there was no excuse
> Bigga was hustling on the corner, making some cash
> When he bumped into some beef that he had from the past
> He watched the guns raised and the bullets fly
> In disbelief as his friends all jumped in their rides
> Left him in the gutter didn't care if he died
> He was rescued by a car with plates that said "gay pride"
> It would have been fatal that shot in your head
> They saved your life though you always said "chi chi fi dead"
> *Chorus*
> Now do you care bout the clothes that they wear
> Would you rather if they left you there
> Do you still care what your friends wanna think if they see you hanging out with

> a queer
> Do you still care
> Does it still mean a lot now you're the one who's needing the help
> Do you still care
> Do you still find hard it to love your neighbor as you love yourself
> Now, tell me why can't you accept me as I am
> Just the way I am now

The above excerpt can be used in learning environments to spur critical reflection on how gender and sexual hierarchies are maintained through local language and behavioural practices. Terms like "chi chi man" (the Jamaican expression for homosexual males or men who have sex with men) may be shirked by a community of learners operating in socially conservative environments because of their pejorative undertone. However, they reflect valid indigenous ways of knowing about the world that are shaped by historical and contemporary realities of people in the Caribbean region. They can therefore be used to enhance learners' understanding of how language reflects, but is also reflective of, particular morals, values, attitudes and beliefs. Given the fact that language, just like identity, is mediated by culture, it too has the potential to reproduce dominance. A critical reading of reggae artistes' lyrics such as this will allow for the cataloguing of emerging vernacular so that learners can unpack their culturally specific meanings. Facilitators of learning can also use songs like these as a pedagogical tool to engage learners in substantive gender analysis. To this end, they serve as fodder for analysis on the material consequences of hegemonic masculinity, femininity and hetero-patriarchy (Luke 2000; Shor 1999; Crichlow 2004).

Stephens also expresses a queer and polyamorous sensibility in her song "It's a Pity". The song is a critique of the politics of respectability[4] peddled by religious and other social actors who pander to bourgeois standards of sexual morality. "It's a Pity" is one of the most forward-thinking songs about exploring and embracing non-traditional sexual or conjugal arrangements in open defiance of bourgeois, normative ideas on sexual proprieties:

> It's a pity, you already have a wife
> And me done have a man inna mi life
> (And I already have a man in my life)
> Rude boy, it's such a pity, yow
> I say, it is such a pity, you already have yuh wife

> And me have a one man inna mi life
> Rude boy, it is a pity . . .
> Who knows? Maybe one day the world will be evolved enough
> We'll share you in a civilized manner between the two of us
> But until then I would a love see you again
> Me know we have fi play it by the stupid rules of sin

In these lyrics, Stephens contemplates women feeling empowered to make decisions that do not necessarily conform to hegemonic sexualities. Importantly, the song is also a reflection of the working-class woman's reality, and is therefore a site for the articulation of a transgressive sexual politics where nonconformist standards of sexual morality and gendered behaviour are embraced and celebrated.

Likewise, Stephens's song "Boom Wuk", when read through a gendered lens, speaks volumes to female autonomy and sexual agency in that it challenges female-identified persons to betray their sexist gender socialization. The song bodes well for female sexual empowerment because socially imposed gender stereotypes of the chaste housewife whose station in life is to sexually please, and therefore win over a man, are replaced by conversations that encourage women to explore their own sexual desires on equal terms with men. In the excerpt below, Stephens expresses a politics where sex is reframed as a mutually pleasurable activity for both men and women, as opposed to a reward offered to men (Weiss 2015):

> It's not the way you walk
> An' it's not the way you talk
> An' it's not your beat-up car
> U definitely ain't no movie star
> It's not the clothes you wear
> An' it's not your nappy hair
> It's not your gangsta flex
> Baby, it's all about de (the) sex

The unnamed lover's ability as an excellent sexual performer or purveyor of "boom wuk" (read: good sex) is the endearing attraction to the woman character in Stephens's song. She is quite able to overlook his apparent shortcomings because he is a source of immense sexual pleasure. This is a transgressive and disruptive stance for women to hold in patriarchal societies, where women's sexual and reproductive labour is usually tied to the material offerings of men or is bartered (unequally), with women benefiting far less than the value of this labour. More often than not, because of the unequal economic imperative behind sexual relations, women are socialized to just "grin and bear" uncomfortable sexual encounters, because sex is all about ensuring men are pleased. She sings:

> Me nuh even understand a why yuh wife a bruk war
> Yuh mighta love me but to me is jus a jook star
> Me jus a cut an' guh thru, fling me kitty pon u an' if de claw dem hol' u good luck star . . .
>
> Lately yuh say yuh get a vybez, seh yuh nuh tink we a guh make it
> Say me only give yuh ratings wen yuh naked
> Here's a good way fi make it work, when u see me lose di pants an di shirt
>
> (I don't even understand why your wife wants to fight with me
> You may love me but to me you are just a quick lay
> I am just going to cut and go through [have sex with you and leave], and if my claws hold you, good luck man . . .
>
> (Lately you have been saying you're getting the feeling that we won't make it
> You say I only pay you attention when you are naked
> Here's a good way to make it work, when you see me lose the pants the shirt)

In the above extract, Stephens elaborates on the psychological and romantic sensibilities of her sexually liberated female character and her ability to separate romantic attachments from living in the presumably mind-blowing joy of the pleasurable act.

Reggae and dancehall, as diasporic African indigenous texts, can also become sites from which to launch ideological critiques of religious conservatism. Stephens's take on spirituality in the song "You Keep Looking Up", for example, is akin to the orientation of most continental, indigenous African religious expressions:

> You keep looking up
> Why don't you look around you
> I am everywhere
> I am the flowers
> I am the tree
> I am the sound floating on the breeze

> I am the wave rocking the seas
> I am even your enemies
> So don't listen to the message of doom
> Dem cyan hold yuh dung wid nuh tomb
> (They can't hold you down with no tomb)
> When you leave the earth your soul just ready fi bloom
> (When you leave the earth your soul is just ready to bloom)
> So kiss your family and tell them that you'll meet them soon
> Don't believe that you're flawed and irreparable
> Cuz a di two a wi a trod and we inseparable
> (Because the two of us are walking and we are inseparable)
> Love me the same whether you rich or you broke
> You are my child whether you sniff or you smoke

This song creates space for a reinterpretation of the gods as present in everything and existing in a unity of beings. These lyrics offer a conceptualization of the gods as immanent in the history and lives of the people. It ruptures the dominant representation of the God of Christianity as a transcendental force in its relationship with society or people. Stephens is lyrically expressing the way that the African Caribbean working-class views God as an ever-present entity in the activities and various spaces traversed by this racialized class grouping. Songs such as "Sunday Morning" are crucial for enacting a politicized and progressive educational agenda in the Caribbean, as they present learners with the possibility of multiple truths that extend beyond the prism of Euro-Western religious hierarchies. Take for instance the verse below:

> I'm ready for a new religion
> For God sakes, it's a sin if I breathe
> I feel like I am in prison
> I'm tired of you trying to feed me your toxic beliefs
> Gradually increasing the doses
> Feeling my soul instead of seeking help for your psychosis
> It might come as a shock to you, but not everybody worships the God of Moses
> That is the same God who is made of love but has no problem with you spreading hate in his name
> Says peace, but has you fighting wars
> Looting and plundering without shame
> Sits while you do crazy stuff to each other and give Satan the blame

All week you looking down on me from the pedestal from which you so
superficially purge
But on Sunday, you smiling at me inviting me to church

Here, we see that Stephens is unconstrained in her critique of the hypocrisy of a gospel that was used as an ideological cover for slavery, genocide and hate, while encouraging its adherents to avoid accountability, attributing their exploitative actions to the authorship of the devil. For Stephens, a new and liberating, non-hegemonic religion is the antidote for the patriarchal "God of Moses". The lines below castigate religious patriarchy for its exclusion and subordination of women. They also call for a new religious paradigm that actively bridges the rhetoric/practice divide (one that extends beyond the spiritual) in addressing the material concerns of the most disenfranchised groups:

And I'm ready, but for a new religion
One which promotes eradicating hunger by eliminating greed
Getting rid of shortage by stomping out the illusion of need
One which directs you to the source rather than depend on it to feed
And one which doesn't condemn me to the eternal flames of hell because
  occasionally I smoke a likkle (little) bloodclaat weed
The same set a people who seh God lives in the sky
Is the same set of people who criticize every time I get high
Dem even have a problem wid mi drinking
And I seh (say) fine
If Jesus had a problem wid (with) drinking, would he turn wata (water) into
  wine?
I'm ready for a new religion
One in which I don't need a mediator between me and my God
Suh (so) sorry Pastor, Bishop, I mean Deacon
I just don't see the need for your job
Mi nah shot up the Bible yuh know
(I am not shooting up the Bible you know)
Cuz see me have a King James version yah (here)
(Because, look, see here I have a King James version)
And me even a look inna it
(And I am even reading it)
See Matthew, Mark, Luke and John yah
But King James, not even one verse from a woman?

Through dialogical engagement about the multiple meanings embedded in songs such as these, facilitators of learning can provoke purposeful readings that develop learners' ability to identify underlying agendas, biases and stereotyping that result in the exclusion of certain voices and perspectives (Statkus 2007). When used as a pedagogical tool, the songs can encourage the creation of more inclusive and anti-oppressive frameworks. Examine for instance the lyrics below:

> And that's the reason why, war cyaan cease
> If yuh nah look like me, me a go pop my piece
> And that's the reason why, we can't get along
> If yuh nuh do it my way then yuh doing it wrong
> And that's the reason why Iraqi babies gonna cry
> And more Palestinians and Israelis gonna die
> That's the reason why the world is in pain
> We say we want peace fi reign but ah bullets again

Here, Stephens conveys the idea that a new social order is needed to counter global hegemony or Western imperialism. She acknowledges, however, that this can only happen when there is acceptance of difference and a realization of our common humanity. The song thus serves as a reminder that the world's problems are all our own. The lyrics can be used to spark the kind of political consciousness needed in Jamaica, the Caribbean and the world, as they encourage civic responsibility as opposed to spectatorship in the face of violence and injustice. In a social context where imperialism's negation of political and ideological differences is rife, this song brings into focus America's destabilization of the democratic socialist experiment of the Michael Manley administration in the 1970s, as a relevant case study today. It could also serve as an entry point into a classroom discussion on the consequences of the structural violence of Euro-American economic imperialism for the African Jamaican working class (Mars 1984).

A song such as "Warn Dem" is a useful learning tool to the extent that it is a representative anthem for youth in various inner-city communities. Much like other popular dancehall songs, the lyrics offer commentary on class exploitation and income inequality experienced by Jamaica's working-class majority:

> When opportunity mean fi wait outside another brother gate
> An when nuh food nuh inna yuh plate, yuh know your life yuh a go hate

Yuh value nah appreciate no matter how yuh hold the fate
Yuh end up crooked and a look it, it nuh pay fi live so straight
Seven years after college all now job nuh come
So yuh overqualified still haffi live inna di slum
Father dead yuh haffi tek care a yuh madda and yuh son
And yuh grip it all a done, yuh load the clip inna yuh gun
It hard fi smile wid everybody weh yuh meet everyday
All wen yuh do good
yuh still a get beat everyday
Nuh ave nutten fi lose, yuh still deh pon di street everyday
If yuh go prison at least, yuh get fi eat everyday

(When opportunity for you means to wait outside another brother's gate
And when there's no food in your plate, you know your life you're going to hate
Your value doesn't appreciate no matter how much you hold on to faith
You end up crooked searching for it, it doesn't pay to live straight
Seven years after college and still no employment
So you're overqualified and still have to live in the slum
Your father is dead, and you have to take care of your mother and your son
And your grip on life is ending, so you load the clip inside your gun
It's hard to smile with everybody you meet every day
All when you do good
You still get beat down by everybody
You have nothing to lose, you are still on the street everyday
If you go to prison at least, you get a meal to eat everyday)

In the Caribbean context, where institutions of higher learning and vocational training centres enthusiastically celebrate matriculating learners, a dismal reality belies this celebratory tone. Members of the working class, even with credentials, are haunted by the spectre of food insecurity, poverty, lack of access to good health care, homelessness and poor-quality education. In such a context, where working-class homes are plagued by chronic unemployment or underemployment, educators may use Stephens's work as texts to help develop learners' capacity to identify the root causes of these forms of structural violence. This can be followed up with exercises that encourage them to explore more equitable economic and social alternatives.

FROM PEDAGOGICAL THEORY TO PRACTICE: ORALITY AS CRITICAL REGGAE/DANCEHALL EPISTEMOLOGY

In the *Pedagogy of the Oppressed*, the late Paulo Freire reminds us that "there is no ... word that is not at the same time a praxis". He further tells us that "to speak a ... word is to transform the world" (Freire 2009, 87). This idea of word-sound and its connection to action is central to already existing indigenous African ontological perspectives in the Caribbean. Within Rastafari ontology, for instance, word-sound is central to its liberation theology. The dialogical engagement, or reasoning, forms a central part of the Rastafari ritual celebration. Reasoning facilitates a coming into awareness that necessitates internal and external changes; changes that challenge the status quo. Elsewhere, Onuora (2013) has written about the Rastafari Nyabinghi circle as a learning event that services the goals of critical literacy theoreticians. Through the ritual activity of reasoning, learners engage in collective knowledge production, critical discussion and interrogation that help them dig deeper into their existential realities. The Rastafari reasoning circle can therefore be seen as a home-grown pedagogical practice that is consistent with the Freirian problem-posing approach. Freire explains the philosophy behind the problem-posing methodology when he states that: "Problem-posing education, as a humanist and liberating praxis, posits as fundamental that the people subjected to domination must fight for their emancipation.... Problem-posing education does not and cannot serve the interests of the oppressor. No oppressive order could permit the oppressed to begin to question: Why?" (Freire 2009, 86).

As was mentioned before, the Rastafari spiritual ritual of Nyabinghi has as its point of departure questioning and dialogical engagement through the practice of reasoning. Consistent with the problem-posing model in Rastafari reasoning circles, a community of learners could problematize everyday issues and subject matters in a similar format. They could critically interrogate how it is that Rastafari as an anticolonial philosophy lends to a reinterpretation of social issues in a way that changes problematic conventions. One of the Rastafari core principles is that words ought to be followed by deeds (action). The assumption is that consciousness born out of the dialogical exchange or "reasoning" is necessarily followed by action. Likewise, a defining feature of reggae and dancehall is orality – the act of transmitting thoughts and ideas verbally, though not necessarily through dialogue. Orality speaks to speech, and the deployment of questions as an interrogative tool is congruent with the type of critical learning that we advocate in this chapter.

Sarah Nixon-Ponder (2001) explains what the problem-posing pedagogical approach looks like concretely:

> Teachers begin by asking a series of inductive questions . . . which moves the discussion of the situation from the concrete to the analytical. The problem-posing process directs students to name the problem, understand how it applies to them, determine the causes of the problem, generalize to others, and finally suggest alternatives or solutions to the problem . . . [it] enables [learners] to bring to the program their experiences, cultures, stories, and life lessons. Their lives are reflected in the thoughtful, determined, and purposeful action.

Instructional techniques that encourage the problem-posing learning approach are therefore crucial to enacting a critical reggae and dancehall epistemology. Learners would read their world better through problem-posing dialogue or "reasoning", as in the case of the Rastafari Nyabinghi ritual. A community of learners could use reggae/dancehall as oral text to stimulate deep thinking about social events that affect their lives. The answers they come up with should create the basis for further questioning in order to get at the heart of learners' social alienation. Through problem posing and questioning, learners arrive at their own solutions to the problems they face. Facilitators could use various instructional techniques to facilitate participation in problem-posing dialogical engagements – small group discussions, role simulation, critical incident reports, role-playing and case studies – for critical thinking and problem-solving. A community of learners could actively employ a critical reggae literacy that involves learners in oral literary criticism through the exploration of topics that connect the lyrics to their lives.

It is not accidental that Bob Marley immortalized Marcus Garvey's ideological liberation message in "Redemption Song" when he called for the oppressed to "emancipate ourselves from mental slavery". Marley quickly reminds oppressed groups that "none but ourselves can free our minds". Critical reggae literacy is inextricably linked to the self-emancipation or self-organization of the oppressed. Consistent with problem-posing questioning is the idea that the people will become the architects of the new, free and just society. Therefore, in overthrowing the hegemony of the ruling class over the worldviews and political sensibilities of the African working class, the racialized class posits its vision and structures of the just and equitable society. Given the people's experience of authoritarianism and the denial of self-determination under liberal capitalist democracies and state socialism, it is reasonable to expect the conscientized working class, informed by critical reggae/dancehall literacy, to create a worldview and society in which they shape and determine the institutions and decisions that impact their lives.

Leslie James (2008, 150) reminds us of the impetus behind the critical literacy of Paulo Freire and the pedagogical thrust of Rastafari as emancipatory projects here:

> One of the intentions of the "pedagogy of the oppressed" is to transform plantation societies into sovereign, autonomous, independent states. Fundamental to this transformation is a decolonization of consciousness which allows one to "emancipate oneself from mental slavery" in order to construct a new world; on my reading, this is also the central task of the Rastafari practice of Reasoning. Thus, both reasoning and the "pedagogy of the oppressed" move beyond protest and also have constructive and integrative functions. That is to say, insofar as both perspectives restore marginalized people to the center of history as agents, both are fundamentally revolutionary and empowering. Insofar as both perspectives remind us that true democracy is more than five minutes in a ballot box every five years, that democracy is also a matter of food, employment, medical care, education, leisure, and an authentic relationship to oneself, they both transcend and denounce popular notions of democracy, and they aid in constructing a new world order rooted in solidarity and freedom.

Reggae is Rastafari music, and dancehall, African indigenous Jamaican music. Therefore, a literacy project such as critical reggae and dancehall is unavoidably implicated in the direction of revolutionary transformation in its offering to the people of an instrument to "sight up",[5] undermine and overthrow the economic, social, cultural and political structures of Babylon. However, given the oppositional character of critical reggae/dancehall literacy, it might find a more welcoming home in social movements controlled and influenced by social spaces, rather than in the educational institutions of the Babylonian system. This is so especially at the primary and secondary levels of the educational system. Yet, the official system of education is not an ideologically monolithic space for ruling class ideas. Within the margins of this site of hegemonic ideational reproduction, progressive educators are able to "corrupt" the minds of learners with transgressive ideas. After all, revolutionaries do emerge from and are cultivated in hegemonic learning institutions.

CONCLUSION

Throughout this chapter, we advocated for viewing reggae/dancehall as a site for bringing about a critical reading of society and for ushering in a politics of subversion in the context of the Caribbean. Through a critical content analysis of select works of Stephens, we have illustrated how reggae and dancehall can help learners in critiquing social values, challenging standards of respectability and facilitating a critical rereading of ruling class ethos. Much like literary texts, reggae and dancehall are oral texts. They are value-laden to the extent that they simultaneously mirror and reject sociocultural biases. They are therefore valid sign systems and part and parcel of the home-grown epistemology that processes, produces and allows for the sharing of thought, as well as progressive critiques of power relations born out of the learners' social world. We have also proposed ways in which the problem-posing critical approach to teaching may fit in the context of the Caribbean in a way that inspires social justice.

While the work of reggae and dancehall artistes like Stephens can be valuable in terms of raising awareness about issues of classism, sexism, racism and homophobia and can be useful in highlighting the violence of these intersecting hierarchies of oppression, we can expect pedagogical contestations to surface within our midst about their usage as an educative tool. Some of the content might be met with resistance from more orthodox facilitators of learning. For educators operating within some educational spaces, using indigenous words (some of which are deemed explicit) and exposing learners to ideas about acceptance of LGBTQ identities may be jarring. Efforts to bring about epistemological equity and social justice will come up against the unfortunate reality of a society that is still plagued by the ideological and social conservatism of our colonial past. Regrettably, these and other challenges (such as the concern about whether revolutionary consciousness or learner awareness of oppressive structures will necessarily lead to action) pose additional barriers for the actualization of a politicized programme of education in Caribbean. These critiques, however, pale in comparison to the fact that the strength in reggae and dancehall lies in their global reach. In the final analysis, if a reggae and dancehall literacy programme provokes the rise of criticality that "permit[s] the oppressed to begin to question: [the] Why?" (Freire 2009, 86) behind hegemonic thinking, educators and cultural workers would have extended reggae and dancehall's global impact beyond the genres' mere celebratory cultural tone.

NOTES

1. The term *neoliberalism* when used throughout this chapter refers to a set of economic principles that result in the amassing of wealth for the ruling class. The foundation of neoliberalism is profit at all cost. Some key aspects of economic neoliberalism are: reduced government regulation or deregulation, privatization of public resources and the selling of state-owned enterprises to private enterprise, and the erosion of the notion of collective and public good or community to make way for individualism and the free market. The effect of this neoliberal agenda is that the poorest people in society are no longer able to secure state or social support, but now have to find individual solutions for their lack of health, poor quality education and social security (Martinez and Garcia 1997, 2).
2. In her writings, Kimberle Crenshaw (1991) uses the concept intersectionality to refer to the various ways in which social identity markers such as race, class, gender, sexuality and abilities intersect to shape people's lived experiences. Intersectionality brings into focus the ways in which systems of oppression interlock and intersect to maintain and produce varying experiences that sustain a larger matrix of domination.
3. The word "sofaraz" ("sufferers" in English) draws from Patwa and is used in this chapter to refer to working-class, racialized peoples and other marginalized groups.
4. Respectability politics, or the politics of respectability, refers to the way in which marginalized groups reinforce bourgeois standards of morality and impose these on their own people to bring them in compliance with elite social values. The policing of dress, speech and sexual orientation and the social regulation of sexual morality are a few examples of how marginalized groups attempt to conform to, rather than challenge, the denial of difference born out of respectability politics.
5. The term "sight up" in Rastafari speak essentially means to see the message or idea being communicated.

REFERENCES

Crenshaw, Kimberle. 1991. "Mapping the Margins: Intersectionality, Identity Politics, and Violence against Women of Color". *Stanford Law Review* 43 (6): 1241–99.

Crichlow, Wesley. 2004. *Buller Men and Batty Bwoys: Hidden Men in Toronto and Halifax Black Communities*. Toronto: University of Toronto Press.

Foran, John. 1997. "Discourses and Social Forces: The Role of Culture and Cultural Studies in Understanding Revolutions". In *Theorizing Revolutions*, edited by John Foran, 197–220. New York: Routledge.

Freire, Paulo. 2009. *Pedagogy of the Oppressed*. New York: Continuum.
Freire, Paulo, and Donald Macedo. 1987. *Literacy: Reading the Word and the World*. South Hadley, MA: Bergin and Garvey.
Gee, James Paul. 1990. *Social Linguistics and Literacies: Ideology in Discourses*. London: Taylor and Francis.
James, Leslie. 2008. "Rastafari and Paulo Freire: Religion, Democracy and the New World Order". *IDEAZ: The Globalization of Rastafari* 7: 138–57.
Johnson, Jake. 2015. "Partners in Austerity: Jamaica, the United States and the International Monetary Fund". Center for Economic and Policy Research, April. http://cepr.net/publications/reports/partners-in-austerity-jamaica-the-united-states-and-the-international-monetary-fund.
Lorde, Audre. 1984. *Sister Outsider: Essays and Speeches*. Berkeley, CA: Crossing Press.
Luke, Allan. 2000. "Critical Literacy in Australia: A Matter of Context and Standpoint". *Journal of Adolescent and Adult Literacy* 43 (5): 448–61.
Mars, Perry. 1984. "Destabilization and Socialist Orientation in the English-Speaking Caribbean". *Latin American Perspective* 11 (3): 83–110.
Martinez, Elizabeth and Garcia, Arnoldo. 1997. "What Is Neoliberalism? A Brief Definition for Activists". National Network for Immigrant and Refugee Rights. January. https://corpwatch.org/article/what-neoliberalism.
McLaren, Peter. 1992. "Critical Literacy and Postcolonial Praxis: A Freirean Perspective". *College Literature* 19 (3/1): 7–27.
Morrell, Ernest. 2002. "Toward a Critical Pedagogy of Popular Culture: Literacy Development among Urban Youth". *Journal of Adolescent and Adult Literacy* 46 (1): 72–77.
Nixon-Ponder, Sarah. 2001. "Teacher to Teacher: Using Problem-Posing Dialogue in Adult Literacy Education". Ohio Literacy Resource Centre. https://www.researchgate.net/profile/Sarah_Nixon4/publication/234598591_Using_Problem-Posing_Dialogue_In_Adult_Literacy_Education/links/5703ef9a08ae44d70ee05b49/Using-Problem-Posing-Dialogue-In-Adult-Literacy-Education.pdf.
Onuora, Adwoa Ntozake. 2013. "Critical Literacy: A Rastafari Perspective". *Caribbean Quarterly* 59 (2): 39–50.
Shor, Ira. 1999. "What Is Critical Literacy". *Journal for Pedagogy, Pluralism and Practice* 1 (4): article 2. https://digitalcommons.lesley.edu/jppp/vol1/iss4/2/.
Statkus, Susan. 2007. "What Is Critical Literacy (and How Do I Use It)?" *Practically Primary* 12 (3): 11–12.
Weiss, Suzanna. 2015. "Six Reasons Telling Women Their Power Is in Their Sexuality Is Not Empowering". *Everyday Feminism*, 14 December. http://everydayfeminism.com/2015/12/power-in-sexuality-problem/.

DISCOGRAPHY

Marley, Bob and the Wailers, vocalist. 1976. "Crazy Baldhead". MP3 audio. Track 6 on *Rastaman Vibration*. Island Records.

———. 1979. "Babylon System". MP3 audio. Track 5 on *Survival*. Island/Tuff Gong.

Stephens, Tanya, vocalist. 2004. "Boom Wuk". MP3 audio. Track 3 on *Gangsta Blues*. VP Records.

———. 2004. "It's a Pity". MP3 audio. Track 7 on *Gangsta Blues*. VP Records.

———. 2006. "You Keep Looking Up". MP3 audio. Track 13 on *Rebelution*. VP Records.

———. 2006. "Sunday Morning". MP3 audio. Track 12 on *Rebelution*. VP Records.

———. 2006. "Do You Still Care". MP3 audio. Track 15 on *Rebelution*. VP Records.

———. 2006. "Warn Dem". MP3 audio. Track 16 on *Rebelution*. VP Records.

CHAPTER 6

"Yuh Cyaan Hangle di Ride"
Tanya Stephens's Critique of Societal Inefficiency

ELSA CALLIARD-BURTON

PEOPLE GENERALLY SEE MUSIC SIMPLY AS A MEDIUM of entertainment (Ibekwe 2013). Tanya Stephens, however, expertly uses the language of her music to skilfully weave her lyrical tapestry, creating masterpieces that highlight areas of economic distress and privation pervasive in Jamaican society. Through her personalized form of critique, she interrogates subjects such as poverty, unemployment, corruption and crime. Her skill with words endears her to an audience that lives vicariously through her because she gives voice to their often-ignored needs, thoughts and concerns. The poor and working-class people generally associated with dancehall music are engaged through her music as she addresses topics with which they are inescapably connected. Stephens utilizes her art form to make postulations on various areas of ineffectiveness and inefficiencies that pervade Jamaican society. The areas of inefficiencies that she critiques pertain to the failure of the government to implement policies that effectively address issues of poverty, unemployment, violence and political corruption. Ineffectiveness is used in this chapter to speak to the inability to fully "hangle di ride", in Stephens's words. The level of ineffectiveness will be measured against the definition of effectiveness given by Pfeffer and Salancik (1978), who define organizational effectiveness as an external standard of how well an organization is meeting the demands of various groups concerned with its activities. Thus, an ineffective organization would be one that is not able to fully meet the demands of stakeholder groups.

In this chapter, I use Stephens's songs "Warn Dem", "The Other Cheek" and "What a Day" to investigate the possibility of popular opinion and inner-city realities to influence government policies in relation to unemployment, poverty and violence. Her lyrical critique of the inability of the government to address these issues is examined based on the theoretical framework of critical social theory. Additionally, I investigate the validity of engaging the recommendations that have been posited in these songs as solutions to the social issues that she discusses. I explore the extent to which music can be more than a means of communication and instead function as a vehicle to effect change. Is it an effective means of communication? How can it inspire change? To whom does it speak, and is the message received as intended?

It cannot be denied that music plays many roles in society, yet we usually do not think much about how music impacts our lives and those of so many others (Garfias 2004). On our good days, it provides entertainment and tells our stories; on our bad days, it soothes our pains and lifts our spirits. Dancehall music, the genre to which Stephens's music belongs, has far-reaching influence as a medium of social and personal commentary, because it is so relatable to many Jamaicans (Morgan 2012). Indeed, Morgan maintains that, by the 1990s, dancehall's influence was recognized as outweighing the combined influence of the church, politicians and the educational system, as it spoke bare-facedly about life. It often presented life in painful, raw, uncensored ways and thereby offered people the chance to explore and discuss topics that were real to them, such as sex and relationships, poverty, and economic hardships. Dancehall music for many persons facilitated the expression of emotions that were often deemed inappropriate, mainly because of the social class with which it was associated.

EXAMINING STEPHENS'S CRITIQUE USING CRITICAL SOCIAL THEORY

I remember as a younger version of myself being hypnotized by some of the lyrics that Stephens chanted and nodding my head in agreement, even while being unable to relate to some of the spicier topics. Listening to some of Stephens's albums, such as *Ruff Rider*, may cause listeners to arrive at the conclusion that the main focus of her repertoire is sex, or the erotic. Certainly, this is a central theme in many of her songs such as "Handle the Ride", where Stephens questions the man's ability to perform as he boasted that he could. She ridicules him as he fails to live up to promises. The critique of sexual prowess or lack thereof described in "Handle the Ride" is juxtaposed in this chapter against the ability or inability of members of the government to "handle" the positions to which they have been elected. In so doing, I highlight the critical and socially interrogative nature of several of her songs. The songs chosen to illustrate areas of governmental or state inadequacies that Stephens interrogates are "Warn Dem", "The Other Cheek" and "What a Day". In addition to exposing the failure of the Jamaican government to fulfil the functions for which it has been elected, they describe the possible repercussions of the continuous economic struggle of members of the working class and offer hope that lessons learnt will result in improvements in the lived realities of Jamaican citizens.

I examine Stephens's music through the lens of critical social theory, which was brought to the fore in 1973 by Max Horkheimer of the Frankfurt School of Sociology. Kellner (1990) states that under Horkheimer's directorship, the school sought to develop an interdisciplinary social theory that could serve as an instrument of social transformation. Critical social theory offers a critique of society with the aim of transforming the lives of humans by emancipating them from historical situations and systems that limit and keep them in bondage (Kellner 1990; Horkheimer 1982; Habermas 1986). Exponents of critical social theory, such as Theodor Adorno, Herbert Marcuse, Leo Lowenthal, Eric Fromm and Jurgen Habermas, all propose that although people can consciously act to change their social and economic circumstances, their ability to do so is constrained by various forms of social, cultural and political domination (Myers 1995). Additionally, Honneth points out that structural domination undermines the resources for appealing to reason when advocating for transforming the conditions that impede freedom (as cited in Datta 2009). What this means is that there are social systems that, instead of enabling lives to be transformed, are used to keep them "dominated" or "enslaved". This may be intentional or due to the ineffectiveness of these systems. In Jamaica's context, these dominations often manifest in the form of political strongholds with conditions of facilitated poverty.[1] Political strongholds often prevent persons from liberating themselves from "mental slavery", to quote Marcus Garvey, because they demand a loyalty that supersedes rational thought, sometimes leading to turf wars and violence (Edmonds 2016).

While there are many differences in the way that critical theorists approach their critique of society, they all believe that, through an examination of contemporary social and political issues, they can contribute to a critique of ideology that would lead to the development of a non-authoritarian and non-bureaucratic politics. In this regard, critical social theory seeks to offer an alternative path for social development (Held 1980). Therefore, examining Stephens's songs within the framework of critical social theory facilitates my investigation of the ways in which Stephens both critiques the structures that enable the oppression of the poor and posits opportunities for people to be emancipated from these oppressive social and economic situations.

THE SOCIAL REALITY OF POVERTY

While the albums *Gangsta Blues* (2004) and *Rebelution* (2006) rose to popularity in the early to mid-2000s, the songs remain relevant even today. Sadly, the fact that they still have currency in the contemporary moment is a clear indictment of our society and our leaders as it becomes clear to us that many of the social and economic issues that were current at the time that the songs were released are still prevalent today. The question therefore resounds: Why do we still struggle with the same social ills and political inefficacies that were prevalent over a decade ago? Perhaps the answer lies in continued inefficiencies wrought by politicians and bureaucrats who "cyaan hangle di ride".

The song "Warn Dem" highlights issues such as unemployment and lack of opportunities that can create environments that are oppressive and restrictive to members of the working class. The resulting hopelessness that is felt by persons who are battered by these socio-economic conditions often induces participation in activities for personal betterment that produce undesirable outcomes for the rest of society. Stephens is not validating criminal or illegal activities but simply stating what exists in many areas where youth feel as though they are trapped "between a rock and a hard place". In "Warn Dem", Stephens sings, "Long time me did a warn dem, dat de youths dem need fi eat some food a dat alone can calm dem" (I have been warning them for a while now that the youth need to earn a decent living). These words underscore the pervasive nature of unemployment in Jamaican society. They also serve as a scathing critique of the government of the day for having failed to heed the signs of discontent among the youth, who are the ones hardest hit by the unemployment crisis.

Data supplied by the Statistical Institute of Jamaica from 2006 to 2018 show that young people in two groups, ages fourteen to nineteen and twenty to twenty-four, consistently exhibit the highest levels of unemployment (STATIN n.d.). The latter prevents the fulfilment of even the most basic material needs, thereby restricting persons from achieving desired changes in their social circumstances. In "Warn Dem", Stephens thus functions as a prophetic voice of the people; in relating the dire circumstances of the poor to those elected by the people, she denounces their failure to implement sufficient corrective social welfare and economic policies and programmes to "calm dem". The words "a dat alone can calm dem" gesture towards the need for improved economic conditions of the poor that would ease the social anxiety felt. In the context of Jamaica, this calm is synonymous with a marked decrease in the level of criminality and antisocial behaviour among youth. The promises that seem to spill so easily from the lips of politicians during election campaigns have not materialized into effective economic and social policies. Politicians thus become the quintessential "Mr Mention" spoken of by Stephens in "Handle the Ride"; they are the ones who "talk bout how much gyal [dem] kill" (the number of girls they have been sexually involved with) but who end up "a write [dem] own will" (having to deal with the backlash for unsatisfactory performance). Mr Mention the politician has not lived up to expectations and must now face the consequences.

EDUCATION AS A VEHICLE FOR SOCIAL CHANGE

Proponents of critical social theory speak of the establishment of conditions under which appropriate strategies for emancipation from oppression can arise (Scott 1978; Habermas 1986; Kellner 1990; Horkheimer 1982). Education is one such avenue through which persons can liberate themselves from poverty and undesirable social situations. But systems of domination retard the power of this instrument of social change, making it seem almost useless to youth who, even with qualifications, remain underemployed or unemployed. The failure of the government to provide adequate employment opportunities, as discussed in "Warn Dem", leads many to question the value of education given that their lived reality has shown that many youth who get access to education often fail to change their economic circumstances. Stephens champions the cause of the youth who bemoan this realization when she sings:

> Seven years after college all now no job no come
> seh yu overqualified still haffi live inna di slum
> faada dead yu haffi tek care a yu madda an yu son
> an yu grip it all a done, yu load yu clip inna yu gun.
>
> (Seven years after college I am still unable to find a job
> say you are overqualified and still have to live in the slum
> your father has died and you have to take care of your mother and your son
> and you've lost your grip on reality, so you load your clip in your gun)

If, as Stephens tells us, there is hopelessness even when the seemingly right road is taken, what option is there for those oppressed by the failure of the systems that are supposedly put in place to help them? How then do we convince "de yute dem" that it is worth their time and effort to pursue education when its benefits seem to continually elude them?

UNEMPLOYMENT AND ITS RELATIONSHIP WITH CRIMINALITY

In higher education, the quality of an institution depends increasingly on its graduates' employability. Describing what should exist in an optimum situation, Knight and Mantz (2003) state that all systems work together to create the higher education environment that produces programmes favourable to the development of employability. In the case of Jamaica's higher education environment, is it that all systems were not working together? Or were they working to create a hegemonic reality that is beneficial to a minority while keeping the majority in certain situations? This is a somewhat disadvantageous position for stakeholders of higher education, seeing that the ability or inability of institutions to assure students of future employment has become increasingly important to their strategic plans and their sustainability. In the United Kingdom for instance, the Quality Assurance Agency has pushed higher education institutions to write specifications for their programmes, which has generally prompted departments to think about the match between pedagogic practices and programme aims (Knight and Mantz 2003). However, in Jamaica, it is difficult for institutions to ensure future employment for students when the national unemployment remains high. In 2016, the unemployment rate stood at 13 per cent; even though the percentage has decreased since then, it remains alarmingly high(Kebede 2016).

Unsurprisingly, youth from varying socio-economic backgrounds experience difficulty in finding employment after completing their studies at the tertiary level. As an educator within the school system in Jamaica, I am aware of several such students who have found it difficult to find employment. At the same time, they are still struggling to repay student loans and cover everyday living expenses. It is even more difficult for students who must navigate the world of work without the social capital afforded to members of the elite class (Simmons 2011, Bourdieu 1986). A solution-oriented employability imperative, according to Morley (2001), which involves implementing policies that would ensure that students are able to find jobs after completing their studies, would help to ensure that students receive a tangible return on their investment. The people's efforts to change their financial and social circumstances seem futile as they are constrained by economic inefficiencies. While Stephens is not an advocate for engaging in criminal behaviour as a response to economic hardships, she recognizes that as privations lead youth to find creative ways to ensure that "dem can eat some food" (earn their bread), a strong warning needs to be issued to alert those in power that the oppressed may very well turn to predatory behaviour as a solution to these economic problems. Stephens, like most of us, understands that the end does not always justify the means; however, very often the socially marginalized only have access to means that are morally, socially or politically problematic in meeting their basic or survival needs.

"Shot dem a drizzle, here comes di storm den" (shots drizzling like rain, here comes the storm then) points to the inevitable undesirable outcomes of poverty being endured by persons in the social situations depicted in the song. It intimates that failure by the government to create an environment for persons to change their situation will undoubtedly result in increased criminal and other nefarious activities. Stephens lends weight to this in earlier lines in the song, when she sings,

> so when di yout dem need a buss gi dem opportunity fuss
> cause if dem siddung an a lust
> den it nuh safe fi none of us
>
> (when the youth need to progress, give them opportunity first
> because if they sit down and lust
> then it is not safe for any of us)

Stephens's premonition here is supported by a study conducted by the Jamaica Constabulary Force's Research, Planning and Legal Services Branch entitled "Youth Victimisation and Offending in Jamaica: An Analysis of Serious Violent Crimes". In it, the authors show that youth involvement in serious crimes has seen a steady increase in the three years preceding the study's publication for those between the ages fifteen to nineteen years old (Hibbert 2014). The study further revealed that in relation to unemployment, 60 per cent of the murder victims in 2013 were between the ages fifteen and twenty-four and were either unemployed or unskilled labourers. Of the 530,393 youths involved in the survey, 51 per cent were males.

MUSIC AS THE VOICE OF THE PEOPLE

We are reminded by Rodriguez (2016) of the need for socially conscious music as an outlet for providing voice to persons who often feel underrepresented and neglected. Stephens, in her role as the griot of those unheard voices, serves up social critique, and, in so doing, carries her message to the "misters" at the helm of power who seem focused on their own political agendas, while ignoring the plight of the everyday people. "Turn the Other Cheek" speaks to the people's refusal to maintain their silence and position as the oppressed. It also criticizes Jamaican politicians who have failed to keep promises that they made to citizens. The line "wid all di highways yu a build a go tru yu neva build a likkle avenue" (with all the highways you are building, you have not paid attention to the small roads) speaks to more than physical infrastructure or pathways. It also hints at the narrow pathways to success and the limited options that are available for the country's most vulnerable. In this line, Stephens offers her assessment of the work being done by the "misters" as being beneficial to only a few members of society: those who can benefit from the metaphorical highways of affluence and success. The "likkle avenue" speaks to the emphasis that ought to be placed on providing opportunities for members of the working class who are most susceptible to the harsh economic realities. The use of the word "likkle" (little) is not accidental. Rather, it reveals the limited and sparse opportunities that vulnerable groups are often prepared to accept as they seek to escape their present unenviable social and economic conditions.

This above critique is continued in the following lines:

> nuh have nutten fi lose
> yu done deh pan di-street every day
> if yu go prison at least yu get fi eat everyday
>
> (you don't have anything to lose
> you're already on the street everyday
> if you end up in prison at least you will get a free meal every day)

The extent of the suffering is underscored here, especially when we consider that some socially marginalized persons would prefer to be behind bars rather than endure hunger pangs resulting from poverty and homelessness. This ideas of seeking liberation through captivity is more than paradoxical. It speaks volumes to the feelings of absolute hopelessness which is the lived reality for many Jamaicans. Giving voice through her music to the despair felt by those who are often disregarded is Stephens's way of underscoring their dejection. Indeed, her words serve as a cry of desperation to those in power to address the social and economic inequities that they have normalized, and have, to some extent, become desensitized to.

CHANGING THE SOCIAL REALITY OF THE POOR

Scholars have argued that social reality is historically constituted, produced and reproduced by people (Myers 2013; Marx and Engels 1969; Freire 1970). Such may be the case in Jamaica, a society many of whose members remain loyal to long-established political parties, regardless of the efficiency of the politicians representing these factions. "The Other Cheek", however, speaks to the people's discontent with the political status quo and hints at the possibility of a change in the political culture. When Stephens asks the question, "Do you expect me to still come out and vote?" and retorts, "no matter what happen we're always broke", she offers a critique of government officials who seem vested in continuing the cycle of implementing ineffective macroeconomic policies that undermine the poor. Stephens gives us the impression that the people have realized the futility of perpetuating the social realities that have been handed down and are now considering using the power that is theirs to wield.

People from marginalized contexts often feel limited in terms of the options available to them to change their situations. Limitation is, however, not synonymous with impossibility and as such Nangwaya (2017) declares that in order for the people to become central actors on the stage of history or in the drama of emancipation, the socially marginalized must be placed in organizational situations where they are equipped with the knowledge, skills and attitude to work for their own freedom and the construction of a transformed social reality. The voter turnout (47.7 per cent of eligible voters) in the 2016 general elections indicates to some extent that there is a high level of discontent among the populace with the status quo. The failed neoliberal capitalist austerity programmes have motivated the people to use the medium of change open to them – their vote (Kebede 2016). The decision that was made by the people exercising their democratic right does not necessarily mean that they have more confidence in the winning party to supply their needs. Rather, it is an indication of their unwillingness to remain with a group that does not seem to offer any improvements in their social and economic circumstances. According to Nangwaya (2017), when the people rise up (not voting is being seen as the people rising up), the expectation is that they are seeking a qualitative change in the operation of the society or the destruction of the existing one. At the same time, the low voter turnout offers governments – both past and present – the opportunity to learn from their mistakes, to take stock of their capabilities and limitations and to pay more attention to the people who wield the power of the vote, regardless of how nebulous this power may seem.

IT'S TIME WE LEARN TO "HANGLE DI RIDE"

Stephens stands as a champion of the masses against a sociopolitical backdrop ripe for inspiration and in a context replete with many reggae and dancehall musicians who are not engaged in social and politic critique through their music. Many artistes seem to have long forgotten the revolutionary power of music as evidenced in the work of Bob Marley, Peter Tosh and Burning Spear – to name a few. Stephens's revolutionary thrust is made clear in her song "The Other Cheek". In it, she warns that failure to alleviate the conditions of poverty and unemployment will result in a national crime epidemic; an epidemic that will force members of the ruling class to face the literal and proverbial music:

> Even the richest man haffi go
> Learn fi tek a stance when
> Dem realize seh dem no safe
> Inna dem mansion
> Is a tough way fi learn seh yuh
> No really secure
> Wen the problems of the poor
> Come kick dung yuh door
> Di yute dem a get 2,000 guns
> Fi every one oonu seize
> Instead of treating the symptoms
> Why don't you cure the disease?
>
> (Even the richest man will have to go
> Learn to take a stance when
> They realize that they are not safe
> Inside their mansions

> It's a tough way to learn that you are
> Not really secure
> When the problems of the poor
> Come knocking at your door
> The youth get 2,000 guns
> For every one seized
> Instead of treating the symptoms
> Why don't you cure the disease?)

Here, the listener is left with a question that was asked over a decade ago, but which is still relevant today: Why not cure the disease? Do we even know how to begin?

A people without a dream is undoubtedly a people without a future. Like Stephens and the proponents of critical social theory, I dream of a society that is committed to emancipation from all forms of oppression, as well as to freedom, happiness, and a rational ordering of society (Scott 1978). Unfortunately, it has become increasingly difficult to dream in a society that is rife with corruption, increasing numbers of persons below the poverty level, mounting costs of education and high levels of criminality. This sentiment is as relevant now as it was when "The Other Cheek" was written. What does that say about our country? What does that say about our future? Can we still dream? I believe that we can and must still dream. The hope expressed by Stephens in lines from "What a Day" is not a futile one, but one that has been born out of harsh social realities:

> I'm tired of the hunger I see on people's faces
> Tired of the animosity between the races
> Tired of corruption in high and low places
> And pricks with money but no social graces
> Tired of being judged for the style in my hair
> And the music that I listen and the clothes that I wear
> Tired of life and death being sold as a pair
> And politicians who keep saying they care
> But maybe hoping for a change is a dream
> Maybe life ain't as bad as it seems.

Through her music, Stephens expresses discontent with the many injustices and prejudices that result in the degradation of society and the creation of unwanted social inequalities – inequalities that, according to Renault (2010), create social suffering. Wilkinson (2005, 164) rightly argues, therefore, that "a critical sociology of suffering is a necessary part of the attempt to engage sociology in the struggle to tell the truth about our world so as to imagine how it can be made to change". What we can learn from Renault and Wilkinson is that by examining the presence of social suffering, and identifying the conditions that result in such suffering, we can, in fact, alter our social reality. Stephens, through her lyrics, weaves a melody that captures the listeners' attention while aiming to emphasize ideal conditions that will resonate with us as persons who are able to eradicate social suffering and create change. She appeals to our conscience, causing us to ponder the question: Can we facilitate that change?

The failure of the Jamaican government to alleviate social suffering and provide equitable economic situations for the working class calls into question their effectiveness. Though admittedly there have been some areas of social improvements, Jamaica still struggles with high unemployment, extreme poverty and rising criminality, which has resulted in the country being labelled one of the most dangerous countries in the world (Schmalbruch 2017). Like Stephens, I look forward to a day when these issues become a thing of the past, and persons can emancipate themselves, not only from mental slavery but also from economic oppression. Isn't it time that we learn how to "hangle di ride"?

NOTE

1. I use the term "facilitated poverty" here to explain the active role state agents play in allowing sections of Jamaica to remain in impoverished conditions, because the harsh living conditions support their political outcomes.

REFERENCES

Bourdieu, Pierre. 1986. "The Forms of Capital". In *Handbook of Theory and Research for the Sociology of Education*, edited by J. Richardson, 241–58. Westport, CT: Greenwood.

Datta, Ronjon. 2009. "Review Essay: Critical Theory and Social Justice". *Studies in Social Justice* 3 (1): 133–43.

Edmonds, K. 2016. "Guns, Gangs and Garrison Communities in the Politics of Jamaica". *Race and Class* 57 (4): 54–74.

Freire, Paulo. 1970. *Pedagogy of the Oppressed*. New York: Continuum.

Garfias, Robert. 2004. *Music: The Cultural Context*. Senri Ethnological Reports, no. 47. Suita, Japan: National Museum of Ethnology.

Habermas, Jürgen. 1986. *Theory of Communicative Action*. Trans. T. McCarthy. Cambridge: Polity.

Held, David. 1980. *Introduction to Critical Social Theory: Horkheimer to Habermas*. London: Hutchinson.

Hibbert, Kimberly. 2014. "Study Reveals Link Between Unemployment and Crime". *Jamaica Observer*, 3 November. http://www.jamaicaobserver.com/news/Study-reveals-link-between-unemployment-and-crime_17858995.

Horkheimer, Max. 1982. *Critical Theory: Selected Essays*. New York: Continuum.

Ibekwe, Eunice U. 2013. "The Role of Music and Musicians in Promoting Social Stability in the Country". *Ujah: UNIZIK Journal of Arts and Humanities* 14 (3): 159–73.

Kebede, Rebekah. 2016. "Jamaica's Opposition Wins General Election as Voters Tire of Austerity". Reuters, 25 February. https://www.reuters.com/article/us-jamaica-election/jamaicas-opposition-wins-general-election-as-voters-tire-of-austerity-idUSKCN0VZ09C.

Kellner, Douglas. 1990. "Critical Theory and the Crisis of Social Theory". *Sociological Perspectives* 33 (1): 11–33.

Knight, Peter, and York Mantz. 2003. *Assessment, Learning and Employability*. Buckingham: Society for Research into Higher Education and Open University Press.

Marx, Karl, and Friedrich Engels. 1969. *The Communist Manifesto*. Trans. unknown, introduction by A.J.P. Taylor. Baltimore: Penguin.

Morgan, Canace. 2012. "Early Globalization and the Roots of Dancehall". Wordpress, 19 April. https://sophia.smith.edu/blog/danceglobalization/2012/04/19/early-globalization-and-the-roots-of-dancehall-dance/.

Morley, Louise. 2001. "Producing New Workers: Quality, Equality and Employability in Higher Education". *Quality in Higher Education* 7 (2): 131–38.

Myers, M.D. 1995. "Dialectical Hermeneutics: A Theoretical Framework for the Implementation of Information Systems". *Information Systems Journal* 5 (1): 51–70.

———. 2013. *Qualitative Research in Business and Management*. London: Sage.

Nangwaya, Ajamu. 2017. "Engendering Revolt in the Anglophone Caribbean Organizing the Oppressed for Self-Emancipation". In *Why Don't the Poor Rise Up? Organizing the Twenty-First Century Resistance*, edited by Ajamu Nangwaya and Michael Truscello, 148–78. Chico, CA: AK Press.

Pfeffer, Jeffrey, and Gerald R. Salancik. 1978. *The External Control of Organizations: A Resource Dependence Perspective*. New York: Harper and Row.

Renault, Emmanuel. 2010. "A Critical Theory of Social Suffering". *Critical Horizons* 11 (2): 221–41.

Rodriguez, Jakob. 2016. "Listen to the Music for Social Commentary". *University Star*, 5 December. https://star.txstate.edu/2016/12/05/listen-to-the-music-for-social-commentary/.

Schmalbruch, Sarah. 2017. "The 20 Most Dangerous Countries in the World". *Independent*, 7 September. https://www.independent.co.uk/news/world/worlds-most-dangerous-countries-colombia-yemen-el-salvador-pakistan-nigeria-a7934416.html.

Scott, John P. 1978. "Critical Social Theory: An Introduction and Critique". *British Journal of Sociology* 29 (1): 1–21.

Simmons, O.S. 2011. "Lost in Transition: The Implications of Social Capital for Higher Education Access". *Notre Dame Law Review* 87 (1): 205–17.

STATIN (Statistical Institute of Jamaica). n.d. "Main Labour Force Indicators 2017–2018". Accessed 22 October 2018. http://statinja.gov.jm/labourforce/newlfs.aspx.

Wilkinson, Ian. 2005. *Suffering: A Sociological Introduction*. Cambridge: Polity Press.

DISCOGRAPHY

Stephens, Tanya, vocalist. 1998. "Handle the Ride". MP3 audio. Track 2 on *Ruff Rider*. VP Records.

———. 2004. "The Other Cheek". MP3 audio. Track 15 on *Gangsta Blues*. VP Records.

———. 2004. "What a Day". MP3 audio. Track 16 on *Gangsta Blues*. VP Records.

———. 2006. "Warn Dem". MP3 audio. Track 16 on *Rebelution*. VP Records.

CHAPTER 7

The Call to Resistance
The Weaponization of Language in the Music of Tanya Stephens

NICOLE PLUMMER

TANYA STEPHENS IS A DANCEHALL ARTISTE WHO PAVED the way for many female performers coming after her. Alongside Lady Saw, she is considered one of the most influential female dancehall acts to have emerged in the 1990s. Her natural and cultivated ability to challenge the deeply held beliefs of her listeners is laudable and, in many respects, revolutionary. Tackling an array of subjects and themes ranging from love, loyalty, pain and heartbreak to fatherhood, politics and street life, Stephens uses wordplay to encourage introspection, as a weapon for resisting commonly held assumptions, and for promoting a revolutionary agenda. This chapter analyses a sample of Stephens's music through the lens of cultural studies, specifically leaning on Stuart Hall's work on language and representation. Grounded in Hall's analysis, it examines how Stephens weaponizes language in her music to challenge gender, class and racial hegemony in Jamaica and the world in general. In many respects, Hall's groundbreaking analysis, which sheds light on the perspectives of minority groups, mirrors Stephens's ability to represent the experiences and perspectives of marginalized groups in a society that often discounts their existence and ridicules their viewpoints.[1] I begin with a discussion of Hall's ideas on representation and the role of language and then undertake an analysis of Stephens's lyrics, focusing on how she uses language as a weapon of resistance against hegemonic structures.

LANGUAGE, REPRESENTATION AND RESISTANCE IN CULTURAL STUDIES

Meanings and representations are derived through language. Stuart Hall (1997c, 61) defines language as "any system which deploys signs, [or] any signifying system". Language is a critical component of culture, to the extent that culture itself can be described as a system of signs. It is through language that we are socialized. It is through language that we learn about ourselves and the communities that surround us. Meaning is coded and embedded within language and presented for our understanding. Language, then, is not only a tool of communication but one of socialization. It is therefore not surprising that one of the primary concerns of cultural studies is language. Chris Barker (2004, 107) contends that "for Cultural Studies, language is not a neutral medium for the formation and transfer of values, meanings and forms of knowledge that exist independently beyond its boundaries. Rather, language is constitutive of those very values, meanings and knowledges. That is, language gives meaning to material objects and social practices that are brought into view and made intelligible to us in terms which language delimits."

Cultural studies' preoccupation with language is demonstrated by the significance placed on textual approaches to understanding or reading cultures, and on whether such textual approaches are fixed (structuralism) or unstable (post-structuralism). Structuralism implies that "signifying practices that generate meaning as an outcome of structures or predictable regularities ... lie outside of any given person" (Barker 2008, 43). Structuralism suggests a fixedness to the language or sign system of peoples. Individuals are products of this static system, merely replicating what they have been exposed to. By contrast, post-structuralism correctly negates the concept of fixedness and is buoyed by Jacques Derrida's assertion that language is unstable, though it acknowledges, similar to structuralism, that meaning and cultural productions lie outside of the individual's construction. Music, food and dress are analysed not so much for their content but for their underlying meaning within the sign system or culture to which they belong. All culture is located within language and is then read textually (Derrida 1976; Saussure 1960).

Language is open to change depending on context and interpretation. As her sociocultural environment and milieu change, so does Stephens as an artiste and an individual. Stephens's wordplay must be understood within the constantly evolving context that she speaks of, and the ideas that she relates combined with her growth and maturity as an artiste and lyricist. As an organic intellectual,[2] she mainly draws her references from the dynamic Jamaican context to emphasize her points and to wield her wordplay as a weapon to challenge hegemonic constructs and representations.

The word "representation" is often used to describe the process by which one object stands for another. Barker (2004, 177) also describes representation more precisely as "a set of processes by which signifying practices appear to stand for or depict another object or practice in the 'real' world". In cultural studies, representation moves beyond its denotative meaning and interrogates the meaning between and behind symbols and the ideas that they represent. It goes beyond merely acknowledging the connection between an object and the symbol that represents it. Cultural studies scholars are particularly keen to notice the instability between objects and the symbols that represent them (Baudrillard 1994; Derrida 1976; Foucault 2002; Hall 1997b; Kristeva 1980). Meaning, they recognize, shifts spatially and temporally. By acknowledging that language is unstable, cultural studies theoreticians acknowledge that representations, and consequently meanings, are unstable. Representations are located within cultural sign systems. Symbols are thus read within that context.

To connect with her audience, Stephens uses recognizable language and symbolism from which they can derive meaning.[3] Meaning is derived through not only what is but also what is not. Hall's work on representation and blackness examines this dichotomy, particularly through the lens of media. The interplay between language and representation is certainly implicit in Hall's analysis of representation. For him, "representation is the process by which members of a culture use language to produce meaning" (Hall 1997c, 61). Hall's definition of representation is clearly constructivist. In other words, meaning is constructed through language and context, which themselves are shifting variables. Stephens's wordplay is evocative and is drawn from the context that is the Jamaican sign system or culture – a variable that shifts due to internal and external hegemonic influences such as globalization, capitalism, patriarchy, racism and ethnocentrism. It is these hegemonic forces that Stephens often resists in her music.

Representation can be a call to action, but it can also be divisive, especially when one considers damaging media representations of people of colour, the poor and LGBTQIA communities. This is the politics of representation, under which representation has a dual meaning. On the matter of representation, Simon During (2005, 23) tells us that it refers to "the way that particular social groups [are] represented, especially in the media . . . [and] second . . . the way in which representative politics disempowered specific interests and identities and reduced political agency". While During's analysis concerned African Americans, in Jamaica, this analysis can be applied to poor Jamaicans of African descent. Persons belonging to these communities are represented in media dually, as culturally rich and ideologically poor, and are framed as subjects of pity and fear, devoid of agency. Mindful of this, Stephens's music presents perspectives from the viewpoint of the disfranchised and maligned, ranging from the young inner-city man demanding respect, to the queer male desiring acceptance, to the mother who gives her partner a "jacket"[4] and to the woman asking her partner to stay at home with her rather than fulfil patriarchal ideals. Stephens uses language in her music to represent inequality and heartache as well as to articulate her rage against the oppressive system that hold some in its thrall. Music and the language therein are therefore Stephens's tools of resistance. She infuses her music, her weapon, with the ideological arsenal of anti-oppression, feminism and collectivism.

"Resistance" is often used to refer to "opposition or insubordination that issues from relationships of power and domination . . . resistance takes the form of challenges to and negotiations of the ascendant order" (Barker 2004, 178). Resistance – the act of opposing an idea, action, ideology or people – is contingent on the cultural, economic and ideological context. That feminism opposes patriarchy, for example, suggests that there is a relationship between what is being resisted and who is doing the resisting. This relationship involves complex relations of power. The subordinate might oppose the culturally, politically and economically dominant group or hegemonic bloc. Therefore, challenges to hegemony are constantly in flux. These challenges differ depending on the time, space and on the subjects being opposed. The Caribbean's long history of enslavement is replete with examples of resistance that demonstrate its relational nature. People of African descent were routinely dehumanized to produce sugar – a luxury product. The profits from sugarcane allowed the master to live a life of relative ease compared to those enslaved. The cane fields then represented this loathsome dichotomy. Accordingly, they were routinely burned during (and even outside of) armed resistance by the enslaved (Beckles 1982; Craton 1982; Hart 1980; Williams 1994). Each enslaved individual was more or less a unit of labour for the planter. Removing oneself through maronnage (grand or petit) or suicide therefore deprived the planter of that labour (Campbell 2012; Heuman 1986; Marshall 2008).

The relational nature of resistance is also evidenced in the cultural resistance carried out by the enslaved Afro-Caribbean people. Duncombe (2007) defines cultural resistance as "the practice of using meanings and symbols, [within] culture, to contest and combat a dominant power, often constructing a different vision of the world in the process". It is also the use of culture "consciously or unconsciously, effectively or not, to resist and change the dominant political economic and social structure" (Duncombe 2002, 5). During the colonial period, African aesthetics, spirituality and culture were routinely devalued. In response to this, many Africans resisted through holding on to what they could of themselves and their homeland. Despite some acquiescence to European culture, Richard Burton (1997) observes that their self-expression, celebrations and spirituality were infused with African influences in direct opposition to their colonizers. Stephens's resistance through her unique wordplay follows this tradition of African cultural resistance. Her artistry is deployed as a cultural weapon to resist hegemonic forces such as capitalism and patriarchy.

WORDPLAY AS RESISTANCE: THE WEAPONIZATION OF LANGUAGE IN TANYA STEPHENS'S MUSIC

Infidelity and the idea of juggling multiple partners have come to form part and parcel of the masculism inherent in Jamaica's patriarchal culture. It is so prevalent that Beenie Man's 1996 song "Nuff Gal" has become a beacon of sorts, signifying Jamaican manhood. Cultural studies scholar Donna Hope (2006, 37) tells us:

> In postcolonial societies such as Jamaica, gender stratification operates in a framework of patriarchy that can be clearly defined as a system or society reflecting values underpinning the traditional male ideal. It is masculism in a political context and it is supported by all the institutions operating within that system or society. Patriarchy is not only male dominance in its strictest sense, but also a persistent ideology of male super ordination that both men and women maintain consciously and unconsciously.

Stephens in her song "1-1-9" opposes infidelity[5] and its attendant disrespect using common gun references:

Funny every time I answer di telephone
All I ever get is a dial tone

*69, you hold my hand
Some bitch on di line, say leave mi man
Dat's the kinda game you play with yuh life
A mussi murda yuh waan mi charge fah

Mi naah call no 1-1-9
Mi love yuh but if yuh ever dis di programme one more time
Yuh gonna wake up in di morning find mi brushing yuh teeth
with ma big Tek Nine
This is a wake up call, bwoy nuh badda bawl
Caa dis a different time, weh me seh, weh mi seh

(Funny every time I answer the telephone
All I ever get is a dial tone
*69, you hold my hand
Some bitch on the line, says leave my man
That's the kind of game you play with your life
Surely, you want me to get charged for murder

I am not calling 119
I love you but if you ever disrespect me one more time
You are going to wake up in the morning and find me brushing your teeth with
   my big Tec-9[6]
This is a wakeup call, boy, don't bother crying
Because this is a different time. What did I say? What did I say?)

Stephens's rage results from being doubly violated. Her partner is cheating on her, and to make matters worse, her relationship and her person are being contemptuously ignored by the other woman who calls her home. Her partner is not only cheating on her, but he is doing so in such a manner that Stephens's status as the main woman is being challenged by his "mistress". Stephens's response to her partner's infidelity is bold, viscerally violent and confrontational. Her "Tek Nine" and Taurus guns will settle the issue. Her graphic imagery and the fear that guns like the Tec-9 instil drive home her message: Your cheating will no longer be tolerated.

Now at her breaking point, it is no surprise that Stephens uses the gun to articulate her rage and to underscore her frustration. Guns are fearsome tools used for protection and defence. They are also used to carry out criminal activities, such as murders and robberies. They symbolize an individual's lethal and legal or illegal authority. In Jamaica, guns represent patriarchy and machismo as well as potency and dominance. Drawing from Barry Chevannes (1999), Donna Hope (2006, 90) maintains that the gun is "the ultimate representation of what it means to be a man". Stepping into the traditional male domain and using the tools of patriarchy to fight patriarchy, Stephens repurposes the gun for her cause célèbre. In so doing, she claims (or reclaims) the upper hand in the situation. With her guns, Stephens demands respect and power in her relationship when she sings:

> Yuh see mi big gun, a it run di yard
> Mi naah tek no lick, yow mi dun wid dat
> Mi nuh waan nuh ice pick, cause mi have mi Glock[7]
> An wen mi taak, nuh badda kin yuh teet
> Hey bwoy, yuh fi tek mi serious
>
> (Do you see my big gun, it controls the home
> I will not take any beating, I am finished with that
> I do not want an ice pick because I have my Glock
> And when I talk, do not bother laughing
> Hey boy, you should take me seriously)

In Jamaica, violence and masculinity go hand in hand within the system of patriarchy. Stephens, in her song, however, does not eschew violence as a way of turning patriarchy on its head. Instead, she grasps what is usually the prerogative of the male – guns and violence – and uses them to assert her authority and reclaim her personhood. Consequently, she rewrites the script using a phallic symbol generally used to assert male dominance, especially amongst disfranchised youth. She asserts power over her male partner to reclaim her personhood. Her "take no prisoner" attitude obtained through her guns, demonstrates a profound indignation, one that is perhaps rooted in the country's failure to protect its women from gender-based violence. In "1-1-9", Stephens refuses to succumb to the beatings her partner usually unleashes on her. Instead, this time, uses her guns as a means of self-defence.

A 2017 *Gleaner* article entitled "'Is She Cause It!' Domestic Violence and Human Rights Abuse in the Jamaican Context, Part 1" relates several stories of violence against women in rural Jamaica, and the stigma and ostracism that the women face as a result. Often, it is the victims who are villainized. Case in point: in one of the stories discussed in the article, a woman who stabs her abuser in self-defence is acquitted of murder but has to leave her community because, according to community members, "she was a woman and she was a murderer". Therefore, she was "no longer welcome" (Smith-Whyte 2017). Similar newspaper articles present violence against women as an ongoing crisis (Wilson-Harris 2016; Campbell 2017). A society governed by the dictates of Judeo-Christian values that position men as the default heads of their households, Adella Campbell (2017) reminds us, "will condone abuse as a manifestation of love. Additionally, inequalities between men and women are still very prevalent, and unfortunately cut across every stratum of society. Abuse is influenced by existing sociocultural, political and economic norms. Women who are affected by this phenomenon are more susceptible to violence; for example, in situations where a woman is economically dependent on her male counterpart for a livelihood."

While Stephens in "1-1-9" is no victim, neither is she as saint. She fights the violence meted out against her with brute force. For her, the adage "an eye for an eye and tooth for a tooth" (Leviticus 24:19–21) rings true. She asserts her agency using violence replete with gun talk – talk that is the norm in many popular Jamaican dancehall songs by male artistes. This could be seen as a controversial and problematic response in the context of a society already riddled with violence and flooded with guns that have been used to wreak havoc on the citizenry (Barrett 2017). Perhaps that is precisely why she utilizes "gun-talk" to resist infidelity and domestic violence. In the Jamaican cultural sign system, guns have long represented masculinity, fear and potency. Guns are subversive and brutal instruments, but they can also allow the powerless to feel a sense of empowerment. In Jamaica, where guns allow disfranchised youth to claim respect and power (albeit towards problematical ends at times), Stephens is merely following suit. One could argue that, in using the gun, she too reclaims authority, control and dignity of which the patriarchal heterosexual arrangement often robs women. She works within violent patriarchal structures to create a bulwark against further incursions that threaten her personhood.

Another interpretation, more within the ambit of textual analysis, is to explore Stephens's gun talk as part of the Caribbean's tradition and culture of theatricality. Caribbean musical performers, ranging from calypsonians to reggae and dancehall artistes, have long relied on theatricality to woo audiences. This theatricality itself is rooted in Afro-Caribbean traditions of storytelling and miming (Alleyne 1984; Burton 1997; Cooper 2004; Lewin 2000; Hope 2006; Warner-Lewis 2003). Scholar Sonjah Stanley Niaah (2010, 4) tells us that "the

DJ used to perform live in the dance as a word artist, a Griot in the broader African sense, one who chants or sings or talks on a rhythm to keep the dance event lively by toasting the fans".

Literary scholar and cultural critic Carolyn Cooper (2004, 147) places gun symbolism within the theatricality of "badmanism" when she states, "there is, as well, an indigenous tradition of heroic "badness" that has its origins in the rebellious energy of enslaved African people who refused to submit to the whip of bondage". Popular movie representations of masculinity in Hollywood action and western films further influenced the "badman" identity and its related gun posturing. Cooper (1994, 430) argues, "'Badmanism' is a theatrical pose that has been refined in the complicated socialization processes of Jamaican ghetto youth who learn to imitate the sartorial and ideological 'style' of the heroes and villains of imported American films." Figurative guns and their mimicked sounds are props that lend credence to lyrical "badman" stylings. Viewed from this perspective, Stephens rebels against the patriarchal system by using the phallic, brutal imagery of a big gun and violent, visually evocative language. Her wordplay forms part of a ritualized rebellious theatrical wordplay that is consistent with Jamaica's history of cultural resistance. The gun is the prop that brings this theatricality to life. Through this theatrical "badman" styling of guns and violence, Stephens transcends feminine borders and inhabits the masculine space.

In "After You", Stephens gives a more conventional "feminine" response as a woman scorned by her husband. Rather than the gun, she uses the justice system to exact revenge. In this song, she maxes out the husband's platinum credit card and goes before the court weeping with the aim of gaining half of his property:[8]

> Yuh neva know what a wife or a lover meant
> So, mi waan half a everyting like di government
> Now yuh can tell yuh friends yuh really have a bitchy wife
> When mi stick yuh up and clean yuh out like Lionel Ritchie wife
> Mi a tek di house, di car, and di children
> Yuh screwdrivers, even yuh power drill dem
> All weh mi nuh need mi still a go tek
>
> (You never knew what a wife or a lover meant
> So, I want half of everything like the government

> Now you can tell your friends you really have a bitchy wife
> When I stick you up and clean you out like Lionel Ritchie wife
> I am taking the house, the car and the children
> Your screwdrivers, even your power drills
> Even things I do not need, I will still take)

Her performance before the judge contains elements of the theatricality present in "1-1-9". It is a performance born of anger, vengeance and desperation. In her Outro, she explains the reasons for the actions of the jilted wife:

> Yuh see weh yuh a cause, yuh know seh mi nuh stay so
> But weh yuh expect mi fi do, all a this a fi yuh fault, cau yuh leff mi nuh choice
> A woman my age wid three kids which man a go pick mi up?!
> I don't have a certificate I done wid my marketable skills
> And when mi tell yuh say mi waan work pon a career yuh neva did rahtid care
> Yuh wife nah fi work and boops yuh breed mi again
> Thirty-six months mi spend a carry yuh pickney inna my gut
> Dat a thirty-six month outta my life when you could a lock and zip it up too
> Heh heh, yuh lucky.
>
> (Do you see what you have caused me to do, you know that I am not like that
> But what do you expect me to do?
> All of this is your fault because you left me no choice
> A woman my age with three children
> Which man is going to want me?
> I do not have a certificate
> I have no marketable skills
> And when I tell you that I want to work on a career you never cared at all
> Your wife should not work and look, I am pregnant again
> Thirty-six months I spent carrying your children in my stomach
> That is thirty-six months out of my life when you could have worn protection
> Hahaha, you're lucky)

Her tone is decidedly scornful and bitter. She feels that she has been left no choice. While in the relationship, she was urged by her partner to refrain from pursuing a career. She has no marketable skills and relied on him for financial support. Now that the relationship has ended, she is left without work experience or any certifiable skill that would allow her to achieve financial independence. This is the tale of a stay-at-home wife who is soon to be ex-wife. In a society where women are often judged harshly for their alleged vindictive or greedy proclivities, Stephens articulates their plight, telling their stories from their perspective. The agency of the soon to be ex-wife and mother is revealed when she appears before the court unabashedly asserting her right to half of the marital property. Not only does Stephens claim the house and car, but she also lays claim to the things that are most central to the validation of her partner's masculine identity – his children, screwdrivers, power drills and money. Money represents independence, influence, dominance and in many instances, virility (Steinem 1995; Hope 2010; Williams, Levy Paluck and Spencer-Rodgers 2010). Amongst other characteristics, the hegemonic male in most societies is expected to be a provider. Thus, wealth is a key indicator of his ability to perform this role consistent with the widely accepted standard and attitudes that a "real" man ought to be the main bread winner (Connell 1987). In fact, much like other social contexts, in Jamaica, the more money a man has, the more powerful he is perceived to be.

Besides money, quintessential to male identity in the Jamaican cultural sign system are the home, children, screwdrivers and power drills itemized by Stephens. In Jamaica, homeownership is an indicator of both wealth and independence. While the image of women with aprons running the kitchen remains a popular trope, so too is the role men play as the individuals who maintain the house. His accessories and even extensions of his identity, then, are his tools – his power drills and screwdrivers, which are also phallic symbols. By taking them from him, Stephens in essence emasculates her male partner. She leaves him without the instruments to "perform" his masculinity.

A clearer picture is drawn in "After You", where Stephens states that she will take half of his money, just like the government. Here, she riffs off the common complaint made by Pay as You Earn (PAYE) workers in Jamaica, who feel that their salaries are heavily taxed by the state. If money and power are correlated, then by evoking the futile ire of the PAYE worker Stephens halves the power of her ex and reduces his masculine financial vigour. By taking his money, house, car, power drills and screwdrivers, she exacts vengeance and wields a newly found power. She further renders his rage ineffectual by revelling in the label "bitchy wife". While there are uneven reclamation efforts to remove the stigma surrounding the word bitch,[9] its pejorative meaning and usage remain. As a result, very few Jamaican women, and women in general, want to be voluntarily labelled as such. In "After You", Stephens does not seem to care and in fact relishes the title in what can be interpreted as another effort to rehabilitate and appropriate the word. If her assertiveness in fighting for what she is due leads to her being called a bitch, then Stephens, rather than flinch at the slur hurled at her by her partner and his cronies, accepts the title. For her, it is a testament of her empowerment – an acknowledgement that she stood her ground and claimed what was rightly due to her.

In the same way that Stephens works within the confines of patriarchy to oppose infidelity and domestic violence, she uses her wordplay to articulate her sexual demands while negotiating with and accommodating dominant hegemonic discourse. It is important to note here that while her tone is militant and her approach assertive, Stephens's heterosexual demands align with dominant dancehall and societal constructs of normative heterosexuality, where men perform their sexual prowess with the vigour of a stallion. This is measured against the woman who is able to absorb, withstand and engage his vigorous performance. Patricia Saunders (2003, 113) therefore asserts, "The few songs by female DJs such as Lady Saw and Tanya Stephens emphasize the prowess of women who 'tek wuk' (take work) or maintain full-time 'wuk' from men while other, less talented women are constantly 'unemployed'. These discourses, while they express a certain measure of empowerment and affirmation of women's bodies and 'pum-pum power', do so within boundaries and discourses handed down to them from above."

In this regard, Stephens uses her platform to reinforce the trope of black male sexual performance, a trope which is rooted in a problematic racist history where the sexualized black female body becomes a performative space of male virility and masculinity. It is in this capacity that in songs such as "Ninja Bike", "Freaky Type" and "Goggle" she maintains the social taboo against oral sex, polices the man's sexual performance and underscores her ability as a woman to "take" that performance.

Stephens's use of wordplay to police male performance is a practice that harkens back to the period of enslavement, when enslaved women used their words as weapons to challenge planter management and engage in verbal duels with each other (Bush 1990; Mair 2006; Shepherd 1999). Warner-Lewis (2003, 285) tells us that "the outspokenness of ordinary African women, both in the plantation and post-plantation Caribbean, is legendary, and orality behaviours such as word-dropping or word-throwing, as well as 'tracing' [the word used in Jamaica], 'cussing out' [the term used in Trinidad], or verbal abuse, are still largely their province". On the plantation, this was articulated both in verbal insubordination in song (Mair 2006). Stephens's lyrical prowess joins this long tradition of feminine wordplay both as a tool of resistance and a way of maintaining social control.

In the songs "Goggle" and "Ninja Bike", Stephens uses common Jamaican motorbike and cowboy riding metaphors to assert her sexuality and police the man's sexual performance. In "Goggle", the man or sexual partner is the rider; the bike he sits astride is the woman, his sexual partner. The man should be skilled enough and big enough (implying penis size) to ensure that he can control or "dally" his "bike". Her lyrics also police certain sexual activities such as oral sex:

> Some man seh dem a rider but dem a slip saggle
> An a claim seh dem a dally but dem a wiggle waggle
> So wen dem want yuh bend dung gyal don't help them out
> Gyal don't gaggle
>
> (Some men say they are riders but they are slipping in the saddle
> And they say that they are riding skilfully on the bike, instead they are riding clumsily
> So, when they want you to go down, girl don't help them out
> Girl don't goggle)

By policing sexual performance and critiquing oral sex, Stephens through her lyrics maintains hegemonic standards of sexual morality.

Referring to women performing fellatio, she uses the word gaggle – the Jamaican word for gag. The women essentially gag on the penis as they perform fellatio. Accordingly, women who have never gagged on a penis are praised, since they did not "bend dung (go down)" or "bow" to a man's will; especially a sexually inept man. A woman who is able to withstand a vigorous sexual performance does not need to accept oral sex. What Stephens wanted from the sexual encounter was the "bashment"[10] promised to her by her partner. He did not live up to his promises, and now Stephens verbally mocks him with her lyrical wordplay derived from the Jamaican cultural sign system in the lines below:

> Seh im know di bashment but im a big fraud
> Cause im have up di flex of a retard
> Long time im unda table a eat hard
> Now mi ave im like a puppet pon a piece a cord

(Said he knew the bashment but he is a big fraud
Because he has the reflexes of a retard
Long time he has been under the table eating hard
Now I have him like a puppet on a piece of string)

The word "flop", which in Jamaica denotes failure, is used in "Goggle" – "A him flop himself and that a big suppen" (he failed himself and that is something big) – as an expression of failure and as a metaphor for her partner's limp penis. This failed sexual encounter leaves the man with his "tail between him leg like shame dog" – a popular expression amongst Jamaican folk. This comparison with a dog is deliberate. A popular rebuke is to compare men to dogs because of their infidelity, amongst other misdeeds. A shamed dog's tail sags as limply as a disappointing man's penis; a happy, healthy dog proudly has his tail in the air. A healthy man is a man whose penis is erect and held in the air, happy at his ability to satisfy his partner.

Stephens also uses literary devices such as onomatopoeia to further drive home her point. Through words like "slerp" (slurp), she provides an explicit visual image of the male performing cunnilingus, contrary to Jamaican hegemonic values and expectations of maleness. The common misconception is that only men who cannot perform or meet their partner's needs in the bedroom through vaginal penetration have to resort to "using their mouth" or tongue to orally pleasure a woman as a way of compensating for any lack or "flop" in their penis. Because of the conservative attitudes surrounding this sexual act, Stephens's having this piece of information puts her in a position of power. She is able to "ave him like a puppet pon a piece a cord", knowing this secret and the social stigma he could attract. This song reinforces conservative Jamaican values that denounce oral sex in general. This is evidenced in the lines, "A weh him pick up dat deh habit deh, a must abroad / But wi nuh support dem tings dey dung a yard" (Where did he pick up that habit? It must have been abroad / But we do not support those things in Jamaica). Here, oral sex is framed as a foreign import as opposed to a commonly accepted, homegrown practice in Jamaica. The song also implicitly taps into the Jamaican folk belief that ingesting a lover's body fluids can tie or bind someone to you indefinitely.[11]

In "Freaky Type", Stephens's tone is less militant against oral sex. She implicitly embraces it, stating, "di freaky type, a dat wi like" (the freaky type, that's what we like). However, yet again, the narrative is that men opt to perform cunnilingus when they are unable to perform in other ways. This is evidenced when she asks, "So unno dweet? / Back weak, so unno gwaan use up unno beak?" (That's how you all do it? Back's weak so you all use your mouth?) Using common Jamaican terms like "weak back" (another way of criticizing men who are unable to deliver strong pelvic thrusts during sex) and animalistic references such as "beak" to describe the mouth, Stephens throws lyrical daggers at men who lack the stamina necessary for penile penetration. Though "Freaky Type" sees Stephens accepting oral sex, she does not, however, reciprocate it. As a consequence, Stephens continues to operate within the confines of dominant masculinity. While her creativity in demanding sexual fulfilment is laudable in a context where women expressing their sexual preference is frowned upon, she still maintains Jamaica's hegemonic sexual discourse. Cooper (2004, 99) sums up the challenges that women are presented with when they incorporate sexualized lyrics in their performances in the conservative Jamaican space:

> The flamboyantly exhibitionist DJ Lady Saw epitomizes the sexual liberation of many African Jamaican working-class women from airy-fairy Judaeo-Christian definitions of appropriate female behavior. In a decisive act of feminist emancipation, Lady Saw cuts loose from the burdens of moral guardianship. She embodies the erotic. But one viewer's erotica is another's pornography. So, Lady Saw is usually censured for being far too loose – or "slack", in the Jamaican vernacular. Or worse, is dismissed as a mere victim of patriarchy, robbed of all agency.

In "Ninja Bike", Stephens uses the motorbike as a metaphor for a penis over which she exerts sexual control and dominance. She is the rider – the aggressor who controls the bike – and her body is not the site on which the male gets to perform his masculinity. On top, as the rider, she is in control of the bike's engagement:

> Me want a man weh hav a big ninja bike fi me ride pan
> Na waan no flim flam
> Weh nuh have de right gear
> Spen de whole night pan yuh divan
> Gi me di right slam
> Cause da gal ya no care
> Big ninja bike fi me ride pan
>
> (I want a man who has a big ninja bike for me to ride on
> I do not want anything fake
> That does not have the right gear

Spend the entire night on your divan
Give me the right sexual performance
Because this girl does not care
Big ninja bike for me to ride on)

Stephens does not want just any bike. She wants a "big ninja bike" or a big penis to navigate. The ninja bike emanates from the Jamaican cultural sign system and is popular among youth. Growing up in the 1990s, many young men and women around me were awestruck by the Kawasaki Ninja and Honda "Hurricane" bikes, particularly because of their horsepower, speed, loudness and size. Similar to guns, ninja bikes were also a way of asserting masculinity and power. Stephens's deployment of this metaphor therefore, like others mentioned previously, is relatable, and thus sharpens her critique of sexually inept men. Not only does Stephens aspire towards riding a big and powerful "bike", she desires one that can go the distance. She plays up the importance of having a male partner who is a "distance runner" (that is, one that can please her for hours on end), using names of places in Jamaica as metaphors that cue listeners into the coordinates she employs as her measure of stamina:

Honda 50 dem a push ova
Dem bike dey caan reach Hanova
Caa nuff man juss get leff inna mi duss
An mi tell dem fi run fi cover (wah me seh)
Before you mek anodda speech
Mek sure yuh bike can reach
Caa mi nuh waan yuh pick mi up
Fi carry me a Negril and broke dung out a Treasure Beach

(Honda 50 is a pushover
Those bikes can't reach Hanover
Because many men will get left in my dust
And I tell them to run for cover [what I say]
Before you make another speech
Make sure your bike can reach
Because I do not want you to pick me up
To carry me to Negril and break down by the time you get to Treasure Beach)

By referencing the Honda 50 in "Ninja Bike", Stephens intimates that she does not want a weak bike; something that cannot go the distance. In referencing

Hanover, Negril and Treasure Beach, located in separate parts of the island, she underscores the point that endurance is critical to her sexual satisfaction. The journey from Negril to Treasure Beach is extensive and gruelling, particularly on a bike. There are sharp corners and hills to navigate with skill. One must be well equipped and experienced to handle the road, the metaphor for Stephens's body. "Ninja Bike" and the song "Nuh Ready fi Dis Yet" can thus be interpreted as part of her instruction manual for potential lovers. Through these songs, Stephens sets up very high standards and is therefore dismissive of partners who fail to live up to the promise of sexual fulfilment.

Consequently, in "Draw fi Mi Finger", Stephens discusses another controversial issue – masturbation – as one avenue to relieve her sexual frustration since the "heat still a linga" (the heat still lingers) after sexually inept men have climaxed. Masturbation remains a taboo subject in Jamaica, particularly amongst the Judeo-Christian populace. And yet Stephens not only castigates her lover for his poor performance, by masturbating she diminishes the need for a male partner to provide a woman with sexual satisfaction. In so doing, she transgresses the rules of masculine and feminine sexual engagement and celebrates self-satisfaction. Rather than feed into the narrative of the temperate, patient, good and faithful woman, Stephens creates room for the sexually liberated woman who knows what she wants and who, according to Perkins (2010, 2), "turns the male-female relationship on its head with the woman being the sexual aggressor and dominant partner". She is not hesitant, coy or flirtatious. She transgresses because she demonstrates stark independence by displaying a willingness to satisfy herself if necessary. It is her body, and she is decidedly in control.

Scholars have argued that Stephens's use of the word "bwoy" (the Jamaican word for boy) in her songs infantilizes males. Donna Hope (2006, 51), for instance, is quoted as saying that "many of my own male interviewees ... felt disrespected by the lyrics of the song and felt that Tanya was too aggressive, uppity and rude".

Stephens's wordplay extends beyond relationship woes and sexuality as she tackles world issues such as racism, queer identity and the conflicts in Iraq and Palestine in "Do You Still Care". She uses storytelling as her tour de force, starting with the racist Bubba:

> Where Bubba Grew Up,
> Kept his tobacco chewed up,

> And when they used to hang ropes, they always kept two up,
> Had crosses burnin all night like the church blew up,
> And if you didn't look like them, they would fuck you up.
>
> Time passed, and Bubba turned forty years old,
> And all them Jack Daniels started taking a toll,
> Seem like Bubba was about to make a final bow,
> None of his friends from the clan couldn't help him now.

Her song, raw and evocative, uses language common to listeners and oft associated with racism: "Nigger" and burning crosses of the Ku Klux Klan. Her description of Bubba's life and circumstances draw on common stereotypes recognizable as characteristics common to men from the southern United States. Bubba (even his name is a stereotype) is a tobacco chewing, Jack Daniels swigging, black people hating and Klansman liking white man. Stephens's thesis is strengthened through common tropes utilized to represent Bubba. Making Bubba an extreme of the southern white man, his predicament is stark – your hate hardly matters when you lie on your deathbed and the only way your life can be spared is by accepting the liver of a human being you hate because of the colour of his skin.

> Family gathered at his bedside, ready to sing the blues,
> When the doctor rushed in and said "I've got some news!!!"
> "The good news is, Bubba, I've found you a liver, only bad news is, it belongs to a Nigger"

When his life is on the line, Stephens in her chorus questions the foundations of the hatred that Bubba had once held dear. By asking the rhetorical question, "Tell me why can't you accept me as I am, Just as I am now", Stephens highlights the futility of hate. Her lyrics are armed with tropes, rhetorical questions and other literary devices that drive home Bubba's racial hatred as an exercise in futility. In the same song, the story of *Bigga* is similar to that of Bubba except that his story takes place in Jamaica or the Jamaican diaspora and explores the futility of homophobia. In Bigga's narrative, she uses common tropes that represent the archetypal black man raised to be tough, heterosexual, promiscuous and devoid of emotions:

> Where Bigga grew up, boys were supposed to be tough
> Girls were trophies every man always kept a few of

When he was hurt and the tears would sting in his eyes
His mother said "Stop di noise, yuh a girl? Real boys don't cry!"
He learned in order to be a man he had to know how to fight
And had some very definitive rules bout what's wrong or right
He never had the luxury of being able to choose
So to him for being different, there was no excuse.

In this song, commonly used homophobic statements – such as "chi-chi (gay man) fi dead" – are presented in her song to highlight Bigga's virulent homophobia. In and through her lyrics, Stephens illustrates how Jamaican patriarchy, supported by its hegemonic male ideal leaves no room for homosexuality. Male homosexuality challenges the masculinist notion that men must have multiple female partners, that they must head households with women in supplemental roles, and that being male means alpha posturing and positioning. Important in this heteronormative construct is the idea that penetration is exclusively penis to vagina and that women take penetration. Men do not. Stephens's lyrics above challenge these prevailing notions. Drawing on common Jamaican words and phrases such as "chi-chi" or the common phrase "Real boys don't cry" used to demean gender nonconforming males, Stephens reinforces her central thesis in this song – hate is futile.

In many ways, the song "Do you Still Care" mirrors the popular biblical tale of the Good Samaritan in Luke 20: 25–37. By drawing comparison to the Good Samaritan – a biblical character and story that many Jamaicans learn about in their infancy – she makes her argument relatable. She is able to represent the issue using stories and common motifs that are endemic in the Jamaican cultural sign system. In the end, her song is about acceptance and freedom; freedom from racism, freedom to love who you choose, freedom from war and the blossoming of human ideals. It presents a kind of utopia. Stephens advances a human rights and social justice perspective in her artistic retelling of the injustice faced by the ordinary black man in a white supremacist context, and a queer man in a heteronormative context. She goes against the grain of Judeo-Christian respectability, in her advocacy for queer acceptance, using the religion's own sign system and its relatable metaphors and stories. Her words seek to break down dominant Eurocentric and Judeo-Christian hegemonic discourse.

In "What a Day", Stephens imagines a day in the world where love and acceptance can reign. She levels a potent critique of conservative church elements and the hypocrisy within the church[12] when she sings:

Tired of leaving church feeling like I've just been robbed
Two hours of rambling not much mention of God
The richest man's the only one who does not have a job
A bunch of righteous freaks extorting worse than the mob

CONCLUSION

Stephens's lyrical genius is undeniable. Like any performer, she inhabits different roles and personas. She is the jilted wife, the sexual aggressor, the lover and the agitator. While she has a romantic side which emerges in songs such as "This Is Love" and "These Streets", she has demonstrated through her body of work that she can also be defiant and militant. Some of her songs assert and reinforce hegemonic discourse, while others operate as a form of cultural resistance that challenges Jamaica's patriarchal institutions and its inequitable regimes of power. Stephens traverses male spaces. When she rides the bike, she is the active party, not a passive site for the performance of masculinity. She demands and initiates high levels of sexual satisfaction. As such, she becomes the sexual aggressor, who, when necessary, rides and reaches her destination alone. Where men chase, she chases. Where they hold, and use guns, so too does she.[13] For fragile masculine egos, Stephens is a problem. She challenges them publicly and privately, seriously and humorously, in brilliant verbal displays, often styling them as "bwoy". It is no wonder Donna Hope's male interviewees wanted to take her down a peg, and Perkins's colleague found her a "man-bashing woman" (Perkins 2008; Hope 2006). In "1-1-9" she uses the gun to defend herself and establish boundaries and lethal authority. She performs and occupies what can only be described as a liminal space that supports and challenges dominant discourse. In this liminality, Stephens works within the heteronormative space carved out by dancehall for heteronormative femininity to thrive. At the same time, her lethal wordplay is like a dagger that cuts into the male ego, policing male bravado, aggression, sexuality and sexual desire. She traverses gendered borders and enters the male arena when she engages in "badmanism". The liminality that Stephens occupies is reflective of her testing, negotiating and even crossing gendered social boundaries while at the same time not completely abandoning them. She challenges what is considered acceptable behaviour, raising issues that are uncomfortable for conservative folks. Perkins (2010, 1) states it best when she writes:

Tanya Stephens, the self-proclaimed "rough rider"... jars the sensibilities of many Christians. When you listen to her... affairs abound; raw, rough sex touted; cheating condoned; female rivalry and fisticuffs encouraged; sex explicitly described; bad words liberally sprinkled; women seduce men; babies are given to the wrong father; genitalia worshipped... and, in the same breath, Christians are castigated as boring, thieving, hypocritical righteous freaks who fail to "practice what [they] preach".

Seeking a utopia where people can be free, she castigates racism and homophobia by allegorically highlighting their uselessness. Stephens speaks from different perspectives and by so doing, she both challenges and reinforces dominant discourses. The cultural studies lens of representation and language, Stuart Hall's work in particular, allows us to explore Stephens's use of language and tease out semantic undercurrents. This postmodernist reading of lyrics is reflective of the deconstructed nature of the relationship between performer and audience. In occupying different spaces and roles, Stephens demonstrates her lyrical genius and her capacity for empathy. This is not always a soft empathy, but one that screams to listeners – listen to the other side of the story. She arms her lyrics with metaphorical bullets; she launches grenades at the male ego with lyrical pizzazz and bombs patriarchal walls meant to confine her as she asks and demands:

> Now tell me why can't you accept me as I am
> Just the way I am now
> Tell me why can't you accept me as I am
> Just the way I am

NOTES

1. The role of traditional and non-traditional media in dehumanizing those deemed the other is well documented. Africans were depicted as thugs, thieves, licentious and ignorant. For more on these representations of Africans, Africa and its diaspora as well as other subaltern groups, see Alexander (2009), Darlington (2011) and Larson (2006). In the Jamaican social media landscape, it is not uncommon for the language, dress, culture and mishaps of the island's poor to be subject to ridicule. Responses to videos of skin bleaching and street dances posted on YouTube are more often than not negative. For more on ridicule and social media in Jamaica, see Osbourne (2016) and Dobson and Knezevic (2017).
2. A Gramscian concept, the organic intellectual emerges within a social class or ethnic group and from there expresses and advocates for the issues of its group

using various tools and skills at their disposal. Tanya Stephens as a black woman from Jamaica's poorer strata advocates on behalf of her gender and those who are economically and racially disadvantaged. For more on the organic intellectual, see Gramsci (2010).

3. Words such as "pickney" from Patwa which refers to child, Honda bikes which are popular across the island, and guns are used in her songs. The *69 a code used to trace phone calls is also familiar to her Jamaican audience as is tobacco chewing to her American and even Jamaican audiences.
4. The term "jacket" refers to children being raised or claimed by men who are victims of paternity fraud. In other words, these men are not the biological fathers of these children.
5. Ironically, in another song recorded later in 2004, "Boom Wuk", Stephens contradicts this position and instead plays the role of the woman on the side who only wants sex with no strings attached. She explains in this song that the sex is so good, she is happy to engage with no emotional or financial ties.
6. The Tec-9 is a self-loading semi-automatic pistol.
7. A Glock is semi-automatic pistol often used by police forces across the world.
8. In Jamaica, this issue was tried in the case *Stoeckert v. Geddes* and settled by the Privy Council in 2004. In this case, Helga Stoeckert lived with Paul Geddes for several decades as his common-law wife. Upon the breakdown of the relationship, Stoeckert sued for and received half of the Geddes estate.
9. See George (2016); Lavoulle and Ellison (2017); Nunn (2015).
10. *Bashment* is a popular term for a very good time or excitement in Jamaica.
11. Menstrual blood and vaginal fluids are thought to be used by some women to tie or bind their male partners to them, in complicated rituals associated with Obeah.
12. Interestingly, in this song, the word "freaks" is used to describe church going folks. However, in Jamaica, it commonly used to refer to persons who do not subscribe to dominant standards of sexual morality. For instance, men who orally pleasure women, and women who orally pleasure men, are considered "freaky types". Stephens certainly challenges the dominant understanding of the word freak in her deployment of this term as a pejorative to describe Christian fundamentalists.
13. Although in another song "Gangsta Gal", she is the woman who holds the gun and bails her man out of prison.

REFERENCES

Alexander, Claire. 2009. "Stuart Hall and 'Race'". *Cultural Studies* 23 (4): 457–82.
Alleyne, Mervyn. 1984. "The World View of Jamaicans". *Jamaica Journal* 17 (1): 2–8.
———. 2011. "Jackets: Made in Jamaica". *Gleaner*, 25 May. http://jamaica-gleaner.com/gleaner/20110525/lead/lead31.html.
———. 2018. "Murder Rate on the Increase in 2018". *RJR News*, 18 February. http://rjrnewsonline.com/local/murder-rate-on-the-increase-in-2018.
Barker, Chris. 2008. *Cultural Studies: Theory and Practice*. London: Sage.
———, ed. 2004. *Sage Dictionary of Cultural Studies*. London: Sage.
Barrett, Livern. 2017. "114 Murders in 20 Days: More Than 1,000 Jamaicans Killed since the Start of the Year". *Gleaner*, 30 August. http://jamaica-gleaner.com/article/lead-stories/20170830/114-murders-20-days-more-1000-jamaicans-killed-start-year.
Baudrillard, Jean. 1994. *Simulacra and Simulation*. Translated by Sheila Glaser. Ann Arbor: University of Michigan Press.
Beckles, Hilary. 1982. "The 200 Years War: Slave Resistance in the British West Indies, An Overview of the Historiography". *Jamaica Historical Review* 13:1–10.
Burton, Richard D.E. 1997. *Afro-Creole Power, Opposition and Play in the Caribbean*. Ithaca: Cornell University Press.
Bush, Barbara. 1990. *Slave Women in Caribbean Society 1650–1838*. Kingston: Heinemann Caribbean.
Campbell, Adella. 2017. "Exposing Violence against Women and Children: A Priority Area for National Action – Part 1". *Jamaica Observer*, 7 May. http://www.jamaicaobserver.com/the-agenda/exposing-violence-against-women-and-children-a_97219?profile=1444.
Campbell, John. 2012. *Beyond Massa: Sugar Management in the British Caribbean 1770–1834*. Wellesley, MA: Calaloux.
Chevannes, Barry. 1999. *What We Sow and What We Reap: Problems in the Cultivation of Male Identity in Jamaica*. Grace, Kennedy Lecture Series. Kingston: Grace, Kennedy Foundation.
———. 2001. *Learning to Be a Man: Culture, Socialization and Gender Identity in Five Caribbean Communities*. Kingston: University of the West Indies Press.
Connell, R.W. 1987. *Gender and Power: Society, the Person, and Sexual Politics*. Stanford, CA: Stanford University Press.
Cooper, Carolyn. 1994. "'Lyrical Gun': Metaphor and Role Play in Jamaican Dancehall Culture". *Massachusetts Review* 35, nos. 3–4 (Autumn): 429–42.
———. 2004. *Sound Clash: Jamaican Dancehall Culture at Large*. New York: Palgrave Macmillan.

Craton, Michael. 1982. *Testing the Chains: Resistance to Slavery in the British West Indies*. Ithaca: Cornell University Press.

Darlington, Patricia S.E. 2011. *Cultural Minority Representation in the Media: A Historic View of Television's Underserved*. Dubuque, IA: Kendall Hunt.

Derrida, Jacques. 1976. *Of Grammatology*. Translated by Gayatri Spivak. Baltimore: Johns Hopkins University Press.

Dobson, Kathy, and Irena Knezevic. 2017. "'Liking and Sharing' the Stigmatization of Poverty and Social Welfare: Representations of Poverty and Welfare through Internet Memes on Social Media". *tripleC: Communication, Capitalism and Critique* 15 (2): 777–95.

Duncombe, Stephen. 2007. Introduction to *Cultural Resistance Reader*, edited by Stephen Duncombe, 1–16. London: Verso.

———. "Cultural Resistance". 2002. *Blackwell Encyclopedia of Sociology Online*, edited by George Ritzer. 15 February. http://www.blackwellreference.com/public/tocnode?id=g9781405124331_chunk_g978140512433 19_ss1-179#citation.

During, Simon. 2005. *Cultural Studies: A Critical Introduction*. London: Routledge.

Foucault, Michel. 2002. *Archaeology of Knowledge*. Translated by Alan Sheridan Smith. London: Routledge.

George, Kat. 2016. "How Female Musicians of the 90s Reclaimed the Word 'Bitch'". *Dazed*. 5 February. http://www.dazeddigital.com/music/article/29629/1/how-female-musicians-of-the-90s-reclaimed-the-word-bitch.

Gramsci, Antonio. 2010. *Prison Notebooks*, vol. 1. New York: Columbia University Press.

Hall, Stuart. 1997a. Introduction to *Representation: Cultural Representations and Signifying Practices*, edited by Stuart Hall, 1–12. London: Sage.

———. 1997b. "The Spectacle of the 'Other'". In Hall, *Representations: Cultural Representations and Signifying Practices*, 223–79.

———. 1997c. "The Work of Representation". In Hall, *Representation: Cultural Representations and Signifying Practices*, 13–74.

Hart, Richard. 1980. *The Slaves Who Abolished Slavery: Blacks in Rebellion*. Kingston: Institute of Social and Economic Research, University of the West Indies.

Heuman, Gad. 1986. *Out of the House of Bondage: Runaways, Resistance and Maroonage in Africa and the New World*. London: Psychology Press.

Hope, Donna. 2006. *Inna di Dancehall: Popular Culture and the Politics of Identity in Jamaica*. Kingston: University of the West Indies Press.

———. 2010. *Man Vibes: Masculinities in the Jamaican Dancehall*. Kingston: Ian Randle.

———. 2017. "Jamaican DJ Weeps after DNA Test Proves He's Not Biological Dad of Two". *Loop Jamaica*. 29 November. http://www.loopjamaica.com/content/jamaican-dj-weeps-after-dna-test-proves-hes-not-biological-dad-two.

Kristeva, Julia. 1980. *Desire in Language: A Semiotic Approach to Literature and Art*. Oxford: Blackwell.

Larson, Stephanie Greco. 2006. *Media and Minorities: The Politics of Race in News and Entertainment*. New York: Rowman and Littlefield.

Lavoulle, Crystal, and Tisha Ellison. 2017. "The Bad Bitch Barbie Craze and Beyoncé: African American Women's Bodies as Commodities in Hip-Hop Culture, Images, and Media". *Taboo* 16 (2): 65–84.

Lewin, Olive. 2000. *"Rock It Come Over": The Folk Music of Jamaica*. Kingston: University of the West Indies Press.

Mair, Lucille Mathurin. 2006. *A Historical Study of Women in Jamaica 1655–1844*. Edited by Hilary McD Beckles and Verene A. Shepherd. Kingston: University of the West Indies Press.

Marshall, Bernard A. 2008. "Maronnage in Slave Plantation Societies: A Case Study of Dominica 1785–1815". *Caribbean Quarterly* 54 (4): 103–10.

Nunn, Gary. 2015. "Power Grab: Reclaiming Words Can Be Such a Bitch". *Guardian Weekly*, 30 October. https://www.theguardian.com/media/mind-your-language/2015/oct/30/power-grab-reclaiming-words-can-be-such-a-bitch.

Osbourne, Dervin. 2016. "Stop Making Fun of Poor People". *Gleaner*, 19 April. http://jamaica-gleaner.com/article/commentary/20160419/dervin-osbourne-stop-making-fun-poor-people.

Perkins, Anna Kasafi. 2008. "'Tasting Tears and [Not] Admitting Defeat': Promoting Values and Attitudes through the Music of Tanya Stephens?" Academia.edu, 12 January. https://www.academia.edu/1831858/Tasting_Tears_and_Not_Admitting_Defeat_Teaching_Values_and_Attitudes_through_the_Music_of_Tanya_Stephens.

———. 2010. "Love the Long Ding Dong: Tanya Transgresses Christian Sensibilities?" Academia.edu, 27 November. https://www.academia.edu/1831865/Love_the_Long_Ding_Dong_Tanya_Transgresses_Christian_Sensibilities?auto=download.

Saunders, Patricia J. 2003. "Is Not Everything Good to Eat, Good to Talk: Sexual Economy and Dancehall Music in the Global Marketplace". *Small Axe: A Caribbean Journal of Criticism* 13 (March): 95–115.

Saussure, Ferdinand de. 1960. *Course in General Linguistics*. London: Peter Owen.

Shepherd, Verene A. 1999. *Women in Caribbean History: The British-Colonised Territories*. Princeton: Markus Wiener.

Smith-Whyte, Oberlene. 2017. "Is She Cause It!' Domestic Violence and Human Rights Abuse in the Jamaican Context Part 1". *Gleaner*, 5 March. http://jamaica-gleaner.com/article/news/20170305/she-cause-it-domestic-violence-and-human-rights-abuse-jamaican-context-part-1.

Stanley Niaah, Sonjah. 2010. *Dancehall: From Slave Ship to Ghetto*. Ottawa: University of Ottawa Press.

Steinem, Gloria. 1995. *Moving Beyond Words: Age, Rage, Sex, Power, Money, Muscles: Breaking Boundaries of Gender*. New York: Simon and Schuster.
Warner-Lewis, Maureen. 2003. *Central Africa in the Caribbean Transcending Time, Transforming Cultures*. Kingston: University of the West Indies Press.
Williams, Eric. 1994. *Capitalism and Slavery*. Chapel Hill: North Carolina University Press.
Williams, Melissa, Elizabeth Levy Paluck and Julie Spencer-Rodgers. 2010 "The Masculinity of Money: Automatic Stereotypes Predict Gender Differences in Estimated Salaries". *Psychology of Women Quarterly* 34 (1): 7–20.
Wilson-Harris, Nadine. 2016. "SHAME! Twenty-Four Women Killed in 2016; Former Victim of Domestic Violence Urges Women to Protect Themselves". *Gleaner*, 18 December. http://jamaica-gleaner.com/article/lead-stories/20161218/shame-twenty-four-women-killed-2016-former-victim-domestic-violence.

DISCOGRAPHY

Beenie Man, vocalist. 1996. "Nuff Gal". Track 2 on *Maestro*. Shocking Vibes.
Stephens, Tanya, vocalist. 1997. "Goggle". Track 3 on *Too Hype*. VP Records.
———. 1997. "Nuh Ready fi Dis Yet". Track 1 on *Too Hype*. VP Records.
———. 1998. "Draw fi Mi Finger". Track 1 on *Ruff Rider*. VP Records.
———. 1998. "Freaky Type". Single. Hi-Profile Records.
———. 1998. "Ninja Bike". Track 5 on *Ruff Rider*. VP Records
———. 1998. "1-1-9". Track 8 on *Ruff Rider*. VP Records.
———. 2004. "After You". Single. Don Corleon Records.
———. 2004. "Little White Lie". Track 6 on *Gangsta Blues*. VP Records.
———. 2004. "This Is Love". Track 10 on *Gangsta Blues*. VP Records.
———. 2004. "What a Day". Track 16 on *Gangsta Blues*. VP Records.
———. 2006. "Do You Still Care". Track 15 on *Rebelution*. VP Records.
———. 2006. "These Streets". Track 18 on *Rebelution*. VP Records.

PART 3

"PUT IT ON YOU"
TANYA STEPHENS'S EROTIC PLAYBOOK

CHAPTER 8

A Lyrical Juxtaposition of Tanya Stephens and Fay-Ann Lyons-Alvarez

ALPHA OBIKA

> Yuh fi pose gwaan[1]
> Wi ah run dis wid or without we clothes on
> Everytime we step out, we take the place by storm
> Ah ready wi ready fi rule the world
> Behold the power of a Girl.
> (Stephens 2003)

THIS CHAPTER EXAMINES THE CONTRIBUTION OF TANYA STEPHENS to the Jamaican music industry through the lens of her lyrics that seek to uplift women while simultaneously challenging the male hegemony of Jamaican society. It seeks to juxtapose selected works of Stephens with Fay-Ann Lyons-Alvarez in order to make a statement about the role these artistes play as pillars of female empowerment in an industry that continues to control and manipulate the perspectives of women. A sample of songs from both artistes was conducted on the broad theme of female empowerment. Empowerment is a message that not only seeks to encourage women to rise above their challenges but also educates men on the value of women. Empowerment of the female in the context of popular culture is very much constructed in opposition to ideals of masculinity. It embodies the thrust of females toward self-determination and social transformation in public and private spaces dominated by a patriarchal hegemony. Drawing on the work of Carolyn Cooper, Donna Hope and other scholars who deal with issues of gender in the context of popular culture, I critically unpack the notion of empowerment. This theoretic engagement will be used to analyse the discourse of the selected songs. While some are inspirational, others appear antagonistic to the patriarchal norms that permeate the music industry.

In 2003 Stephens released the masterful track "Power of a Girl" on a compilation album titled *Shanty Town* (Pow Pow Productions 2006). Although Stephens was the only female artiste featured on the fifteen-track reggae album, by the time of its release, she was already a prominent figure in Jamaica's dancehall arena. Her presence alongside artistes like Sizzla Kalonji, Luciano and Anthony B showcased her versatility and unique ability to move between genres in Jamaican popular music. It was also symbolic of her status and talent in transgressing barriers of gender and public appeal in the male-dominated Jamaican music industry. Indeed, Stephens may be seen as a symbol of empowerment for women in a patriarchal context, reflected and reinforced by popular music.

While Samuel Fure Davis (2012, 123) locates Stephens as "the leading contemporary Jamaican female voice", her dominance must be viewed in a broader context of the wider society. Hope (2006, 51) tells us that "women like Tanya upset the traditional patriarchal structure of masculine dialogue into which the dancehall courtier or conqueror plays". The Jamaican music industry is viewed as reflective of a system of oppression that strategically hinders the progress of women. Against this paradigm, Hope (2015, 200) refers to the "prevailing hegemonic systems that limit the role of women to that of sexual recipient or domestic furniture". The patriarchal hegemony affects societal worldviews in the modern-day Caribbean and manifests itself in the output of the cultural and creative industries, of which the music industry is a fundamental component.

The culture inherent in the dancehall space epitomizes the objectification of women as sexual objects. According to Cooper (1993, 156), "it is the sexuality of women, much more so than that of men, which is both celebrated and devalued in the culture of the dancehall". The female body continues to be a subject of contestation and politicization in the arena of calypso and soca of Trinidad and Tobago as much as it is in Jamaica's dancehall spaces. Indeed, while Hope (2006 and 2015) and Cooper (1993) assess the politics of sexuality and gender dynamics of dancehall music, much of their analysis can be extended to the realities of the calypso and soca music industries. In a sense, Jamaica's Dancehall Queen and Trinidad and Tobago's Soca Jammette[2] are cousins.

Although centred around the Caribbean diaspora carnivals, Trinidad and Tobago's music industry presents a poignant example of a burgeoning sector captivating regional (Caribbean) and international audiences. Calypso and soca are the two prominent forms of popular music in the twin-island republic. Both genres, like their Jamaican counterparts (reggae and dancehall), deal extensively with themes that reflect a dominant, male-centred Caribbean ideology. The fact that many of the storytellers are male no doubt influences the stereotypes evident in the music. The representation of women is therefore seen through the male gaze. Gottreich (1993, 3) argues that themes of female exploitation and control epitomize typical approaches in the lyrics of calypso and soca, noting that "traditional (male-composed) Calypsos are generally disparaging in their portrayal of women. Images of women in Calypso range from physical characteristics of dirtiness and ugliness, to woman's unfaithfulness, her being overly sexual, or not sexual enough, to her manipulativeness and her greedy nature. Prominent throughout these images is the advocation of the need for violence to control her."

While Gottreich's analysis presents a one-sided view of calypso that fails to portray the nuances and subtleties of Trinidad and Tobago's culture, it does reveal an aspect of male hegemony that cannot be ignored. Not all male-composed calypsoes depict women in a negative light. However, Gottreich's point is further emphasized when one observes the history of calypso tents[3] in Trinidad and the treatment of women who aspire to participate in its early history. Research conducted by Rudolph Ottley (1992, 174) reinforces this fact; he notes that "according to a large percentage of female calypsonians, male calypsonians are treated with more respect and paid better wages than themselves. They also contend that some tent managers also attempt to seduce some female calypsonians as a means of listing them as members of their cast."

These derogatory ideas about women in the popular music of Trinidad and Tobago have a long history rooted in the dominance of male calypso performers and the virtual absence of female counterparts. One notable exception, however, was Calypso Rose (Martha Lewis) in the 1950s (Gottreich 1993). Despite her relatively early emergence, Ottley (1992, 174) tells us that "it was not until the early 1970s and 1980s that women as a group ventured to become calypsonians". Calypso Rose blazed a trail for emerging female calypsonians and soca artistes. Lyons-Alvarez would not only walk in the footsteps of her female predecessor but also in those of her father, Austin "Super Blue" Lyons, a veteran and icon of soca music in Trinidad and Tobago. Lyons-Alvarez is part of a "soca royalty" due to her marriage to fellow Soca artist Ian "Bunji Garlin" Alvarez. As explored below, while the path of Lyons-Alvarez is different from Stephens, her experience echoes with similarities once we examine the role that Stephens has played and continues to play as one of the most respected artistes in Jamaica and the Caribbean.

POWER OF A GIRL: STRENGTH AND RESILIENCE, CHALLENGING THE PATRIARCHY

The song "Power of a Girl" is a clarion call for women to recognize their strengths and exercise control of their destiny. However, unlocking the innate power that women possess necessitates a rejection of the stereotype that females are merely irrational, sexual beings. Dispelling this depiction of women is central to Stephens's quest:

> Make them know the body comes with ah mind
> Ah we nuh deya fi no bump and grind
> A nuh we sole purpose inna life is skin out or cock up or wine we waistline
> Make de man dem know how we feel
> Ah long time we ah get ah raw deal
> We did ah beg and send out we appeal
> An dem never wah take we fi real.
>
> (Let them know the body comes with a mind
> And we are not here only for sex
> It's not our sole purpose in life to move our waistline
> Let the men know how we feel
> Long time we have been getting a raw deal
> We begged and sent out an appeal
> And we were not taken seriously.)

The defence of women's rights is a central theme here, where voice is given to the concerns of females, who Stephens argues in the song, have been given "a raw deal". The suggestion is that the traditional, coy, "lady-like" approach has not been successful in representing how women feel. Therefore, women have been taken for granted and oppressed. "Power of a Girl" appears almost as a roadmap to liberating women from the oppressive relationships with men that have largely led to their submission. Stephens tells them, "You have the right to stand up and fight, time to defend your role." The tone of assertive encouragement present within the lyrics embodies the solution for women to exert more power in society and is suggestive of the possibility of collective action to achieve this outcome. While Stephens is careful not to negate women's sexual expression in the bedroom, she encourages them to assume more power both in the personal space and the public realm when she sings, "make dem know de body comes with a head / we exist outside a di bed" (let them know that our bodies come with a head / we exist outside of the bed).

Empowerment is a central theme of many of Stephens's songs, which have a simultaneously mirroring effect. While extolling the virtues of standing strong in the face of adversity, she is constantly enacting and re-enacting the values of strength and resilience to survive in the Jamaican and global music industry.

The quest for sexual dominance in the personal space and the public realm is a recurrent theme in dancehall music and is one that Stephens tackles head on. Cooper (1993, 155) states that "for the female DJ, as much as for the male, sexual prowess is an essential element of the kudos of the entertainer, but female sexuality is imagined in terms of the male gaze". In a male-dominated music industry this has the effect of proffering the male perspective at the expense of female representation. Stephens therefore plays a critical role in representing the perspectives of women while also challenging the hegemony that privileges men in Jamaican popular music.

According to Marshall (2006, 3) women in Caribbean post-slavery societies have been historically "portrayed as innately promiscuous and predatory Jezebels".[4] The hierarchy within the slavery and post-slavery society placed the black woman at the lowest level, possessing the least power. Marshall more explicitly reveals the reality of "jezebelization" of the black woman when she writes, "The icon of the sexually denigrated Black female not only effectively legitimated the maximum exploitation of her reproductive labour but also exonerated white men who abused her from guilt. The rearticulation of this history of racialized sexual subordination contributes to the inferior socio-economic and political position of women in the Caribbean region. The representation of Jezebel in Caribbean societies today reproduces myths that have existed since the sixteenth century."

The black woman was therefore subjected to multidimensional violence of a physical, sexual and psychological nature, which sought to disempower her spirit for the purpose of the plantation society. This racist ideology, mainly propagated through the white male, also meant that the subjugation was symbolic of a patriarchy representative of male dominance. This paradigm persists across the modern-day Caribbean and is emblematic of the manifestations of female sexual and racial oppression in popular culture whereby "the depiction of Caribbean women as promiscuous, prostitutes and libidinous is evident in Soca and Dancehall scenes" (Marshall 2006, 5).

Oppressive notions of female identity feature prominently in soca and dancehall music. In fact, calypso songs from earlier periods boldly portray stereotypes that only serve to restrict the independence and growth of women. Thus, in his song "Women Will Rule the World", Attila the Hun (birth name Raymond Quevedo), a calypsonian from the early 1900s, emphasized the patriarchal view of women at the time:

> I'm offering a warning to men this year
> Of modern women beware (*twice*)
> Even the young girls you cannot trust
> For they're taking our jobs from us
> And if you men don't assert control
> Women will rule the world

According to Gordon Rohlehr (1990, 224), "it is clear from calypsoes such as this one that the very veneration of women's role as wife, mother and helpmate was part of an ideology of control which was designed to deny women the possibility of successful movement beyond the home and the family". The calypso genre therefore reflected popular beliefs, attitudes and values toward women and their role in society. This lays a foundation for understanding calypso and soca music and the portrayal of women as sexual objects for the pleasure of men in the modern era. In the soca music industry of Trinidad and Tobago, Lyons-Alvarez has had to face challenges as a female entertainer in a male-dominated sector. She is a symbol of female empowerment due to her strong resistance to stereotypes of women. Songwriter, recording artiste, performer and businesswoman are just some of the labels that can be used to describe her. A *Newsday* article published in 2015 lauds Lyons-Alvarez as a soca legend in the making:

> In 2009 Fay Ann copped the International Power Soca Monarch and International Groovy Soca Monarch[5] titles, and in so doing created history as the first female to win the Power category, and the first individual (male or female) to win the Power, Groovy and People's Choice awards in the same year. She also went on to win the Road March[6] that year, becoming the first Soca artiste to win that "triplet" of titles. (*Newsday* 2015)

Lyons-Alvarez is considered "soca royalty" mainly because of her hard work and many achievements, but also due to the influence of her father, Austin Lyons, also known as Super Blue.[7] Lyons has won many titles over his thirty-eight-year career, including the Soca Monarch and Road March titles. This longevity and many accomplishments no doubt paved the way for the emergence of his daughter. Crediting her father, Lyons-Alvarez is quoted as saying, "My dad gave me advice on how to write and today I write for myself, which is one of the biggest tools. Because I can write for myself, I can feed myself and take care of my family" (Luke 2012). The accolades obtained have positioned her as one of a few female soca artistes in an industry heavily dominated by their male counterparts. Lyons-Alvarez is a symbol of female empowerment in Trinidad and Tobago and the Carnival diaspora.

Barratt (2015, 97) has argued that Lyons-Alvarez "is one of the few female soca artists who writes all of her songs and in 2004, she was recognized by the Copyright Organization of Trinidad and Tobago with awards for New Songwriter of the Year, Female Songwriter of the Year and Song of the Year". The importance of song writing cannot be overstated as a direct vehicle to presenting the perspectives of women in the public realm. Lyons-Alvarez is therefore equipped to represent the views of women in a male-dominated soca industry. In 2009, she captured the International Power Soca Monarch and Road March titles with the song "Meet Super Blue". While paying homage to her father, the song is a message to the world that she is a newer, stronger and more resilient version of him:

> Dey trying to flop me
> Tell them ah keep moving doh stop
> Ah know they cyah stop me
> Tell dem ah keep moving doh stop
> Long time dey whah drop me
> Tell dem ah keep moving doh stop
> So dey underrate me
> Tell dem ah keep moving doh stop
> Let these people know I am not my fadda
> Bad like him, but truth be told
> Like me there will be no other
> Dis is not a sham
> Who God bless don't put asunder

If yuh believe that this is true
Meet Super Blue.

(They are trying to make me fail
Tell them I'll keep moving and I won't stop
I know they can't stop me
Tell them I'll keep moving and I won't stop
A long time they want me to drop
Tell them I'll keep moving and I won't stop
So they underrated me
Tell them I'll keep moving and I won't stop
Let these people know I am not my father
I am good like him, but the truth be told
There will be no other like me
This is not a sham
Who God bless don't put asunder
If you believe that this is true
Meet Super Blue.)

"Meet Super Blue" is a statement of her ability to captivate audiences through mastery of soca music. It embodies her determination for success despite constant criticism.

The tenacity of Lyons-Alvarez is exemplified by her winning "both the Groovy and Power Soca Monarch titles in 2009, just a few weeks before giving birth to her daughter, Syri" (Luke 2012). Performing in a fully pregnant state, Lyons-Alvarez "disputed perceptions about pregnant women, and by continuing to work, she challenged social norms that view pregnant bodies as being in a state of disability and those that view expectant mothers as only waiting for the birth of their child" (Barratt 2015, 105). This moved audiences around the country to rally behind the song, making it a Carnival anthem in 2009, and cementing her place among the legends of the art form.

Interestingly, while Lyons-Alvarez draws on the name and legacy of her father in "Meet Super Blue", she is careful to establish her own identity when she sings, "Let these people know I am not my fadda, Bad like him, but truth be told, Like me there will be no other" (Let these people know I am not my father, Good like him but truth be told, Like me there will be no other). While acknowledging the path laid for her, she makes a strong statement that her route will be different. As a trailblazer, she is aware of her resistance to the dominant forces in the music industry who expect conformity to societal norms, as seen in this excerpt of from the same hit song:

> Been hearing them lately
> Tell dem ah keep moving doh stop
> She doh act like ah lady
> Tell dem ah keep moving doh stop
> Make no apology
> Tell dem ah keep moving doh stop.
>
> (I've been hearing them lately
> Tell them I'll keep moving and I won't stop
> She doesn't act like a lady
> Tell them I'll keep moving and I won't stop
> I'll make no apology
> Tell them I'll keep moving and I won't stop.)

Her defiance of the patriarchy is described as unladylike behaviour, for which she is unapologetic. The expression "Meet Super Blue" encapsulates her inherited legacy and simultaneously her innate strength.

Lyons-Alvarez has much in common with the reggae and dancehall icon Stephens. The comparison through a discourse analysis of both artistes' songs supports the claim that they both embody the positive values of African Caribbean women who struggle for existence in male-dominated postcolonial societies. Both Stephens and Lyons-Alvarez have constructed female archetypes that are willing to move beyond the scripted oppressive roles that are outlined for them in patriarchal society. These two artistes are articulating and demonstrating to society that women's moral agency, intellectual autonomy and self-actualization can only be realized by way of walking on the path of human equity, justice and self-determination. Both the songs "Power of a Girl" and "Meet Super Blue" express ideas of female empowerment and a world in which women's bodies are not valourized while their minds are devalued, and in which ideas of ladylike behaviour are not used to constrict their human potentialities and full participation in society.

HANDLE THE RIDE: SEXUAL ASSERTION AND SATISFACTION

Dancehall music is a battleground for sexual dominance between the sexes. Hope (2006, 48) asserts that "in the male-dominated dis/place, this negotiation for elevated status and identity is translated into the lyrical and stylistic courtship, conquest and dominance of female sexuality, femininity and women". This is evident in the constant lyrical quest by male protagonists to court and control the "punaany".[8] The following lyrics of "Pum Pum Conqueror" by Spragga Benz (Carlton Grant) exemplify the obsession with the female anatomy and attendant sexuality:

> Pum pum conqueror, pum pum conqueror
> Pum pum fat, pum pum slim
> Pum pum bushy and pum pum trim
> Pum pum black, pum pum brown
> Pum pum heavier than a hundred pound
> Pum pum conqueror, pum pum conqueror.

The prevalence of "pum pum"[9] conquering songs catalysed the emergence of female artistes who sought, through their own lyrics, to challenge the misogynistic objectification. While Lady Saw (Marion Hall) was touted as the "Queen of Slackness" (Hope 2006, 50), Stephens also took up the helm of subverting the sexual trajectory imposed by male dancehall performers. According to Hope, "Tanya Stephens's release of the dismissive 'Yuh Nuh Ready fi Dis Yet' in 1996 pushed at the gendered boundaries of dancehall discourse when she berated the self-praising man for his lack of sexual prowess and his inability to satisfy women" (51). Stephens's subversion of the status quo also takes place in songs like "Handle the Ride" and "Big Ninja Bike". Rendered on the Lecturer Riddim,[10] "Handle the Ride" highlights the ironic claim of male dominance while revealing male sexual vulnerability. The notion of patriarchy itself seems volatile, as Stephens exclaims, "You couldn't handle the ride" (1997). Here she exposes the hypocrisy eminent in the public show of sexual bravado and virility by men, while in reality many are deemed sexually inferior performers in private. The song uses an effective mix of metaphors and personifications to paint a vivid picture of female sexual assertiveness and strong expectation of sexual satisfaction. For instance, John, the protagonist of the song, represents the male sexual organ, while the champion, "Philly" (or well-bred horse), is the woman personified. In the song, John loses the encounter with the Philly and dies. The intro to "Handle the Ride" introduces John and reveals his predicament:

> Aye John, what kinda idiot ting dat ya keep up pon mi man?
> Bout yuh back bad?
> Mi lose off of you enuh!
>
> (Aye John, what kind of idiotic behaviour is that?
> Saying that your back is bad?
> I have lost the bet placed on you!)

In addition to revealing the farcical claim of male sexual dominance, the male ego is at the centre of the discourse Stephens engages in. The failure of John to admit he lacks stamina is met by an unapologetic Philly who is not afraid to move at full throttle:

> Tell your friend dem you wicked and brutal
> But now you end up in the hospital
> Talk bout how much gyal you kill
> You never stop till you write your own will
> Now you gone a doctor fi pill
> You should ah hear when mi tell you fi chill.
>
> (You told your friends that you are wicked and brutal
> But now you are in the hospital
> You talk about how much girls you dominated sexually
> You never stopped until you wrote your own will
> Now you are going to the doctor for sexual enhancement pills
> You should have listened when I told you to relax.)

The demise of John is compounded by the frailty of the male ego that Stephens exposes as an ironic reality in patriarchal society. The public persona of John must maintain a position of strength to mask the reality of weakness. While not seeking to destroy John, Stephens takes the approach of a teacher who seeks to educate men about the proper ways of treating women. "Handle the Ride" is part of a discourse that highlights women's power, to create or destroy, to please or to hurt. Respect for women appears to be one of the ultimate goals of the discourse around female sexual assertion and satisfaction captured in this song. Stephens also highlights women as active as opposed to passive participants in sexual intercourse, explicitly undermining the idea that men are the directing force during this pleasurable episode. However, this sexual dominance cannot be oversimplified and must be seen in the broad context of Stephens's diverse repertoire.

Stephens's champion Philly in "Handle the Ride" can be likened to Lyons-Alvarez's "Heavy T Bumpa". The soca song won the Groovy Soca Monarch competition in 2009, because of its captivating analogy of female sexual strength epitomized by the bumper of heavy T vehicles.[11] Heavy or extra-heavy T vehicles represent female derrieres and function as the central tool for the rhythmic gyration of the waist[12] while soca is played. Lyons-Alvarez pays homage to the female posterior as a symbol of strength, but she goes further to empower full-bodied women who may have ordinarily been body shamed or ignored by the Euro-Western male-centric version of what a beautiful female body should look like. "Heavy T Bumpa" emboldens women of all sizes (but especially encourages full-bodied women) to express themselves proudly, while challenging the male claim to dominance in both the public and private spheres: "No man cyah mash up meh structure, true for de gyal with the heavy T bumper." "Heavy T Bumpa" gives women "licence" to have fun:

> Make de man dem want it
> Turn round your bumpa and flaunt it
> In your low-rise jean, Bumpa lookin mean
> Have man behaving real drastic
> Now, move over skinny bumpa gyal
> Move over narrow bumpa gyal
> Flat bumpa get left behind
> Kill dem with de Heavy T wine[13]
>
> (Make the men want your bottom
> Turn around your bottom and show it off
> In your low-rise jeans, your bottom is looking good
> You have the men behaving desperate
> Now, move over small bottom girls
> Move over narrow bottom girls
> Flat bottom girls will get left behind
> Give them your big bottom wine)

The song also reveals another layer that must be peeled away to highlight its significance. While Lyons-Alvarez subverts traditional Western notions of beauty epitomized by slim bodies in empowering women who do not conform to this stereotypically imposed norm to be proud in their skin, the lines

> Move over skinny bumpa gyal
> Move over narrow bumpa gyal
> Flat bumpa get left behind
> Kill de with the Heavy T wine

embolden full-bodied women while seemingly body shaming women with smaller bodies. Although referencing a vehicle, "Heavy T Bumpa" has similarities to Stephens's "Handle the Ride", particularly in expressing the male's inability to manage or control the woman's body as an instrument of sexual pleasure or an entity desirous of sexual intimacy:

> Most man cyah ride with it
> So dey get park up one side with it
> Say dey cyah hold on so they cyah stay long
> So they slip, slip, slip and slide with it.
>
> (Most men cannot wine on a big bottom
> So they get pushed to the side
> They say they cannot hold on or wine long on the bottom
> So they slip, slip, slip and slide with it.)

The paradox present in the comparison of female bodies to animate and inanimate objects as a show of strength is that it plays into the very objectification and sexualization of female bodies by men that is being challenged. The display of sexual agency and ownership by the female protagonists in the songs presented is part of a narrative of reclamation and empowerment that is not without its nuances and contradictions. Nevertheless, themes of female strength, resilience and sexual assertiveness are portrayed in the lyrical characterizations in both "Heavy T Bumpa" and "Handle the Ride". Both songs are successful in connecting to women and gaining the attention of men. With respect to men, they are indicating that bodily erotic pleasure must centre women's satisfaction and active participation. Additionally, the songs confront the ritualized subjugation of female bodies by the patriarchy. Finally, as female artistes in industries dominated by males, both Stephens and Lyons-Alvarez exert a powerful presence through the statements of power, agency and self-confidence expressed in their lyrics.

LITTLE WHITE LIE: COMPLEXITY OF HUMAN NATURE

While Stephens espouses the virtues of strength, resilience, sexual assertiveness and autonomy by women, her portrayal does highlight some degree of vulnerability. This trait does not define the woman, but it exists and reveals itself every so often in her lyrics. The complexity is not couched as a female idiosyncrasy but instead can be observed in her songs as a general part of human nature. "Little White Lie" is one such song that depicts a situation in which the mother (protagonist) is withholding the truth about the actual biological father of her child from her partner, who believes that he is the father. The truth is also withheld from the child, which is both a source of shame and hurt to the mother in the lines:

> You got your daddy's smile, you got his eyes
> I feel my heart breaking every time you cry
> I'm gonna burn in hell, but it's no sacrifice
> Your stability is worth a million lies
> I see your daddy, in everything you do
> And if you could talk, I'll bet you'll talk like him too
> But he can't be your daddy, I hope you understand
> The man who thinks he's your father
> Is a much better man
> Maybe one day, you'll end up crying on Ricki Lake
> But baby it's a chance your momma's willing to take.

The lyrics are sung as a lullaby to her sleeping child. The guilt about the lie the mother has perpetrated is reflective of what is commonly referred to in Jamaica as "jacket".[14] Stephens reveals the plight of women participating in this phenomenon, a lie that is couched in a socio-economic dilemma wherein the eventual pain and hurt that would be caused from discovering the truth in the long term are worth maintaining the current position of familial stability for the child's sake in the short term. The question here is not whether the justification has merit in the context provided. What matters is that Stephens brings to light a complex social issue from a woman's perspective, thereby giving voice to a sensitive matter that creates tension in a patriarchy that scorns such situations. The power of a mother's love is also represented, not as a weakness, but as a strength:

And so I lie, baby I try, and it kills me inside
But I'm gonna live with this until the day I die
And I hurt, baby, oh how I hurt
But I know what you're worth, yeah
So I'm gonna live with this
Until I hit the dirt.

The song utilizes slow reggae instrumentals to emphasize the emotions depicted in the lyrics. The storytelling ability of Stephens is highlighted through the connection to real life experiences and portrayals of women's perspectives. In dealing with the contradictions of human nature, Stephens succeeds in painting a true representation of feminine realities. This is evident in songs such as "It's a Pity" and "Tek Him Back".

"It's a Pity", undoubtedly a classic, reveals the dilemma of a woman caught between her current relationship and the man she desires. While the song appears to privilege monogamy and faithfulness by the suggestion that the protagonist has "a one man" in her life, there is a strong undercurrent of regret evident in the phrase "It's a pity". In this song, the protagonist harbours thoughts of infidelity and promiscuity, typical of male sexual behaviour. Stephens therefore challenges the prevailing paradigm, which projects monogamy on the female while tolerating de facto male "polygamy". At the same time, the words "pity" could be interpreted as a pejorative, one that implies Stephens's (unwitting) pandering to dominant paradigms where monogamy is the prevailing norm, especially for females. Monogamy, in a sense, becomes the enemy of female empowerment, which is creatively constructed to subvert structures of power that serve to disempower women.

Male sexual promiscuity has typically been celebrated in dancehall music. Hope (2006, 47) tells us that "the concept of a wukka man (worker man) who have "nuff gyal inna bungle" (many girls in a bundle) is one that is actively subscribed to by men who are precariously placed on the lowest ledge of the race/class/gender nexus". While the range of men in Jamaica subscribing to polygamous relationships certainly extends beyond the dancehall space, Stephens gives voice to the female point of view, suggesting that women also harbour thoughts of engaging in multiple relationships, as seen from this verse in "It's a Pity":

I woulda like one of these mornings to wake up and find
Your face on a pillow lying right next to mine

I woulda cut out the partying the smoking and the rum
And buss a extra wine and make we seal up a son
Well every time mi fantasize, me see your lips, me see your eyes
Your trigger finger do something, a left the rude girl hypnotized
For you it's just a thing, just another little fling
But for me this is heaven and the angel them a sing.

(I would like one of these mornings to wake up and find
Your face on a pillow lying right next to mine
I would stop partying, smoking and drinking rum
And have sex with you and give you a son
Every time I fantasize, I see your lips, I see your eyes
Your finger does something to me, and leave the rude girl hypnotized
For you it's just a thing, just another little fling
But for me this is heaven and the angel them a sing.)

The woman presented in "It's a Pity" can be compared to the protagonist of "Tek Him Back", who has successfully broken up a monogamous relationship. Stephens sings, "Couple of times you used to call me pon de phone, cuss me how fi lef your husband alone" (A few times you used to call me on the phone, curse me and telling me to leave your husband alone). Extolling the financial and sexual worthlessness of the man, the woman begs the wife to take back her husband: "Wifey, please, come tek him back" (Wife, please, come and take him back). Stephens highlights the role of the "matey",[15] who is a product of the quest for financial and sexual satisfaction by any means. This juxtaposes the good girl versus bad girl image, showcasing multiple dimensions, enriching the portrayal of women in Jamaican popular culture.

"Little White Lie" closely approximates "Denial" by Lyons-Alvarez. Although categorized as soca, "Denial" has a typically "calypsoesque" lyrical structure and rhythmic pattern. There are three verses and a well-developed chorus that allows for the development of the story, while utilizing a calypso/groovy soca beat and instrumentals. The vocal style varies between calypso and rhythm and blues, which enhances the transfer of emotions evoked in the song. The theme of human complexity is once again presented from a female perspective, which itself is empowering. The lyrics of "Denial" lay bare a relationship based on deception, where both female and male have been actively attempting to deceive the other through a series of lies. Within that context, Lyons-Alvarez presents deception from the woman's angle, expressing guilt at the hidden truth. The approach of feigning innocence through denials of specific accusations shows vulnerability and an attempt to preserve a façade of faithfulness:

> Whey yuh was when ah call yuh phone this morning
> Ah don't know what yuh talking bout
> And every question ah ask yuh stalling
> Ah don't know what yuh talking bout
> And who's the man drop yuh home last night in ah Lancer
> Ah don't know what yuh talking bout
> And when ah call yuh phone yuh take long to answer
> Ah don't know what yuh talking bout
> Ah tried and I tried, and still denied
> De truth inside, so ah answer
> Ah don't know what yuh talking bout
>
> (Where were you when I called your phone this morning
> I don't know what you are talking about
> And every question I asked you are stalling
> I don't know what you are talking about
> And who is the man who dropped you home in a Lancer vehicle
> I don't know what you are talking about
> And when I called your phone you took long to answer
> I don't know what you are talking about
> I tried and I tried, and still denied
> The truth inside, so I answered
> I don't know what you are talking about.)

The female protagonist in "Denial" fails to conceal her infidelity expressing regret for being caught, rather than for cheating. The implicit admittance of guilt in the response "Ah don't know what yuh talking bout" (I don't know what you are talking about) is a reflection of both the individual and the unstable relationship. Some semblance of dignity is eked out with the phrase "Ah started off with good intention", but this fails to absolve the protagonist of wrongdoing. At the same time, the song also places blame on the male partner, who employs his own series of weak denials.

The transition from female to male denials suggests a reciprocal infidelity, which destroys the relationship. In the first verse, the woman asks the question, "Whey yuh was when ah call yuh phone this morning?" (Where were you when I called your phone this morning?) In the second verse, the role of interrogator is switched to the male, who also asks the same question only to receive the same response that he gave the female, "Ah don't know what yuh talking bout" (I don't know what you are talking about). What occurs is the subversion of roles, which ultimately challenges female stereotypes of monogamous individuals who are victims of the patriarchal hegemony. In "Denial", Lyons-Alvarez apportions some blame to the female while indirectly making a connection to the actions of the male that can be described as causal. Nevertheless, "Denial" is successful in relating real-life scenarios involving a domestic female-male situation. Through this composition, Lyons-Alvarez brings to light issues from the woman's perspective, thereby privileging the female voice. Empowerment in this context may also be derived from the woman's quest for self-satisfaction, inside or outside of a stable relationship. The protagonist essentially breaks the traditional code of female monogamy, which typically limits and polices the sexual autonomy and self-determination of women. The subversion of denial is craftily employed to challenge patriarchal notions of a woman's role as victim and the man's as perpetrator. This strategy is similar to the approach that Stephens employs in "Little White Lie".

The complexity of human relations explored thus far in the lyrics of Stephens and Lyons-Alvarez has dealt with the deliberate subversions of male narratives that position men as active enforcers of patriarchy and women as passive recipients of patriarchal domination. The irony here is that women have revealed that they can be unfaithful, polygamous individuals, equally obsessed with the sexual prowess of men and their ability or lack thereof to perform sexually. The female artists in this context have reimagined sexual prowess from a female gaze. Despite its contradictions, this subversion is in itself an act of empowerment.

The repositioning of the sexual narrative by Stephens and Lyons-Alvarez continues in such songs as "Boom Wuk" and "Pressure", respectively. "Boom Wuk" is explicit in affirming the female gaze and the subsequent objectification of the male subject. The first verse sees the female telling the male, "Baby, it's all about the sex", a statement that reduces the masculine subject to a sexual object to be used for female sexual satisfaction. The chorus reverses the "pum pum" conquering ways of the male to what could be considered the "ding dong/buddy conquering" female:

> Me just love off your boom wuk[16]
> Love the way you have me pum pum stuck
> Pon de big buddy,[17] pon de big stick

Tell me tan, when me bum flick
Love de long ding dong.¹⁸

(I love how you have sex with me
I love the way you make my vagina feel
On the big penis, on the big penis
Tell me to turn when we have sex
I love the long penis.)

In this chorus, the "punaany" or "pum pum" narrative typical of male dancehall artistes is reversed to include a discourse on the "ding dong", or the "buddy". This no doubt reinforces Cooper's (1993) assertion that sexual prowess is as important to the female dancehall performer as it is to her male counterpart. In fact, the male protagonist in "Boom Wuk" is uncomfortable with this sexual subjugation, as evidenced in the lines "Lately, you seh you get a vibe, seh you nuh tink we ah guh make it / seh mi only give you ratings when yuh naked" (Lately, you say you are getting a vibe, you don't think our relationship will survive, and I only admire you when you are naked).

In contrast, the sexualization of the male through his sexual prowess in "Pressure" by Lyons-Alvarez is more subtle. In the context of soca music, double-entendre is an important instrument for the transference of meaning. Subtlety is a device used in sexual discourse prevalent in soca and calypso. "Pressure" utilizes sexual imagery that is understated but certainly implied by the clear instructions, as is clear in the following lyrics:

Turn it round, put pressure on it
Up and down, put pressure on it
In and out, put pressure on it
Round about, put pressure on it.

"It" in the chorus refers to the woman's posterior, which is an essential tool in the soca space. Lyons-Alvarez takes the role as instructor guiding the man's actions to ensure her satisfaction. The motions captured mimic sexual movements performed in public spaces where soca is played. The female protagonist asks the man to "Press harder, press harder, harder", which simultaneously challenges the masculine sexual prowess while asserting feminine power. The objectification of the man continues in a similar vein as Stephens's "Boom Wuk" when Lyons-Alvarez instructs the man to:

> Stop talking, be about it
> Come closer, push up on meh
> Watch me wine and check up on it
> I won't lie, I'm not shy.

The clear instruction renders the man voiceless and relegates him to the status of the silent or junior partner in the process. Through "Pressure", the woman is claiming her sexuality in the soca space. While the result of the woman's performance is mutually beneficial, the process is controlled, managed and directed by the female protagonist. This process of sexual reclamation of the female body is a central theme of Lyons-Alvarez's songs and certainly connects her to Stephens in this regard.

CONCLUSION

The chapter began as a lyrical exploration into the music of both Stephens's and Lyons-Alvarez's music with the purpose of aligning their discourse as part of an approach geared toward female empowerment. My argument that the work of both artistes reflects the broad theme of female empowerment emanates from a critical examination of the range of topics covered and the implication of their music for women's lived experiences. Based on the themes, similarities can be drawn that position both as symbols of a movement toward balance in male-dominated music spaces. The patriarchal dictates of postcolonial Caribbean society make it imperative that female opinions, views and perspectives be heard. Both Stephens and Lyons-Alvarez are part of that movement. At this juncture, an acknowledgement must be made that even with their similarities, both artistes are different, operating in differing spaces with distinctive ideologies and unique challenges. Reggae and dancehall in Jamaica are quite different from calypso and soca in Trinidad and Tobago. However, Cooper (1993, 191) quite rightfully draws comparisons between the creative indigenous energies of the Caribbean region, despite social, economic and political issues that seek to limit sustainable development: "the Governments of the region may not be federated, but the people of the Caribbean share a common capacity to make sweet music out of the industrial waste of our societies". Calypsonians and reggae musicians are singled out among the "devalued 'low culture' artistes and artisans" who create music to "service the local needs, but increasingly cater to the international mass market in exoticised 'world culture'". This certainly applies to the popular musical artisans in the Caribbean and is also reflective of the current mass appeal of music in the region. The quest for cultural identity is the context against which the critical analysis of gender relations in the popular musical art forms must be closely examined.

Stephens is a living musical icon in Jamaica and the Caribbean diaspora, whilst Lyons-Alvarez is an award-winning soca artiste on the path to becoming an icon. In the spaces where they operate, these artistes have accepted the responsibility to be positive influences not only on the women who seek to emulate them but on their audiences in general. Some of the approaches adopted by female artistes could be interpreted as negative, contradictorily employing sexualizing and objectifying narratives for their own purpose. The case of Stephens and Lyons-Alvarez presents a deliberate subversion of female stereotypes for the purpose of empowerment. They challenge the ideological mores and societal norms that continue to subjugate, suppress and sideline women. Stephens in particular has displayed longevity and resilience that puts her in a class by herself. Her versatility and willingness to represent the views of women assertively and unapologetically means that credit must be given. An attempt was made to locate her work within a growing body of artistic discourse around gender issues in a Caribbean context. The comparison was made through an extensive process of listening, transcription and lyrical analysis. The themes of strength, resilience, challenging the patriarchy, sexual assertion, and autonomy and human nature were threads of commonality that made the critical assessment possible. As Stephens's catalogue continues to grow in the years to come, one can only envision her playing a greater role as a symbol of empowerment, not only for females specifically but for Caribbean people in general.

NOTES

1. Girl, be proud of how you look and show off.
2. "Jammette" is a colloquial term used in Trinidad and Tobago to describe a woman of "loose morals". She is also an overtly sexual woman. In the dancehall culture of Jamaica, "skettel" is the term used to categorize this type of woman.
3. A calypso tent is a place where calypsonians performed calypsoes, typically during annual Carnival celebrations in Trinidad and Tobago.
4. According to Marshall (2006, 4), "the name Jezebel signifies a sexually perverse, cruel and deceitful woman".

5. The International Power Soca Monarch and International Groovy Soca Monarch competitions are the biggest and most prestigious competitions for soca music in Trinidad and Tobago and the world.
6. According to Mark Lyndersay (2018) in *Caribbean Beat*, "the modern Road March must be the anthem of wining, that rhythmic gyration of the waist, often done in concert with a partner or two". In existence since 1930, the Road March Competition is essentially the driving force behind Trinidad and Tobago's Carnival.
7. Austin Lyons is a ten-time Road March Competition winner ("Road March Winners: Trinidad and Tobago Carnival: 1998–2010", http://www.caribbeanchoice.com/carnival/roadmarch.asp) and a seven-time International Soca Monarch Champion ("International Soca Monarchs Hall of Fame, 1996–2018", http://www.tntisland.com/ismhof.html).
8. According to Hope (2006, 48), "'punaany' is a Jamaican colloquialism for female genitals; the vagina".
9. "Pum pum" is another Jamaican colloquial term for the vagina.
10. "Riddim" is defined as "a passage of music (meaning the music and the audio)" (Ashbourne 2012, 44).
11. Heavy T in Trinidad and Tobago refers to heavy or extra heavy truck. In order to drive a Heavy T vehicle, one must possess a Heavy T licence.
12. Rhythmic gyration of the waist is commonly referred to as wining in Trinidad and Tobago and the wider Caribbean.
13. The act of gyrating one's waist to soca music. This act could be done alone or with a partner.
14. "A child that is raised by a male who doesn't know that he isn't the child's biological father. (Usually the result of his wife/girlfriend cheating on him)" (Jamaican Patwah 2018).
15. This term refers to a woman "engaged in an extra-marital or extra-relationship affair with another woman's spouse" (Hope 2006, 55).
16. "Boom wuk" is a Jamaican colloquial term for sex.
17. "Buddy" is a Jamaican colloquial term for penis.
18. "Ding dong" is also a colloquial Jamaican term for penis.

REFERENCES

Ashbourne, Peter. 2012. "From Mento to Ska and Reggae to Dancehall". In *Global Reggae*, edited by Carolyn Cooper, 37–48. Kingston: Canoe Press.

Barratt, Kai. 2015. "The Redefinition of 'The Jamette' by Female Soca Artistes in Trinidad". PhD dissertation, University of the West Indies, Mona.

Cooper, Carolyn. 1993. *Noises in the Blood: Orality, Gender and the "Vulgar" Body of Jamaican Popular Culture*. London: Macmillan.

Davis, Samuel F. 2012. "Reggae in Cuba and the Hispanic Caribbean". In *Global Reggae*, edited by Carolyn Cooper, 95–126. Kingston: Canoe Press.

Gottreich, Anna S. 1993. "'Whe' She Go Do': Women's Participation in Trinidad Calypso". Accessed 24 September 2018. http://ufdcimages.uflib.ufl.edu/CA/00/40/01/29/00001/PDF.pdf.

Hope, Donna P. 2006. *Inna di Dancehall: Popular Culture and the Politics of Identity in Jamaica*. Kingston: University of the West Indies Press.

Hope, Donna P., ed. 2015. *Reggae from Yaad: Traditional and Emerging Themes in Jamaican Popular Music*. Kingston: Ian Randle.

Jamaican Patwah. n.d. "Definitions of "Jacket" (Slang)". *Jamaican Patwah: Patois and Slang Dictionary*. Accessed 6 October 2018. http://jamaicanpatwah.com/term/Jacket/1016#.XARKwmhKjIV.

Luke, Aba A. 2012. "The Layers of Fay-Ann: Learning from Life's Lessons". *Trinidad and Tobago Guardian*, 2 May. http://www.guardian.co.tt/article-6.2.421534.6fe9894621.

Lyndersay, Mark. 2018. "How to Win the Road (March)". *Caribbean Beat*, January/February. https://www.caribbean-beat.com/issue-149/how-to-win-the-road-backstory#axzz5X1YeFco3.

Marshall, Annecka Leolyn. 2006. "Jezebels, Soca and Dancehall Divas: The Impact of Images of Femininity upon Social Policies and Gender Relationships in the Caribbean". Presentation, SALISES Seventh Annual Conference, Sherbourne Conference Centre, Barbados, 31 March.

Newsday. 2015. "Fay Ann Lyons-Alvarez Building her Empire from the Ground Up". *Newsday*, 25 January. https://archives.newsday.co.tt/2015/01/25/fay-ann-lyons-alvarez-building-her-empire-from-the-ground-up/.

Ottley, Rudolph. 1992. *Women in Calypso*. Arima, Trinidad: R. Ottley.

Rohlehr, Gordon. 1990. *Calypso and Society in Pre-Independence Trinidad*. Port of Spain: G. Rohlehr.

DISCOGRAPHY

Lyons-Alvarez, Fay-Ann, vocalist. 2009. "Heavy T Bumpa". Track 1 on various artists, *Best of the Best Soca Grooves*. JW Production.

———. 2009. "Meet Super Blue". Accessed 12 January 2019. https://www.youtube.com/watch?v=s9_foyrgAFQ.

———. 2011. "Pressure". *Pressure*. Accessed 12 January 2019. https://www.youtube.com/watch?v=zGLjBC_BZ54.

———. 2012. "Denial". Track 13 on various artists, *I Am Soca: 2012*. Platinum Trini Entertainment/Bungalo Records.

Quevedo, Raymond, vocalist. 1999. "Women Will Rule the World". Track 3 on *Fall of Man: Calypsos on the Human Condition 1935–1941*. Rounder Records.

Spragga Benz (Carlton Grant), vocalist. 2000. "Pum Pum Conqueror". Track 13 on *Spragga Benz*. VP Music Group, 2000.

Stephens, Tanya, vocalist. 1997. Vinyl. "Handle the Ride". Track 1 on *Handle the Ride*. Brickwall Records.

———. 1997. "Yuh Nuh Ready fi Dis". Track 1 on *Too Hype*. VP Records.

———. 1998. "Big Ninja Bike". Track 5 on *Ruff Rider*. VP Records.

———. 2003. "Power of a Girl". Compact disc. Track 1 on *Power of a Girl*. Pow Pow Productions.

———. 2004. "Boom Wuk". Compact disc. Track 3 on *Gangsta Blues*. VP/Tarantula Records.

———. 2004. "Little White Lie". Compact disc. Track 6 on *Gangsta Blues*. VP/Tarantula Records.

———. 2004. "It's a Pity". Compact disc. Track 7 on *Gangsta Blues*. VP/Tarantula Records.

———. 2004. "Tek Him Back". Compact disc. Track 8 on *Gangsta Blues*. VP/Tarantula Records.

———. 2005. "After You". Compact disc. Track 11 on *Drop Leaf Riddim*. Don Corleon Records.

———. 2006. "Power of a Girl". Compact disc. Track 9 on *Shanty Town*. Pow Pow Productions.

CHAPTER 9

The Collision of RastafarI and the Erotic in the Work of Tanya Stephens

SARA SULIMAN

TO PEOPLE OF AFRICAN DESCENT, DISCOURSE ON LIBERATION is not a luxury but a central tenet to our livelihood. Many pan-Africanist movements, including Rastafarianism/ RastafarI, have centred racism against the external oppressor in this ongoing discourse over other forms of oppression. However, the interrogation of how these oppressive dynamics play out within our own communities (particularly when it comes to gender and sexuality) continues to move at a much slower pace, and with ample resistance. This has been compounded by patriarchal styles of leadership that have perpetuated the suppression of the erotic. The erotic, as defined by the literary icon Audre Lorde, is an infinite feminine resource within each of us that intuits the full spectrum of the human expression and necessitates authentic and uninterrupted access to our deepest desires (Lorde 1984). Although RastafarI was built on a foundation of progressive resistance against white supremacy, it failed to facilitate an open discourse on gender equity and transgressive sexuality.

Vivienne "Tanya" Stephenson has been instrumental in popularizing lyrics that challenge this dichotomy between RastafarI and sexual equity. The context has certainly demanded that women create spaces to resist the patriarchy and establish control over their sexuality in a way that ruptures the moral strictures of bourgeois culture as well as those found in the scared text of the Christians – the Bible. Stephens challenges monogamy while favouring polyamory in songs like "It's a Pity". She also challenges heteronormativity and homophobia in songs such as "Do You Still Care?" and confronts what RastafarI deem to be taboo sexual acts such as cunnilingus in songs like "Please Me". This chapter highlights how her music continues to be a voice of defiance, in a context that distorts the erotic and consequently stifles the free expression of the deepest desires of both women and men in favour of an orthodox patriarchy.

RASTAFARI AND LIBERATION THEOLOGY

The RastafarI movement was named after the Ethiopian emperor Haile Selassie I, born as Ras Tafari Makonnen and widely known in RastafarI circles as "His Imperial Majesty" or "HIM". The birth of RastafarI dates back to around 1933, when Leonard Percival Howell, thought to be the "First Rasta" (or at least one of the earliest leaders of the Rastafarian movement) began selling five thousand postcards – each for a shilling – of HIM as alleged passports to Ethiopia two years after his coronation in Addis Ababa, Ethiopia (Dunkley 2012). The 1930s saw the emergence of preachers declaring the divinity of HIM as a manifestation of the reincarnated promised Messiah (Kitzinger 1966). The movement called to reclaim the undermined potential of diaspora Africans, whose enslavement across the Atlantic and estrangement from the motherland was considered a primary factor in dismantling the collective sense of self and identity. The movement called for a return to Africa, inspired by the repatriation thrust of Garveyism and Marcus Garvey's alleged prophecy that blacks would return to Africa liberated with the crowning of an African king (Julien 2003). Consequently, Rastas today view Africa as the prophesied "Zion" or "Promised Land" to which they shall return (Kitzinger 1969). During this time, Rastas lived in the economic margins of Jamaican society, mostly in camps in Kingston and Montego Bay, in large dwellings on government wasteland known as "the Dungle". They were not respected by or included in the Jamaican mainstream middle class (Kitzinger 1966; Kitzinger 1969). Not surprisingly, many struggled to gain access to employment or consistent sources of income. Furthermore, the widespread use and cultivation of marijuana popularized a criminal image of the community, which rendered it a repeated target for police raids. This alienation was also propagated by the heightened suspicion of mainstream capitalist Jamaican society and the political and economic structures it inherited from colonial British rule (Kitzinger 1969).

The period between the 1950s and 1970s saw a global widespread discourse on liberation of people of African descent. This period coincided with major global events, including the independence of African and Caribbean nations from colonialism and the emergence of radical civil rights and black liberation movements among the African American populace in North America (Rollins 1986). The energy of this Black Power era, together with open discourse on decolonization grounded the Rastafarian political cause and the movement's call for social justice. During this period, Jamaica itself gained independence from British rule in 1962. Coincidently, the Organisation of African Unity, the predecessor to the African Union, was founded in 1963 under the leadership of Selassie alongside other African leaders and was a global symbol of the emerging sovereignty and empowerment of African people (Padelford 1964). However, during this time, the bubbling hostility by mainstream Jamaicans and inflicted police brutality on the Rastafarian community continued, culminating in the infamous "Coral Garden Massacre" in April 1963.

Rudolph Franklin, a militant Rasta leader of the time, was reported to farm illegally in a land under dispute with the Kerr-Jarrett family, which resulted in the police attacking him and the farm multiple times. In one of the attacks in 1961, the police shot Rudolph multiple times. Rudolph miraculously survived after being treated in a hospital, but he was subsequently imprisoned for six months for possession of ganja. Upon his release, and with ongoing harassment by the public and police against the Rastafarian community, Rudolph's camp set the Ken Douglas Shell station on fire. This resulted in the police attacking him and his camp again. This second attack led to an altercation that resulted in the deaths of two policemen, including one Corporal Clifford Melbourne, and three Rastamen and Rudolph himself (Blackford 2017). In retaliation, a police operation, known afterwards as the "Coral Garden Massacre" (under the authorization of then prime minister Alexander Bustamante) was dispatched, leading to the arrests and detention of over one hundred and fifty bearded men thought to be Rastas. They were beaten and their locks and beards forcibly shaved as a form of punishment and public humiliation (Blackford 2017).

Rastafarian ideology is rooted in a nuanced pan-Africanist interpretation of the Bible's Old Testament. This understanding claims the African lineage of the Messiah as a descendant of King Solomon and the Queen of Sheba, who are both claimed to be African descendants in the Rastafarian interpretation of biblical scriptures (Kitzinger 1966). This interpretation is evident in the lyrics of Rastafarī reggae artistes, such as Sizzla Kalonji in "Rock Stone", suggesting that they (African people) are in fact the children of Israel in the narration of Jewish history:

> Mi nah lie, true mi hail Selassie I dem wah fi war I
> Read mi Bible turn to peace and praise Tafari
> Goodbye Babylon goodbye, goodbye
> Open up, Zion door
> Mount Zion, Ethiopia for sure
> Children of Israel, children of Israel

The RastafarI political ideation rejected political structures inherited from the "evil" colonial "Babylon" (status quo) system, which included governments and other social institutions, in favour of the self-sufficient provision of services from within the RastafarI community. For instance, RastafarI, ideally, reject any alignment with the church or Jamaican government (Kitzinger 1969), irrespective of their proposed political agenda. They also reject social structures that may provide services to their communities, such as health care and labour unions (Kitzinger 1966). This rejection of structures that provide health care has had a direct impact on the well-being of RastafarI women, as will be discussed later in this chapter.

TANYA STEPHENS, RASTAFARI AND GENDER ROLES

In the track "Sunday Morning", Stephens criticizes the toxic potential of Christianity and its continuous attempt to mould people into a rigidly prescribed code of conduct: "I'm tired of you trying to feed me your toxic beliefs, gradually increasing the doses." In this line, Stephens confronts the evident hypocrisy of organized religion, namely Christianity, and how it has been consistently deployed to justify prejudice and shaming of women, under the name of God. She continues this scathing indictment when she sings, "that is the same God who is made of love but has no problem for [the] use of hate in his holy name".

Rastas reject the mainstream Eurocentric interpretations of biblical scriptures and apply a pan-African nuanced analysis instead. Paradoxically, Rastafarian ideology does not steer far from Christianity in its orthodoxy, particularly around women's behaviour, as both versions equally centre the male figure as the righteous saviour and beacon of enlightenment (Rowe 1980). Maureen Rowe theorizes that the Jamaican cultural landscape is divided into several worldviews, including one that is "occupied by African continuities (Rowe 1998, 73–74)". There exists, however, aspects of Jamaican culture that reside in a grey area where there is a blend of European ideals and retained African behaviours, which cannot be historically traced to African cultural traditions. Indeed, there are remnants of belief systems imparted by the colonial rule of African nations themselves. Because of these influences, two definitions of maleness emerged. The European ideal of maleness centres capitalism and derives the masculine worth from wealth and the capacity for material provision to the family. In contrast, maleness in African tradition derives masculine worth simply by virtue of being male. RastafarI adopted the African version of this theory of maleness as an intrinsic quality to entitle men to respect and authority as a birthright, irrespective of their ability to provide materially.

In a corollary to the belief that "women are not Rasta in heart" (Kitzinger 1966, 9), authority and leadership must rest with the male Rastas who are endowed with the knowledge and physical strength to manifest the prophecies of RastafarI. Women, on the other hand, remain on the periphery of the movement, serving primarily as catalysts for the actualization of their kings (Kitzinger 1966). It is understood that "a good Queen obeys her husband in all things that is righteous onto God" (Kitzinger 1969, 8); hence a woman is only crowned a "Queen" by virtue of her socially recognized relation or cohabitation with a Rastaman. On the other hand, the Rastaman is worthy in and of himself and has absolute God-given rights, irrespective of his attachments to women. The suspicion that women are disloyal to RastafarI stems from the belief that women are transient members of that community and would be tempted to betray the cause by seeking opportunities for "hypergamy" (upward social and economic mobility) mainly outside the Rastafarian community, considering its financial plight and marginalization from economic opportunities in the surrounding Jamaican society (Kitzinger 1966).

The perception that "dawtas" (daughters or Rasta women) do not fully embrace RastafarI theology is evident in the lyrics of the late reggae artiste Gregory Isaac's song "Not the Way". In it, he justifies why women need the assistance of their "Kingman" to "sight up" (acknowledge or accept) Jah and become initiated into RastafarI:

> Cause the dawtas always take a little longer
> to sight up the father
> Cause the dawtas always take a little longer
> to do the works of Jah Jah
> Never let her go astray
> Try show her the right way

Rasta teachings emphasize the notion that "the lord in the beginning created male and female to replenish the earth (Kitzinger 1969, 250)". This idea reinforces the traditional belief that the worth of a woman correlates with her capacity to bear the Rastaman's children, so he can fulfil his duty to repopulate Africa and "replenish the Earth". As a result, Rasta teachings are not subtle in controlling the reproductive freedom of women (Rowe 1998). One example is the overt condemnation of contraception and abortion, spurred by widely believed conspiracies that white medicine invented these interventions to curb the numbers of Africans and their mission of repopulating the motherland. Practices like contraception and abortion are also believed to negate the "nature" of men and women and the divine duty they ought to fulfil. The lyrics of Alpha Blondie in "Abortion Is a Crime" clearly reflect this anti-choice sentiment:

> Yes, a foetus is alive . . .
> Don't make them cry, cry
> Cry from their mother's womb
> Why should they pay for the sins
> They haven't done
> Feel, you got to think
> Jah say don't let the children cry
> Feel, you got to feel
> Jah say don't let his children cry
>
> Abortion is crime.
> Abortion is a bloody bloody crime
> Abortion is a crime

"Nature" in RastafarI is a very important concept, referring to the subtle inner consciousness and intuitive knowledge one has of God and the inherent purpose of existence beyond rational comprehension. Sex is an important component of this inner knowing, and "losing one's nature is to become impotent" (Kitzinger 1969, 251). Within this expected role, the RastafarI rejection of health care structures derived from Western medicine, together with their self-alienation from broader Jamaican society, means that qualified health care providers or qualified midwives rarely support Rasta women, even through the difficult task of childbirth. Ironically, Rastafarian men are extremely health conscious and believe in their duty to maintain healthy vessels (bodies). They also believe in pursuing natural and non-invasive remedies, particularly herbs, to cure illnesses (Kitzinger 1969). However, compounded by the belief that women are unclean, particularly during menstruation and childbirth, Rastafarians do not exist in a framework where men support women through these roles despite the pride RastafarI males take in their ability to provide healing (Lake 2012). The division across gender lines permeated the organization of the Rastafarian community, as documented in the 1960s, where some Rasta camps used to exclude women altogether even as they welcomed their sons who would grow in Rasta surroundings; surroundings which reproduced the marginalization of women, even those who gave birth to these very children (Kitzinger 1966).

THE EMERGING INDEPENDENCE OF RASTA WOMEN IN RASTAFARI

During those years, brethren actively suppressed any activities carried out by the sistren, who were perceived to be impressionable followers of the "evil" Western feminist movement. In the 1970s, inspired by the national politicized discourse on decolonization and civil rights, many young women joined the RastafarI movement and its gatherings. However, these younger women were disconnected from elder Rasta women who were also founding members and supporters of the movement since its inception. Younger RastafarI women were taught in isolated camps dedicated to indoctrinating the youth. This isolation effectively functioned to distance a generation of female youth from having a first-hand knowledge of the gendered experiences of their predecessors, who were part of the movement since its formative years.

The anxiety of brethren over the increasing power of the female collective potentially stemmed from the increase in the number of women joining the movement in the 1970s, in a global context where the international discourse on feminism was steadily advancing, especially among radicalized liberation movements, not unlike Rastafarianism. Ironically, the response of the brethren in the movement was to increase the frequency of teachings of the RastafarI doctrine and to use these teachings as a basis to reprimand members who displayed behaviours perceived to be inconsistent with the conventional philosophies of RastafarI. These punishments were applied disproportionately to the sistren out of fear that the growing women's empowerment would threaten the traditional modes of the movement's male-centred leadership. There was also increased hostility towards gatherings of women not performed under the guidance of a "Kingman" (Rowe 1998).

This response of increased policing and control ironically resembles that of colonial white-supremacist institutions which, in response to perceived rebellion bubbling in their colonized nations, exerted further policing and punishment as a means of protecting the existing power hierarchies. Furthermore, for a movement rooted in liberation from injustice, the role it played at the time to advancing woman liberation was not only inadequate but often stifling and counterproductive. However, the higher numbers of women gradually meant that more were joining as wives and mothers within Rastafarian family units. Since the politicized and Afrocentric education of children was central to the advancement of the movement, women elicited a newly established respect by the brethren, which manifested in their being upgraded from "dawtas" (daughters) to "Queens" who raise the family alongside the "Kingmen". They were, however, to do so quietly, carrying the lion's share of both the physical and emotional labour[1] of the Rastafarian family unit and community at large (Rowe 1998). In this way, narratives of gender roles reinforced patriarchy and the inequitable burden it places upon women, even within a supposedly progressive framework such as that of RastafarI (Dwyer 2013).

Stephens's song "Weather Change (So Many Men)" aptly captures this inequitable gender politics within RastafarI:

> All some weh say dem a Rasta dem a di worst pon di planet
> Di behaviour weh dem have woulda mek Selassie I vomit
> And a pose like dem a big man
> Mi know why dem nuh nyam pork
> cause some a dem a pig man
> Give dem self-righteous instructions
> Like dem a praise a child fi truth
> Why?
> Because him father one bag a yute
> Dat nuh cute
>
> (Even some who say they are Rastas, they are the worst on the planet
> Their behaviour would make Selassie I vomit
> And they pose as if they are the big man
> I know why they don't eat pork
> Because some of them are pigs, man
> Giving their self-righteous instructions
> Like they are really praising a child

Why?
Because he has fathered many youth
That's not cute)

In these lyrics, Stephens specifically condemns the entitlement of RastafarI males to superiority over women. Her depiction of men in RastafarI as "the worst pon di planet" targets how they hide behind so-called righteous Rastafarian teachings to justify patriarchy and domestic violence, behaviours that would revolt their very own symbol of "morality", HIM himself.

RACIALIZED WOMEN AND THE EROTIC

The renowned feminist educator and poet Audre Lorde has put forth the concept of the erotic as a source of feminine power, referring to it as "a resource within each of us that lies in a deeply female and spiritual plane, firmly rooted in the power of our unexpressed or unrecognized feeling" (Lorde 1984, 53). The concept of the erotic has been distorted, primarily in patriarchal schools of thoughts, to mostly reflect a superficial and unilateral focus on sexuality, that is, pornography and the physical sensations associated with it. The erotic in Lorde's writings rejects this distorted depiction and reclaims it as the deeper non-physical wells of power from where women (and men) derive their intuitive wisdom. In her view, "the erotic offers a well of replenishing and provocative force to the woman who does not fear its revelation, nor succumb to the belief that sensation is enough" (Lorde 1984, 54). It is where the sense of self and the creative force of the feminine begin, untainted by the physical desires of men, who wish to predominantly engage with the sexual aspects of the feminine. The erotic expands the realm of experience to encompass everything from superficial sensations to the most irrational feelings of the soul that connect the physical and non-physical planes.

From a feminist perspective, the erotic has been misappropriated as a patriarchal tool of oppression. Within this paradigm, women who attempt to exercise freedom to openly express pleasure in the sensation, or who wish to expand this expression beyond directing their energy solely to the servitude of men, are trivialized, chastised and kept at the periphery of society. This is done so as to not threaten the "supremacy" of the man and his masculine models of dominance. This tension between the feminine power, which derives its power from intuitive knowledge and feelings, and the masculine counterpart, which relies mostly on logic and physical domination, has existed since ancient times (Lorde 1984). Consequently, the erotic as a form of feminine empowerment has been viewed with suspicion. An empowered woman, who is truly connected to her deepest and most chaotic feelings and desires, establishes knowledge of these desires from an intuitive source and cannot be misled by the propaganda that reduces her power to a subordinated labourer or provider of non-reciprocal sexual pleasure.

Thus, women's empowerment through connection with the erotic, is in fact incompatible with the notion of female compliance to male dominance, particularly when achieved through the objectification of women as providers of sexual pleasure and traditional feminized labour. Further, this point of view rejects arrangements that only revolve around women supporting men as the sole agents of societal leadership and transformation. Moreover, outside of this sexual role of women, the socialization and prevalent economic demands on women, particularly women of colour, enforces an idea that the feminine creative forces may only exist to fulfil the bare necessities of serving others (hooks 1993). The physical labour of women, as well as the relevance of this labour to the comfort of family and men, has been the currency upon which the worth of a woman has and continues to be valued. This leads to a meaningless reproduction of labour without acknowledgement of the needs of the female labourers (Rowe 1980). In fact, black women learn from an early age how to market their bodies and sexualities as "a commodity that can be exchanged in the sexual marketplace" (hooks 1993, 115). Thus, the notion that black women can reclaim their energy to be spent on self-loving acts of creativity and exploration outside the traditional demands of provision of food and comfort to family and community, or outside of offering sexual pleasure to male partners when in heterosexual arrangements, is extremely radical. Indeed, this idea challenges thousands of years of indoctrination. Embodying the erotic also means that denying women their deepest desire for joy in all aspects of life, and relegating their worth to the measuring sticks and external directives of the patriarchy, can easily become deeply unsatisfying and inconsistent with the knowledge established through authentic connections with the self and others. This realization of internal power and freedom threatens to destabilize the male-dominant status quo and to redefine the power dynamics at home and in the broader society.

Other writers engage the concept of the erotic, where this well of intuition and feelings is described as the power of "the goddess" or "the divine feminine" (Bashford 2018, 33–37). This reflects a similar concept: that women are the guardians of intuitive wisdom, which derives mostly from the non-physical plane and runs counter to the vertical and aggressive frameworks of distorted and toxic masculinity. In alternative readings of the story of Mary Magdalene, she is shown to possess the well of wisdom which Yeshua ben Joseph (Jesus) frequents through sexuality and intimacy to nourish his own true nature and fulfil his divine purpose. This well is symbolic of a subtle inner alchemy (that is, the erotic) Mary inherited from ancient goddesses, including the Egyptian goddess Isis (Kenyon and Sion 2002). This beautiful depiction of divine love between Yeshua and Magdalene has been distorted by a largely patriarchal church, whose interpretation depicts Magdalene as a prostitute unworthy of societal respect.[2]

The lyrics of Stephens's song "Power of the Girl" also emphasizes the empowerment of women who are worthy of affection for qualities they possess which do not fall in the realm of sexual pleasure. She sings, "We exist outside of the bed. Sometimes we rather talk instead." Coincidentally, the concept of nature in RastafarI also refers to the expansive set of irrational intuitive feelings one has as guidance to one's divine purpose from birth to death, in which sex is but a singular manifestation of one's duty in this physical reincarnation on Earth (Kitzinger 1969). Paradoxically, although this intuitive nature parallels the erotic as explained by Audre Lorde, since it encompasses the infinite dimensionality of the human's most subtle feelings, it is largely attributed to the men of RastafarI alone. This is consistent with the notion that Rasta men are the custodians of divine knowledge, thus leaving women estranged from access to nature and the erotic, which had originated to honour their authentic feminine selves in the first place. Just as the erotic has been distorted to mean pornography, the mystic concept of nature has been sexualized in a way that reduced it from the original intended infinite concept into the call to perform sex as a means of reproduction. This reduction of nature to mean consistency with one's calling for sex to manifest God's purpose of proliferation on earth has served to effectively trap women in the culture to a singular dimension, consequently undermining their potential to meaningfully participate in all facets of the Rastafarian spiritual movement.

THE EROTIC IN THE MELODIES OF REGGAE MUSIC

I was about thirteen years old, visiting my extended family in Ethiopia for the first time, when I became more consistently exposed to reggae music as a soundtrack in the background of family gatherings, or through the radios in the narrow alleys of Mercato (the marketplace in Addis Ababa). This was unsurprising in light of the strong foundational role of Ethiopia in reggae and RastafarI. Kwame Dawes (2004) ascribes the magnetism of reggae music to its slow repetitive circular melodies, which command slow and evenly dispersed sensual movements. When reggae emerged as the indigenous soothing sound of the Caribbean islands, so did the sensual dances, starting with the "rub-a-dub" style, which simulates sexual intimacy between man and woman. This erogenous capacity of reggae music existed at odds with its roots in the ethos of RastafarI; a relatively conservative movement firmly based on dated biblical patriarchal ideals from the Old Testament, preaching old-fashioned righteousness despite its progressive revolutionary mission.

Reggae music resolves this paradox by seamlessly merging the contrasting activist political messages of RastafarI with explicit "unholy" intimacy, thus providing a rhythmic sensual outlet for a largely conservative Protestant mainstream in Jamaica (Dawes 2004). The "Natural Mystic" in reggae symbolizes the unison of the grounded earthly mind, with its focused political mission to overthrow Babylon and neocolonialism from the psyche of African people, with sex in service of procreation. It also symbolizes the spiritual mind, which is interwoven with the metaphysical plane and extends love and intimacy from a natural inner knowing of oneness. In this spiritual mind, sex and intimacy are expansive expressions of emotions, a longing to love and celebrate black bodies as a radical assertion of a lost identity in postcolonial Jamaica, and a home to heal the intergenerational trauma carried by blackness across the Atlantic. In this vein, the vast multidimensional universe of reggae is the perfect backdrop music of the multilayered self in a quest to heal its distorted identity, as it "privileges and sees beauty in blackness" (Dawes 2015).

In this way, reggae mirrors Lorde's concept of the erotic, where the listener grapples with the infinite deeper experiences of joy and tribulations through living between the loud cries of megaphones in political rallies and the rhythmic intimacies and sacred sexualities of the bedroom. This exquisite capacity of reggae to speak the unspoken and to subconsciously transform the psyche of listeners renders it an ideal tool to infuse radical messaging around the plight of women in Jamaica and the global RastafarI community at large. Dawes states that "reggae's continued existence, its mutations and evolution and in many instances its welcome departure from a patriarchal sensibility towards one that contends with the feminine are exciting to see" (2015). Hence, in contrast to rigid RastafarI teaching camps, reggae can provide a flexible progressive platform to facilitate the discourse on feminism and sexual liberation.

COUNTERCURRENTS OF SEXUALITY IN REGGAE AND THE VOICE OF TANYA STEPHENS

Perhaps one of the earliest indications of how the sexuality of women has been perceived in the Rastafarian culture dates back to its most renowned co-founder, Leonard P. Howell. Howell was found to cohabitate with thirteen concubines during a police raid on the community in 1941 (Kitzinger 1969). Polygyny has been widely accepted as a reserved right of males in RastafarI (Rowe 1998). "Dawtas" and "Queens" are expected to act in accordance with their roles as supporters and catalysts for Rasta men in realizing the RastafarI political mission to expand in numbers and destabilize Babylon. It is customary for the man to say, "I like you to bring forth a child for me" (Kitzinger 1966, 37) before intercourse, thus emphasizing the primary purpose of sex with the societally recognized "Queen" to be one of reproduction, not pleasure; and certainly not her pleasure. The organization of the RastafarI community is reminiscent of traditional African arrangements that extend into the modern time, where the prevalence of polygyny among men is high but generally denied to women.[3] The prevalence of the "small house" phenomenon in Zimbabwe, for instance, exemplifies this arrangement (Mutseta 2016). The small house institution refers to an extramarital relationship in which the married man engages in an extended affair with a woman who is not socially recognized as the primary wife (Mutseta 2016). In both RastafarI and African communities, these arrangements are a testament to the emergence of the postcolonial grey cultural space (Rowe 1998). This space is a paradoxical hybrid of traditional belief systems that endow males (but generally not females) with the right to polygyny. It is also reflective of the Christian-inspired colonial court system, which only acknowledges monogamous marital contracts by law.

Stephens challenges such strict male-centred marital arrangements and asserts the right of women to openly discuss possible unconventional frameworks to inform their sexuality. In her song "Tek him back", she attempts to negotiate with the wife of a man with whom she is having an affair. As the song opens, Stephens calls the wife to initiate an open dialogue, but the wife's irate response affirms her subscription to the traditional rules of obligatory monogamy: "Tanya who tek meh man and gwaan like she waan broke fight pon mi pon top". In a radical feminist style, Tanya affirms her own empowerment to "just tek" any man she wants, while also acknowledging the wife's hurt feelings:

> any man we see and we waan we jus tek
> gyal talk too hard get ah kick inna she neck well
> couple of times you used to call me pon de phone
> cuss me how fi left your husband alone
> ah jus now me ah fully understand
> why me really need fi leave your man

Throughout the song, Stephens stresses the right of women to negotiate the terms of their unorthodox sexual arrangements and explore possible polyamorous relationships, where they can all have sexual access to the same man, primarily for the purpose of pleasure. In an extramarital affair such as the one in "Tek him back", the man may not fulfil her interest in intimacy beyond sexual pleasure, because the charm and attraction may have simply emerged from the illusion of his unavailability:

> cuz one gyal treasure is anudda gyal trash
> me notice certain likkle trend datta gwaan
> man alwayz look betta inna de nex gyal arms
> but im neva fail soon as de nex gyal gone

Polyamory is a "style of consensual, non-monogamous relating whereby everyone is aware of the relationships involved" (Barker 2014, 16). Historically, the most common arrangement in African, Caribbean, and RastafarI communities is polygamy, often practised by men alone (polygyny) (Rowe 1998). This polygynous arrangement is rarely, if ever, discussed openly and honestly. It is certainly not discussed from the perspective of the women in question. In affirming the woman's right to choose the terms of her intimate relationships, Stephens challenges the RastafarI paradigm in which men reserve the right to negotiate the terms of pleasure and intimacy in sex. She affirms the right of women to seek sexual pleasure, in whichever arrangements they desire, as an end in and of itself, not just a means of procreation. While any RastafarI women may have embraced the conservative strictures of the movement around the purpose, act and end of sexual intimacy, Stephens's pronouncements may be a way for many RastafarI women to experience the fulfilment of erotic possibilities.

In the album *Gangsta Blues*, Stephens humorously tells a story about a woman's interaction with a man who treats her with respect and dignity, in the track "Damn You". In it, she describes his pre-intimate interaction as a "delightful representation of the masculine gender". However, as the night progresses, the sexual experience becomes woefully unfulfilling for the female narrator and she does not shy away from expressing her disappointment. The man falls asleep before she communicates her dissatisfaction to him, which in itself is symbolic of his lack of interest in understanding her experience of pleasure and an indication of his ambivalence to the mere possibility of her desiring it. At this point, the track skilfully slides into the song "Good Ride", where Stephens describes in detail what her sexual expectations actually are:

> Man to the way you move
> Skilled wit your fingers
> You na haffi indulge
> Inna nuh cunnylingus
> Wen yuh dally two time and put on a wheely
> You nuh haffi ask if me feel
> Gi we some good ride
> Whoa ooa
> Just back out di bike
>
> (Man, because of the way you move
> Skilled with your fingers
> You don't have to indulge in cunnilingus
> When you bob and weave and put on a wheely
> You don't have to ask if I feel
> Give us some good ride
> Whoa ooa
> Just back out the bike)

There are numerous examples where Stephens's lyrics demonstrate the woman's assertiveness to not only communicate her desires, but also demand sexual pleasure and reciprocity from her male partners. Some songs such as "Please Me" directly demonstrate this point. In others, such as "Ninja Bike", she communicates a set of expectations regarding the ninja bike – a metaphor used to describe the male sexual organ or penis – she deems acceptable for sex:

> Me want a man way have a big ninja bike fi me ride pon
> Na waan no flim flam
> Way nuh have de right gear
> Spen de whole night pan you divan
> Gee me de right slam
> Cause da gal ya no care
>
> (I want a man who has a big ninja bike for me to ride on
> Don't want no flim-flam
> That don't have the right gear
> Spend the whole night on your divan mattress
> Give me the right sex
> Because the girl does not care)

It is uncommon for women to be direct in stating that the objective of an interaction with a man is simply sexual pleasure. In light of the expansive non-sexual definition of the erotic, one may claim that Stephens's focus on demanding sexual pleasure arguably also reduces relationships between men and women to a physical transaction and ignores the deeper nonphysical dimensions of intimacy. The immediate apparent contradiction between the demand for pleasure and the erotic can be resolved if we understand that the original intention of Lorde through the erotic is to liberate the deepest connections with one's feelings and desires. Thus, the authenticity of black women and the deep desire to respect their deep and undisturbed connection with their, often suppressed, nature demands that we shape the discourse on the politics of black female bodies. In doing so, black women like Stephens are undoing millennia of social conditioning, while radically affirming the beauty of the bodies of black women. Black women have historically been estranged from being safely loved, being instead valued merely for their labour to serve others. As bell hooks (1993) explains in response to Lorde's exploration of the erotic, "it gives us permission to talk publicly about sexual pleasure" (hooks 1993, 85).

The embodiment of the erotic calls us to recognize sex as a holistic experience of deep feeling and connection with ourselves and with our partners. As black women, we are intricately familiar with how our bodies are policed from a young age either to conform to the societal rules of respectability on one extreme or to reduce our worth to fit the narrow context of our sexual desirability on the other. Consequently, we learn early on how to navigate either dimming or hyper-sexualizing ourselves so as not to offend this distorted erotic. bell hooks articulates how self-love and loving our own flesh in a world that demonizes the bodies of black women is a non-negotiable prerequisite to our empowerment. She continues to say that we should not shy away from requesting physical reciprocity from our partners. From the lens of the erotic, these partners ought to engage with all of our layers, in a mutual sharing act of love. As hooks puts it, "Empowered by a healing eroticism, black women are able to envision and engage in sexual encounters that do not diminish our well-being" (hooks 1993, 94).

SLACKNESS AND RESPECTABILITY POLITICS IN DANCEHALL AND REGGAE MUSIC

Explicit eroticism, or "slackness", in reggae music and subsequently dancehall was introduced early on by pioneer reggae artistes, such as General Echo and Yellowman, in the early 1980s (Stanley Niaah 2006). Dancehall evolved as a separate branch of reggae music with the introduction of "programmable drum machines, synthesizers, sequencers, samplers and desktop computers", which hugely expanded the range of "riddims" (rhythms and beats) (Troeder 2010, 95). The catchy beats of dancehall quickly dominated music in Jamaica and gained worldwide acclaims in the early 1990s with pioneers like Shabba Ranks, Buju Banton, Lady Saw, Beenie Man, Lady Patra and Stephens herself, as well as many others (Troeder 2010).

Roots reggae music is generally deemed "respectable", especially in its representation of sexual interaction between men and women, although nuanced and subtle iterations of kinky sex are interwoven into the songs of founding roots reggae artistes like Peter Tosh in "Ketchy Shuby" and Bob Marley and the Wailers in songs like "Kinky Reggae" and "Stir It Up". In contrast, dancehall is stereotypically perceived as a misogynist and violent offshoot of reggae, where vulgar and explicit eroticism does not hide behind the lyrical innuendo of roots reggae. For example, in the song "Dancehall Queen" by Beenie Man and Chevelle Franklyn, Beenie Man says, "If a mi alone I would turn you in mi lover / Gal yuh a mi nail mi want fi knock wid mi hammer" (If it were me alone, I would have turned you into my lover / Girl you are my nail, I want to knock you with my hammer).

Carolyn Cooper (2004), however, problematizes the gross generalization of these stereotypes through a closer analysis of the lyrics of Shabba Ranks and Bob Marley, as archetypes of dancehall and roots reggae musicians, respectively. In a sense, both genres serve important political functions in Jamaican culture: reggae has been a medium to disseminate the "conscious" Rastafarī ideology of rebellion and black empowerment, while dancehall signifies the "politics of noise" (Cooper 2004, 75) by disturbing the peace and postcolonial complacence of mainstream Jamaica in a difficult social and economic climate. With respect to gender, the two styles represent clashing representations of women and their bodies, with reggae symbolizing righteousness and respectability and dancehall popularizing vulgarity and objectification – both perhaps seeking dominion over women's sexuality through different routes. However, if one were to claim that reggae music, as a vehicle of conservative Rastafarī ethos, liberates women and their sexuality through its respectable outlook, they would overlook reggae's undertones of repression of the sexual expression of women and its omission of the necessary discourse around their pleasure and reciprocity in sex and intimacy. Thus, Rastafarī's emphasis on righteousness and purity neglects the responsibility of Rasta men as lovers to please their "Queens" (particularly within their assigned gender roles), while leaving these men free to practise polygyny and seek pleasure outside these societally recognized arrangements. This may well be a consequence of the suspicion with which the men of Rastafarī view a woman as the "alluring entrapper/fallen Eve" (Cooper 2004, 83) who is not "Rasta in heart" (Kitzinger 1969, 252).

Consequently, Rasta men maintain the motive to suppress women's expression of sexuality, as it threatens their righteousness and the gender-based organizational structure of their Rastafarī 'kingdoms'. Ironically, this view is consistent with the Christian interpretation of Eve as the temptress responsible for seducing Man, an act that subsequently led to their expulsion from the Garden of Eden. Cooper's (2004) alternative analysis of Marley's lyrics in the reggae song "Pimper's Paradise" reveals this paternalistic undertone in which Marley expresses pity for the woman who loses innocence and indulges in self-destructive "seductive" behaviours. Marley equates this tendency with the abject commodification of her body:

> Pimper's paradise
> Don't be just a stock
> A stock on the shelf
> Stock on the shelf

Marley indirectly infuses Rastafarī politico-religious ideation in his judgemental narrative of this deviant woman who is a "pimper's paradise". Intriguingly, the lyrics imply that male pleasurable sexual fantasies, or "paradise", is explored in the homes of women whom they deem objectified as a mere "stock on the shelf". This notion indirectly showcases the compartmentalization of sexuality in the Rasta man's realm: sex with the righteous "Queen" for the purpose of birth, nurturing the family and replenishing the "Promised Land", and on the other polarity, erotic sexual fantasies and pleasures to be explored with the "whores" who live on the margins of Rastafarī communities. In this narrative, although the Queen is revered, she is denied that essential tenet of sexual relations as an objective of her sexual experience – pleasure.

In contrast, the prevailing perception of the lyrics of Shabba Ranks, and many other contemporary dancehall artistes, is that they are misogynists who aggressively objectify women. Cooper (2004) radically argues that the lyrics of dancehall artistes like Shabba can be interpreted as a validation of the average black working-class woman, which had before been rarely affirmed and celebrated in mainstream Jamaican culture. In an era where Eurocentric beauty standards have colonized the mainstream lens on the female body, the depictions of black women's bodies as beautiful and desirable as they "bubble" and "bruk out" is a radical affirmation of black beauty.

This validation of the everyday black women contrasts with depictions of the Rastafarī culture in film, where black women have been largely absent while the discourse centres masculinity as the essence of Rastafarī communities (Dwyer 2013). Women are left on the periphery, which is justly reflective of the reality of Rastafarī cultural organization as narrated by Rasta men themselves. Dwyer critically examines the movie *Brooklyn Babylon* (2001) as one example portraying the forbidden love between a Rastaman (Solomon, abbreviated as Sol) and a white Jewish woman (Sarah). This cinematic representation is depicted as clashing with the puritan nature of both Rastafarī and Judaism, as ethno-specific cultures that discourage admixture with members of outside cultures not conforming to their respective ideations. Although this rebellious destabilization of puritanism may seem progressive, it comes at the expense of erasing black women in the narrative, or portraying them with tired stereotypes which favour the coupling of the Rasta man with a white woman but not the reverse (Dwyer 2013).

The omission of black women in depictions of forbidden cross-cultural love is not unique to RastafarI films but extends to Caribbean, Continental African and African American cinematic portrayals at large. These representations tend to normalize a narrative of undesirability of black women's bodies. However, this gendered erasure becomes particularly problematic in the context of RastafarI philosophy, which is supposedly rooted in promoting social justice ideals, particularly for the historically oppressed people of African descent. This ethos neglects a necessary intersectional analysis that centres black women who face compounded micro-aggressions from within and without RastafarI communities.

Interestingly, despite these prevalent dated sentiments on women and sexuality in Caribbean popular culture, the men of RastafarI generally speak respectfully of women, calling them "Sisters", "Empresses" and "Queens" (Julien 2003). According to Julien (2003), catcalling and sexual harassment are largely absent within the RastafarI camps themselves. Women are revered as long as they stick to their expected gender roles. Therefore, it is not surprising that mothers and motherhood are held in high regard in RastafarI. The conflict in gender dynamics arises when women no longer abide by the guidelines to be submissive and obedient and instead want to vocalize their opinions, at which point they are perceived as antagonistic and rebellious (Julien 2003; Lake 2012). Even more radically, the culture does not offer a safe space should women choose to be in sexual relations with other women. In the current times, any intellectual engagement with a political or religious movement would have to interrogate the intersectionality of race, gender, sexual orientation, ability, class, and other social identity markers. An analysis that represses one aspect (gender and sexuality) to highlight the inequalities in another (race) is one that is largely incomplete and inconsistent with the progressive mission of the RastafarI movement itself.

"QUEERING" RASTAFARI IDEATION AND REGGAE MUSIC

Despite its reformist rebellious roots, RastafarI ideology continues to place many restrictions on sexual relations between men and the women in the RastafarI community. For instance, women may not be approached during their menstrual cycle, as that renders them dirty and unholy. In addition, oral sex is strongly condemned in the culture, especially because of its perceived approximation to homosexuality, even when intended to please the woman (Julien 2003; Lake 2012). For instance, the popular song "Heads High" by dancehall artiste Mr Vegas perpetuates the same negative attitudes towards oral sex, and implicitly homosexuality. Even Stephens has pandered to the anti-oral sentiments in "Good Ride", when she states, "Yuh na haffi indulge inna no cunny lingers". Implicit in the statement is the notion that her partner can generate sexual pleasure without needing to resort to cunnilingus. However, this is not necessarily a moral condemnation of this way of rocking her world. This is evidenced in one of her other songs, "Freaky Type", where Stephens certainly enjoys her partner's tongue.

The negative attitude within dancehall towards homosexuality is consistent with the RastafarI belief system, which strongly condemns "Sodom" and considers it a great sin and deviation from the holy RastafarI nature (Kitzinger 1969). More generally, homophobia in Jamaica is thought to have arisen as a result of "buck breaking".[4] Although sexual abuse of female slaves is well documented, historical records of buck breaking against enslaved African males are scarce and inconsistent. Anal and oral sodomy was thought to be motivated by the colonizer's mission to emasculate and disempower the enslaved male (duCille 2018). Alternatively, the idea may have been disproportionately popularized to justify homophobia in the Caribbean. This homophobia has extreme manifestations, ranging from physical violence to even murder against gay men, and includes "corrective rape", where men violently rape gay women in a violent attempt to correct their sexual orientation (Gaskins 2013, 434). These crimes are largely neglected by law-enforcement authorities, who also subscribe to this homophobic paradigm (Allyn 2012).

The sentiment of dancehall artiste Mr Vegas is echoed strongly by reggae artiste Shabba Ranks, who called for the crucifixion of homosexuals in 1992; it is also found in Buju Banton's lyrics for "Boom Bye Bye" in the same year. Buju Banton's song has been interpreted as a call for the murder of "Batty Bwoys" or homosexual men (Troeder 2010). Similar sentiments are still prevalent in the music of more recent dancehall artistes, although out of fear of being denied opportunities to make a living abroad, these performers have toned down homophobic songs or used metaphoric or ambiguous language to peddle anti-LGBTQ (lesbian/gay/bi-sexual/transsexual/queer) sentiments. In contrast, Stephens has taken a strong stance against the popular displays of homophobia that remain very prevalent in Jamaican culture and music.

Queering refers to the act of questioning how gender and sexual identity are portrayed in literature, music, and popular culture and the historical constructions that inform normativity and power dynamics in that depiction (Somerville

2007). It is the literary practice that calls into question what we consider "normal", particularly when dissecting how these constructs served historical roles to assert certain power dynamics which rely on women being confined to serve specific gender and sexual roles. Heteronormativity refers to the assumption that heterosexuality is the acceptable norm for sexual relations in society. Thus, queering RastafarI is calling its roots in patriarchy and heteronormativity into question, especially since the movement preaches equity and liberation.

Long before the global discourse on sexuality had reached its advanced level today, Stephens artistically articulated the prejudice experienced by queer individuals navigating a violently homophobic Caribbean society. In "Do You Still Care", Stephens wrote the lyrics from the lens of a young Caribbean man "Bigga", who as a young boy had been socialized to conform to specific qualities that constitute acceptable manhood. This toxic masculinity is learned from qualities displayed by male role models in his community, which included the number of female sexual partners a male has, since polygamy is perceived to be a compelling gauge of manhood. Hence, this young boy feels conflicted when he notices a "gay pride" banner on the vehicle of a group of men who save him from a potentially fatal encounter on the streets. The lyrics underscore how the mere association with the potentially queer rescuers would impact him in that context, even though their own sexuality was only inferred from their display of solidarity with the gay community.

Bigga's dilemma is an indication of the extent to which homophobia prevails in the Caribbean: the mere association with a queer ally, irrespective of their own sexual orientation, would subject the individual to estrangement and prejudice. In the context of Bigga's near death experience, the lyrics call into question whether it is still worth holding on to the prejudice. Stephens's critique in this song is in stark contrast to the lyrics of reggae artiste Capleton's "Bun Out di Chi Chi", which reflect the pervasive sentiment of homophobia in Jamaica:

> Blood out ah chi chi, Bun out ah sissy,
> Batty dem ah fuck and ah suck too much pussy,
> Blood out ah chi chi, Blood out ah shitty,
> Say dem ah deal with too much
>
> (Blood out the gays, burn out (purge) the sissies
> Homosexuals fuck (one another) and suck too much pussy
> Blood out the gays, blood out a shit
> Say they deal with too much)

Or the lyrics of the song "My Crew, My Dogs" by contemporary dancehall artiste T.O.K.:

> From dem a par inna chi chi man car
> Blaze di fire mek we bun dem! (Bun dem!)
> From dem a drink inna chi chi man bar
> Blaze di fire mek we dun dem! (Dun dem!)
>
> (Those who hang out in a gay man's car
> Blaze the fire, let's burn them! (Burn them!!)
> Those who drink in a gay man's bar
> Blaze the fire, let's kill them! (Kill them!!)

In queering reggae music, Stephens brings the discourse around sexuality back to the drawing board, calling all male-centred sexual dynamics into question. This process can thus facilitate the discourse on queering the RastafarI philosophy. The bodies of black women have been historically demonized in their darkness and voluptuousness as the uglier contrast to the slender bodies of white women, which formed the ideals of a beautiful body image (Gentles-Peart 2018). Thus, any movement that affirms the right of black female bodies to love, pleasure and respect is inherently radical and challenges centuries of white supremacist indoctrination. This is particularly so because black women have been denied the right to choose when it comes to who provides that love and the right to negotiate the cost at which it is exchanged, often in the form of physical and emotional labour (hooks 1993).

Queering in this instance not only refers to choosing same sex lovers but, more importantly, affirms the right of black women to the choice of who provides love and how that love is received. Queering RastafarI necessitates an interrogation of how these dated beliefs around women and sexuality have served the patriarchal organization of the community, fuelling a need to forestall a feminist discourse. In other words, Rasta men have benefited and continue to benefit from the subordination of women in RastafarI, restricting them to heterosexual arrangements. Thus, allyship necessitates a willingness to give up the privilege offered by these inequitable social arrangements. In calling out the men of RastafarI on their frail solidarity with the empowerment of RastafarI women, an important angle is affirming the right of women, and incidentally queer men, to the choice of partners. The collective desire of Rasta men to maintain a patriarchal social order in RastafarI communities, even when masked in the rhetoric of liberation against white supremacy, can insidiously maintain gender-based oppression by constantly diverting the discourse from internal inequities to the "external" enemy. Power dynamics in sexual relationships are one critical and often overlooked area in this framework. Are we (African people) ever truly free if women are denied the right to the sexual arrangements they desire?

CONCLUDING THOUGHTS AND REFLECTIONS

From my own lens as an East African woman, I continue to find the reverence for Emperor Haile Selassie I rather peculiar and fascinating. Selassie undoubtedly served a crucial historical role in safeguarding Ethiopian land from Mussolini and the Italian occupation in 1935. His call for African unity and the establishment of the Organisation of African Unity, and his dedication of Shashamane to repatriate African descendants in the West (namely Jamaican Rastafarians), are all testaments to his commitment to the political solidarity and economic prosperity of Africa and the fragmented African diaspora.

However, the reasons behind my hesitation to revere him or ascribe messianic qualities as the promised "Black Jesus" are many.

I recently visited Shashamane on a trip to Ethiopia with family in 2015. The five hundred acres of land have not survived the decades of neglect, and certainly do not represent the sacred image upheld by the RastafarI community as "The promised land". The location's decrepitude is symbolic of the need for renewal of some of the foundational Rastafarian ideals and the need for Rastafarians to employ an intersectional political analysis in keeping with the times. Although this brief visit and jaded reflection certainly do not hold weight to discredit the prophecies of RastafarI, the knowledge of the extent of suffering Rastafarians have endured in Jamaica, and elsewhere, for this potential heaven on earth is perhaps distracting from the original intent to reclaim the African identity, where Zion could be more powerful as a metaphor for the collective return to the self within, rather than leaving for a physical space.

Second, although Selassie was an undeniable symbol of African unity and the advancement of the pan-African cause, he was, and still remains, a representative of the "royal" Amharic elite as a putative descendant of King Solomon, which propagates a belief of supremacy of Amhara heritage over other Ethiopian ethnic identities. This symbolism of Amhara-led nationalism has continued to marginalize other Ethiopian groups, including but not limited to the largely Muslim Oromo and Jewish Falasha. This has arguably fuelled some of the extreme ethnic conflicts that remain a topic of heated discussion in Ethiopia today. Thus, Selassie's external representation of African unity appears disingenuous and incomplete when examining his meagre efforts to build internal unity at home.

Lastly, and relevant to this chapter, the prevalent Rastafarian portrayal of Selassie as the King of Kings (Stepman 2016) certainly reinforces a model of pan-Africanism that centres masculinity in the liberation of Africans. To men in RastafarI, he is "the King of kings, Lord of Lords, the Conquering Lion of the Tribe of Judah" (Kitzinger 1969, 249). The model is consistent with the African patriarchal interpretation of maleness as a sufficient intrinsic quality to warrant respect and obedience, particularly by women, whose primary role is to support men in their actualization of the divine mission to achieve justice for African descendants.

Ironically, although the RastafarI ethos is rooted in the fight against oppression, particularly when imparted by white supremacist and colonial structures, it largely fails as a male-dominated institution to acknowledge its inherent debility in advancing the liberation of women. The exception of course is courageous Rasta women and other Jamaican women who have forwarded the cause, with very few brethren serving as allies. I remain conscious of the diversity of the African diaspora, and my ancestral narrative was not one that carries the imprints of the transatlantic slave trade and the identity fragmentation resulting from this displacement. Hence, I may not fully appreciate the necessity for this "back-to-Africa" movement, or the means to heal the generational trauma and psychological turmoil experienced by the black man since he was stolen from the continent. Nonetheless, one is left to question whether a heteronormative male-dominated framework for social justice, based on the worship of a male deity as the symbol of masculinity and black martyrdom, could ever serve to advance gender equity and female liberation. These contradictions are particularly apparent considering how reinforcing archaic gender roles for men and women is fundamental to serving the broader RastafarI doctrine. The dialogue ought to continue, with foundational beliefs continuously revisited and re-evaluated, although answers may not be easy or reductionist and are likely to require new anti-oppression paradigms.

In Stephens's song "Sound of My Tears", she reminds us that "acknowledgement is the first step towards a solution". She also sheds light on our collective societal hypocrisy in challenging our own internal prejudice in "What a Day", when she sings:

> What a day when men
> finally live what they teach
> and love ain't just a concept we preach
> and blood no longer runs in the streets
> oh oh oh, what a day?

Stephens's music is faithful to her ideals and beliefs, irrespective of external validation. Her lyrics express a diverse array of emotions and desires and counter the monolithic representation of black women in both reggae and dancehall. This vast representation of the layers of black women certainly mirrors Lorde's concept of the erotic, since it is through this authentic and uninterrupted access to one's nature and inner truths that Stephens manifests creativity in the form of socially conscious music that has left an imprint in the psyche of Jamaica and reggae enthusiasts worldwide. Claiming this rightful space to open a dialogue on many social issues, including the plight of women in RastafarI, has certainly rendered her a beacon for change, as she extends our inner reflections and critique as a community where social movements fall short. Stephens is undoubtedly a pioneer and has paved the way for more artistes to use their platforms to live and speak their truth through music.

NOTES

1. Emotional labour refers to the largely unacknowledged time and effort one spends to support relationships and regulating one's feelings, mostly by shutting down one's needs, in favour of facilitating the goals of the collective (Grandey 2000).
2. It is important to note here that this is necessary in order to reduce the erotic to objectified sexuality, which serves to facilitate the patriarchal mission of the church in asserting male-dominance and subordination of women.
3. Accurate estimations are unavailable since most courts deriving legislations from Christianity only recognize one primary "legal" marital contract (Fenske 2015).
4. "Buck breaking" refers to the practice of gay white enslavers sexually abusing the enslaved black men in front of other slaves of both genders, as a means of asserting power and domination.

REFERENCES

Allyn, Angela. 2012. "Homophobia in Jamaica: A Study of Cultural Heterosexism in Praxis". Marlboro University. 1 July. http://dx.doi.org/10.2139/ssrn.2097180.

Barker, Meg. 2014. "Polyamory". In *Encyclopedia of Critical Psychology*, edited by Teo Theo. Springer, New York.

Bashford, Sophie. 2018. *You are a Goddess: Working with the Sacred Feminine to Awaken, Heal and Transform*. Carlsbad, CA: Hay House.

Bing, Steve, and Charles Steel, producers. 2013. *Marley* (documentary). DVD. Directed by Kevin Macdonald. Magnolia Pictures.

Blackford, Richard. 2017. "Behind That Coral Gardens Incident". *Jamaica Observer*, 17 April. http://www.jamaicaobserver.com/columns/Behind-that-Coral-Gardens-incident_95932.

Cooper, Carolyn. 2004. *Sound Clash: Jamaican Dancehall Culture at Large*. New York: Palgrave Macmillan.

Dawes, Kwame Senu Neville. 2004. *Natural Mysticism: Towards a New Reggae Aesthetic in Caribbean Writing*. Leeds, UK: Peepal Tree Press.

———. 2015. "Natural Mysticism: Reggae and Caribbean Poetics". Warton Lecture on English Poetry, the British Academy, London, 23 April.

duCille, Ann. 2018. "Blacks of the Marrying Kind: Marriage Rites and the Right to Marry in the Time of Slavery". *Differences: A Journal of Feminist Cultural Studies* 29 (2): 21–67.

Dunkley, Daive A. 2012. "Leonard P. Howell's Leadership of the Rastafari Movement and His "Missing Years". *Caribbean Quarterly* 58 (4): 1–24.

Dwyer, Asheda. 2013. "Left Waiting in Vain for Your Love: Situating the (In)Visibility of Black Women of Rastafari as Lovers, Partners and Revolutionaries in Brooklyn Babylon and One Love". *Caribbean Quarterly* 59 (2): 25–38.

Fenske, James. 2015. "African Polygamy: Past and Present". *Journal of Development Economics* 117:58–73.

Gaskins Jr, Joseph. 2013. "'Buggery' and the Commonwealth Caribbean: A Comparative Examination of the Bahamas, Jamaica, and Trinidad and Tobago". In *Human Rights, Sexual Orientation and Gender Identity in the Commonwealth: Struggles for Decriminalisation and Change*. Institute of Commonwealth Studies, School of Advanced Study, University of London: 429–54.

Gentles-Peart, Kamille. 2018. "Controlling Beauty Ideals: Caribbean Women, Thick Bodies, and White Supremacist Discourse 1". *Women's Studies Quarterly* 46 (1): 199–214.

Grandey, Alicia A. 2000. "Emotion Regulation in the Workplace: A New Way to Conceptualize Emotional Labor". *Journal of Occupational Health Psychology* 5 (1): 95–110.

hooks, bell. 1993. *Sisters of the Yam: Black Women and Self-Recovery*. Boston: South End Press.

Julien, Lisa-Anne. 2003. "Great Black Warrior Queens: An Examination of the Gender Currents within Rastafari Thought and the Adoption of a Feminist Agenda in the Rasta Women's Movement". *Agenda: Empowering Women for Gender Equity*, 57: 76–83.

Kenyon, Tom, and Judi Sion. 2002. *The Magdalen Manuscript: The Alchemies of Horus and the Sex Magic of Isis*. Louisville, CO: Sounds True, Inc.

Kitzinger, Shelia. 1966. "The Rastafarian Brethren of Jamaica". *Comparative Studies in Society and History* 9 (1): 33–39.

———. 1969. "Protest and Mysticisim: The Rastafari Cult of Jamaica". *Journal for the Scientific Study of Religion* 8 (2): 240–62.

Lake, Obiagale. 2012. "Cultural Ideology and RastafarI Women". In *Rastafari in the New Millennium: A Rastafari Reader II*, edited by Michael Barnett, 222–35. Syracuse, NY: Syracuse University Press.

Lorde, Audre. 1984. *Sister Outsider: Essays and Speeches*. Trumansburg, NY: Crossing Press. http://www.aspresolver.com/aspresolver.asp?BLWW;1000060639.

Mutseta, Alex. 2016. "The 'Small House' Phenomenon in Zimbabwe's Urban Space: Study in Glen Norah-Harare". *Open Science Journal* 1 (2): 2–30. DOI: https://doi.org/10.23954/osj.v1i2.484.

Padelford, Norman. J. 1964. "The Organisation of African Unity". *International Organization* 18 (3): 521–42.

Rollins, Judith. 1986. "Part of a Whole: The Interdependence of the Civil Rights Movement and Other Social Movements". *Phylon* 47 (1): 61–70.

Rowe, Maureen. 1980. "The Woman in Rastafari". *Caribbean Quarterly* 26 (4): 13–21.

———. 1998. "Gender and Family Relations in Rastafari: A Personal Perspective". In *Chanting Down Babylon: The Rastafari Reader*, edited by Nathaniel Samuel Murrell, William David Spencer and Adrian Anthony McFarlane, 72–88. Philadelphia: Temple University Press.

Somerville, Sibohan. B. 2007. "Queer". In *Keywords for American Cultural Studies*, edited by Bruce Burgett and Glenn Hendler, 187–91. New York: New York University Press.

Stanley Niaah, Sonjah. 2006. "'Slackness' Personified, Historicized and Delegitimized". *Small Axe* 10 (3): 174–85.

Stepman, François. 2016. "King of Kings – The Triumph and Tragedy of Emperor Haile Selassie I of Ethiopia". *Afrika Focus* 29 (2): 122–23.

Troeder, Werner. 2010. *Reggae: From Mento to Dancehall; Music, History, Artistes, Producers, Discography*. Kingston: LMH Publishing.

DISCOGRAPHY

Alpha Blondy and the Solar System, vocalist. 1994. "Abortion Is a Crime". MP3 audio. Track 1 on *Dieu*. VP Music Group.
Banton, Buju, vocalist. 1992. "Boom Bye Bye". Vinyl 12" audio. VP Records.
Beenie Man and Chevelle Franklyn, vocalists. 1997. "Dancehall Queen". MP3 audio. Track 1 on *Dancehall Queen* (soundtrack). Universal Island Records.
Capleton [Clifton George Bailey II], vocalist. 2002. "Bun Out di Chi Chi". MP3 audio. Track 5 on various artists, *Reggae Gold 2002*. VP Music Group.
Isaacs, Gregory, vocalist. 1982. "Not the Way". MP3 audio. Track 7 on *Night Nurse*. Island Records.
Marley, Bob, vocalist. 1980. "Pimper's Paradise". MP3 audio. Track 7 on *Uprising*. Tuff Gong Records.
Marley, Bob, and the Wailers, vocalist. 1976. "Crazy Baldhead". MP3 audio. Track 6 on *Rastaman Vibration*. Island Records.
Marley, Stephen, Capleton and Sizzla, vocalists. 2016. "Rock Stone". MP3 audio. Track 17 on Stephen Marley, *Revelation Pt. II: The Fruit of Life*. Ghetto Youths International.
Stephens, Tanya, vocalist. 1998. "Freaky Type". Track 16 on various artists, *Strictly the Best, Vol. 21*. VP Records.
———. "Ninja Bike". MP3 audio. Track 5 on *Ruff Rider*. VP Records.
———. 2003. "Please Me". MP3 audio. Track 7 on various artists, *Riddim Driven: Tai Chi*. VP Music Group Inc.
———. 2004. "Damn You". MP3 audio. Track 4 on *Gangsta Blues*. VP Records.
———. 2004. "Good Ride". MP3 audio. Track 5 on *Gangsta Blues*. VP Records.
———. 2004. "It's a Pity". MP3 audio. Track 7 on *Gangsta Blues*. VP Records.
———. 2004. "Sounds of My Tears". MP3 audio. Track 14 on *Gangsta Blues*. VP Records.
———. 2004. "Tek Him Back". MP3 audio. Track 8 on *Gangsta Blues*. VP Records.
———. 2004. "What a Day". MP3 audio. Track 16 on *Gangsta Blues*. VP Records.
———. 2006. "Do You Still Care". MP3 audio. Track 15 on *Rebelution*. VP Records.
———. 2006. "Power of a Girl". MP3 audio. Track 9 on *Shanty Town*. Pow Pow Productions.
———. 2006. "Sunday Morning". MP3 audio. Track 12 on *Rebelution*. VP Records.
———. 2006. "You Keep Looking Up". MP3 audio. Track 13 on *Rebelution*. VP Records.
———. 2014. "Unapologetic". MP3 audio. Track 15 on *Guilty*. Sanctum Entertainment/VPAL Music.
———. 2015. "Weather Change". MP3 audio. Track 1 on various artists, *Essential Dancehall, Vol. 2*. Tad's Records.
T.O.K., vocalist, 2001. "Chi Chi Man". MP3 audio. Track 3 on *My Crew, My Dawgs*. VP Records.

CHAPTER 10

"It's a Pity Yuh Already Ave a Wife"
The Possibilities and Pitfalls of Tanya Stephens's Civilized Man Sharing

CHAZELLE RHODEN

> It's a pity yuh already ave a wife
> An mi done have a man inna mi life
> Rude boy, it's such a pity
>
> (It's a pity you already have a wife
> And I already have a man in my life
> Rude boy, it's such a pity)

THE EPIGRAPH TO THIS CHAPTER COMES FROM TANYA Stephens's 2004 hit "It's a Pity". In these lines, which serve as a chorus, Stephens bewails the societal norms that constrain her relationship. Her romantic involvement with the man to whom she sings is adulterous, thus relegating her desire for them to have children and parent them within a committed partnership to wishful thinking. Through the verses, she mulls over what allowance might exist within Jamaican societal customs to fulfil this dream but perennially comes up short: she could give her current partner what many Jamaicans call a "jacket", a child born from adultery, a situation which forces the mother to lie about the child's true paternal identity to maintain her primary relationship. Although this option would allow her more satisfying relationships with both men, Stephens considers it sinful to lie to her child. She also decries the role of mistress – a "matey" in Patwa – for the intensity of her feelings merits a more capacious arrangement with her lover. Moreover, knowing that her community would view a transgression of such magnitude with disdain, she clarifies her intentions, stating they are not to disrespect her lover's "queen" and his children, or to disrespect her "king". The "queen" and "king" here in popular Jamaican parlance refers to the matrimonial or common-law partner or to the partner with whom there is the strongest commitment. Stephens ends her ruminations by identifying the source of her predicament. She lays blame on the "stupid rules of men", a diagnosis that problematizes the edifice of heteronormative familial arrangements. Stephens does not stop there, but moves her critique to envisage a solution. In an upbeat syncopation, which to me communicates her hopefulness for a different future, Stephens speculates:

> Who knows? Maybe one day the world will be evolved enough
> We'll share you in a *civilized manner* between the two of us
> But until then I would love see you again
> Me know we have to play it by these stupid rules of men.

It is Stephens's idea of "civilized sharing" that captures the attention in this chapter. Marked as amenable to her desire for fulfilling relationships and families with both men, "civilized sharing" is capacious in holding the new kinds of sexual, romantic and familial relationship structures that would need to exist for her to exercise such freedom. Venturing further, on the other hand, then, would be an "uncivilized" type of sharing. Remembering how she rejects the social role of mistress and refuses to turn her child into a "jacket," the wifey-matey or wife-mistress relationship structure can be viewed as a kind of uncivilized sharing. This chapter presents an examination of the benefits to be had from "civilized sharing" as juxtaposed with the less emancipatory "wifey-matey" relationship structure that is commonly practised within Jamaican society. I ask: Does this "civilized sharing" hold the potential to resolve the violence, hurt and other consequences that are entrenched in and emerge out of Stephens's notion of "uncivlized sharing"? Toward this end, I account for the lessons learned when I put Stephens's critique of the "wifey-matey" arrangement in conversation with my mother's lived experiences navigating this relationship dynamic. Therefore, Stephens and my mother provide most of the theoretical grounding for what follows.

To begin, we must unravel the construct of the "wifey-matey" gender roles. So, it is worthwhile to pay attention to the ways in which Jamaican women engage in the "wifey-matey" relationship dynamics and to consider the consequences that arise when they do so. These are questions that scholar Heather Russell (2010) responds to in her article "Man-Stealing, Man-Swapping, and

Man-Sharing: Wifeys and Mateys in Tanya Stephens' Lyrics". Russell skilfully illuminates how Stephens's work reflects the psychology of the Jamaican "wifey" and "matey". The word "wifey" is used to refer to a woman who is the legitimate female partner, whose partnership is validated through marriage or common-law union. A "matey", on the other hand, is defined by Russell (2010, 290) as "'the woman on the side', the mistress, or illegitimate partner who stands outside of the socially sanctioned domestic sphere". Russell identifies the way in which various social institutions (sex, marriage and socio-economics) influence the creation of these "wifey-matey" gender roles. She also discusses the processes that occur as a result of "wifey-matey" contestations, which she coins "man-stealing", "man-swapping" and "man-sharing". Each concept represents the desire for, exchange of, and/or sharing of men as part and parcel of the need to acquire resources in a severely constrained economic environment. The purpose of "stealing" a man or "sharing" him with his wife is, of course, to (at the very least) materially benefit from such a transaction.

Another way to understand the "wifey" and "matey" gender roles is through the concepts of respectability and reputation. "Respectability is the value system of the colonizers. It emphasizes marriage, the home, self-restraint, work, education and also reinforces social hierarchy. . . . [Its main institutions] are the church and the school. . . . Reputation is the counter-system of respectability. It is based on equality and personal worth as opposed to respectability, which maintains social hierarchy" (Boucher 2003, 85). Scholarship on the respectability-reputation value system posits that women and men heed different social norms as a means of accumulating socio-economic capital. Lisa Boucher has intervened to rethink Peter Wilson's *Crab Antics: A Caribbean Case Study of the Conflict between Reputation and Respectability* (1973), which positioned women as traditionally upholding the respectability value system, and men as upholding the reputation value system. Boucher counters this by pointing out that Caribbean gender roles do not fit neatly within this dichotomy; nor do they fit the colonial prescriptions of family structure. I find Boucher's thesis generative as it renders legible the quotidian efforts of black Jamaican women who tap into both the reputation and respectability value systems and the "wifey-matey" roles are a key example of this. Following Boucher's intervention, in this essay, I see Jamaican women who occupy the space of the "wifey" as performing within the respectability value system. This is so as she often carries out the self-restraining labour of compulsory monogamy as a means of establishing a form of self-value and worth. The "matey", on the other hand, mostly performs within the reputation value-system. Unlike the "wifey", she is unfettered by the institution of marriage and can more freely move in and out of romantic relationships for immediately personal and material gain.

Stephens engages with wifey-matey roles in other songs, where she often represents the friction that arises between the two. To parse out these contentions, I first consider Stephens's portrayal of the "wifey-matey" interaction. I then proceed to focus on my mother's own lived experience.

LIVED EXPERIENCES OF "WIFEY-MATEY"

In highlighting the complexities of the "wifey-matey" relationship dynamic evidenced in Stephens's work, Perkins contends that "one minute she [Stephens] is the matey setting out like a goalie or a Red Cross volunteer to 'save' or to 'rescue' the husband from a bad marriage that is 'killing' him" (2008, 12). In this instance, the wifey is blamed for not playing her sexual role and the husband is absolved from any obligations to his marriage. He is instead positioned as having no agency or willpower, so that the matey (Stephens) has to come to his aid.

There are, however, other instances where the transgression of "man-sharing" or "man-stealing" happens naturally; where people have lapses in judgement and succumb to sexual urges and romantic connections outside of their primary partnerships. There are also other times when this transgression is calculated. Stephens relates this occurrence in her song "Tek Him Back", where the matey begs her lover's wife to take back her husband because he is unable to provide for her financially. As such, he is of no material value to her:

> A tell me bout im ave a drop-top and a yacht
> Mi cyaan believe a gyal like me fall fi dat!
> If me neva did so vex me wuda find it funny
> Wen me ready fi spend an fine out him nuh ave nuh money
> Free paper wa me geh him meh have to turn down buddy
>
> (Telling me about him having a drop-top car and a yacht
> I can't believe a girl like me really fell for that!
> If I wasn't so vexed, I would find it funny
> When I am ready to spend, and find out he has no money
> Free access I gave him
> I even refused the sexual advances of other men)

Here, the logic behind what Russell (2010) calls "man-stealing" becomes apparent, as the man is commodified as a source of economic and social capital. For the matey, he becomes a tool for economic survival or upward social mobility from whose capital she is able to build her reputation (personal worth). This is especially important for her given the fact that her extramarital relationship pushes her outside the scope of respectability. In "Tek Him Back", the man is not able to perform this commodified function, and so the matey wants to return him in exchange for her freedom; the freedom from having to "turn down buddy".[1] Instead, she wants to be able to pursue other opportunities for economic mobility vis-à-vis the sexual exchange. Stephens's work illustrates the role of economics in "man-swapping" and shows us that it is not only men who leave their wives for other women: women also swap men in pursuit of material gain and, to a lesser extent, pleasure. This opposes the normalized discourse surrounding "swapping", as it is more commonly accepted that husbands will acquire mistresses. One hardly hears about wives openly acquiring new lovers. Therefore, the matey stands as a female figure that defies the norms on which gender is allowed to participate in swapping.

The economic impetus behind the phenomenon of man-sharing and man-swapping is further explained in Andrena McMayo's letter to the editor of the *Gleaner*. In it, she reminds us that the Jamaican economy disproportionately favours men over women. Women are paid less than men and continue to face underemployment, which limits their chances of survival (McMayo 2014). More recently, gender rights advocates in Jamaica, such as Nadeen Spence, have called for mechanisms to be put in place so that current equal pay laws have more teeth (Clarke 2019). In dire economic contexts like Jamaica, it is easy to see how men play a utilitarian role in providing women access to resources most are unable to attain on their own.

I now turn my attention to the role of the wifey. Stephens's portrayal of the latter is clearest in the song "Gangsta Gal", a duet with dancehall artiste Spragga Benz. In this song, the protagonist supports her gangsta man's criminal activity by hiding his "piece" from the police, oiling his weapon and, when necessary, bailing him out of prison. Interestingly, scholar of theology Anna Kasafi Perkins (2013, 7) tells us that "this [gangsta] gal's facilitative role seems to conform to the conservative view of a woman who is to cook and clean for her man". However, I further understand this "facilitative role" as one that parallels the archetypal "ride or die chic" glorified in the music of hip-hop and R&B artistes – musical genres consumed by Jamaicans on a large scale – in songs such as Beyonce and Jay-Z's "Bonnie and Clyde". These songs revere the black woman who tolerates abuse, emotional neglect and disrespect from her partner, even at the expense of her own health and personal safety (Maddox 2018). In the case of the wifey, she overlooks her husband's infidelity to keep her socially sanctioned relationship intact, thereby retaining her air of respectability. This is arguably also driven by her inability to survive financially on her own and by her reluctance to suffer a potential fall in her socio-economic standing. In some cases, this means that she must even make accommodations for the husband's newly acquired familial arrangement.

MY MOTHER'S STORY AS A "MATEY" AND A "WIFEY"

My childhood memories of witnessing my mother occupying varying roles within the "wifey-matey" relationship framework has shaped my interpretation of "wife-matey" dynamics taken up by Stephens in her oeuvre. I proceed by pointing out the many areas of overlap between Stephens's wifey and matey and my mother's experience of this domestic situation. My intention is to use my mother's experiences to contribute a more textured (re)presentation of what it may mean to live through the gender roles. My mother's story renders the ramification of "wifey-matey" contestations palpable and prompts me to deeply consider the complex ways in which Stephens treats this issue.[2]

Growing up, I did not realize that my mother was my father's "mistress". I had heard mention of a Mrs Rhoden in conversations, and my father did go to his own home every night. However, as a child, it was difficult to understand the complexity of these matters. In her song "Still a Go Lose", Stephens lays the blame for the husband's adultery at the feet of his wife:

> A worry bout me so much yuh nah see wen a
> Next gal a groove im
> You know a you kallis you wah blame me fi dis
> Wen a you did abuse im
> A seh me rek yuh life?
> Nuh im present di chice?
> All mi do a choose im
>
> (You are worrying about me so much you are unable to see when

Another girl is having sex with him or interested in him sexually
You know you are careless, you want to blame me for this
When you abused or neglected his care
You say I wrecked your life?
Wasn't he the one to present the choice?
All I did was choose him)

Just as Stephens believed that the wife was to be blamed for her husband's infidelity due to her carelessness and her inability to cater to her husband's needs, my mother justified her twenty-seven-year-long relationship with my father (essentially her "man-stealing") by describing the various ways in which my father's needs were not being met at home. I recall her emphasizing his deplorable health condition when they first met. She would often say, "Wen me tek up wid dat man im did have a bad stomach. Tru im neva did a eat pon time and im love di coffee and chaaclit im develop ulcer. A mi cook good food gi im an' im get better" (When I met that man, he had digestive issues. Because he never ate on time and he loved coffee and chocolate, he developed an ulcer. I cooked good food for him, so, he got better).

My mother viewed my father's primary partner as underperforming in her role as a "wifey". In her mind, this validated her own place in his life since she was able to fulfil the domestic duties his wife seemingly neglected, such as cooking a proper meal for him to come home to. As my father's "sweetheart", there were many ways that my mother simultaneously gained and lost respectability and reputation. She was aware that under her church's veneer of indifference to her relationship status, there existed contempt and disrepute. At the same time, she was able to gain access to a network of the town's elite, since my father was a local politician. This bolstered my mother's social capital and her reputation. With my father's financial support and social network, she rose to become a grassroots philanthropist in her own right, providing material aid to those in the community she saw as less privileged. Interestingly, my mother used her new social position as a mediator, redistributing some of my father's wealth to the local community. When my mother and father ended their relationship and she no longer had access to the financial support he provided, she would come to rely on the social capital she had amassed while they were together. She later drew on this social network to provide for me.

After twenty-seven years together, my parents finally "lef" (broke up). I was ten. It was night. My mother said to me, "Your father won't be coming back here". That was it! Before that, I had never seen the sun catch my mother in bed. Months leading up to that night, my mother had introduced me to her new friend. He would visit at night after my father had gone home. My father once asked my mother's best friend to help him get her back. The friend declined, responding, "Yuh cyaan give har wat she want. Yuh cyaan married to ar" (You can't give her what she wants. You can't marry her).

Some months later, my mother wedded the man who started to visit our home after that evening on which she told me my father would no longer visit. The small ceremony took place at the same Baptist church that had scorned her extra-marital affair with my father. As my father's "sweetheart" (mistress), my mother had gained socio-economically. However, the respectability gained through her new marriage was imperfect, because she had already sullied her reputation by being in a previous relationship with my father – a married man. Instead of continuing an errant relationship with a man who could provide economic stability, she chose to legally marry another man. She would later become divorced – though not by choice. The marriage was rocky and short-lived. The divorce papers were delivered by courier from the United States. Years later, my mother would enter a common-law union with a man who perpetually cheated. Ironically, she became the "wifey" spoken of in Stephens's songs.

It is clear from the account of my mother's experience that "wifey-matey" relationship dynamics are complex, as they simultaneously hold possibilities for upward social mobility and disempowerment. The women involved are always presented with a win-lose situation. In response to this, Stephens, in "It's a Pity", longs for a relationship structure that is less deleterious and compromising for the women involved as they grapple with realities around sexual desire. Here, Stephens dreams of an ideal world that is "evolved enough", where both wifey and matey can engage in man-sharing in "a civilized manner". It is to the idea of "man-sharing in a civilized manner" that I wish to call attention.

Russell (2010, 16) urges us to consider how

> replacing patriarchal values and institutions within the realm of domestic relations with more gender equitable ones remains a worthwhile goal and a monumental task to be arduously pursued by those of us who are feminists invested in such social transformations. In the meantime, however, in societies like Jamaica where what may be referred to as an informal polygamy to varying degrees is the norm, perhaps Stephens' notion of formalizing the "man-sharing" that is already taking place, provides, not only from a materialist perspective, a mechanism by which

the entire society is forced to confront, bear responsibility for and formalize the existent complex of domestic arrangements. In societies like Jamaica, marked by stark social class boundaries and entrenched sex/gender codes which are ensnared in the propagation of neo-colonialism, most often in the end, it is both the wifeys and the mateys that ultimately lose.

I therefore see Stephens as responding to Russell's call for social transformation as the singer champions an alternative arrangement that can serve to reconcile the tensions that are wound up in the "wifey-matey" construct. Russell views Stephens similarly, but argues that Stephens proposes the formalization of the informal polygamy that already operates in Jamaica. I agree that Stephens's dream of a civilized world, in which she may freely share the man who garners her attention in such a way that is least harmful to his household and to her own, is indeed a gesture toward bearing responsibility for the complexities of the "wifey-matey" relationships. However, I do not think it is accurate to say that Stephens advocates for a formalization of informal polygamy. In my mind, formalizing man-sharing as it exists within the "wifey-matey" framework – in other words, allowing men either legally or socially to have multiple wives – would not sufficiently attend to some of the tensions and negative consequences inherent to the "wifey-matey" relationship dynamic. My main concern is that formalizing man-sharing would centre state-sanctioned marriages and common-law arrangements rather than deal effectively with the "wifey-matey" dichotomy. Consequently, the violent institutions of colonialism, sexism, patriarchy and classism which create the inequitable gendered contestations remain unchallenged. I am further led to wonder about the potential of extending this formalized sharing to women as a way of rectifying the gender imbalance that emerges from man-sharing. Would variations of polyandry – where women would be legally or socially permitted to have multiple husbands – tend to the aforementioned social and economic inequalities and violence?

Given these limitations, I suggest that we not place as much attention on formalization or normalization of the informal polygamy practised locally. Instead, my own interpretation of Stephens, as informed by the nuances of my mother's experience and my uncertainties around formalization, impel me to wonder what it may mean, look and feel like to move towards building relationships within the domestic space that seek to break away from the ramifications of the "wifey-matey" arrangement stated. Stephens's album *Rebelution* (2006) is replete with signposts for such an inquiry. Throughout the album, she foregrounds a commentary on the ailments that inhibit the realization of her social utopia. In this compilation, Stephens speaks out against homophobia and racism, brings to the fore issues of unplanned parenthood, critiques economic systems that perpetuate poverty, and unmasks various forms of structural violence in Jamaican society. These issues are entangled with the "wifey-matey" relationship structure and should be considered in any attempt to reimagine our relationship structures.

Any model of Stephens's civilized sharing must correspond to the socially progressive ideals she articulates in *Rebelution*. This would mean promoting gender equity in a way that challenges hierarchical cultural and social institutions, particularly those that lead women to be reliant on man-sharing to meet their material needs. Stephens's civilized sharing would permit women the space to move out of the confines of respectability, in which social institutions reinforce social hierarchy. Nowhere is this more apparent than in the song "It's a Pity", where Stephens articulates her desire to step outside the socially acceptable domestic and monogamous romantic space. Here, she centres her needs as a woman and not her male lover's. One may easily think Stephens is therefore proposing the formalizing of polygamy, where social power is given to a specific gender. However, in the narrative of "It's a Pity", Stephens aspires to challenge the prevailing idea that males should hold more social power within romantic and sexual relations than women. She instead dreams of a world where she can engage romantically and sexually with a man without disrespecting the other woman involved in the romantic circle. This counters polygamy, in the sense that both women and men are equally able to form other domestic and romantic relationship paradigms outside of the "respectability" of state-sanctioned monogamous and polygamous marriages and outside of the more informal common-law structure. They are instead, in Stephens's ideal world, allowed more latitude to structure their sexual and domestic lives.

In other areas of Stephens's repertoire, the "wifey's" sexual and economic liberation is celebrated, allowing for a more expansive view of what is permissible within this role. In songs such as "Home Alone", the woman no longer declares an enduring loyalty to a male partner who is ignoring her sexual needs and other expectations. She forthrightly gives him many chances and pleads with him, but when he refuses to relent, she draws on her ex-lovers and gives him "bun".[3] In this song, we see a different "wifey"; one who is not passive and facilitative but is ready to leave her partner when he fails in his role as a husband.

Another issue that must be confronted within the man-sharing or man-swapping phenomenon and that ought to be considered in Stephens's utopia of civilized sharing is the way in which these relationship forms have the potential to fuel gender-based violence and specifically violence against women in Jamaica. We see in the Jamaican context common occurrences where men respond violently in situations of domestic conflict, often justifying their violent behaviour by "their women" cheating on them or exploiting them for financial gain. The violence is even more inflamed when these men learn that they are given "jackets".[4] In rural parts of Jamaica, which is where I was raised, these justifications for violent behaviour often translate into motives for homicide perpetrated by men against women with whom they are involved. Often, violence is also meted out by men against other men because they have, or are suspected to have had, affairs with women the aggressor is involved with (Whyte-Smith 2017).

In Stephens's ideal world, men and women would be able to move beyond the limiting domestic structures that are informed by Jamaica's colonial sensibilities of respectability and instead move towards relationship structures conducive to more flexible practices. This would certainly auger well for the protagonist in "It's a Pity", who desires to raise a child with a man who already has a primary partner. It would also eliminate the potential of condemning a "love child" born out of that relationship arrangement to a life of scorn, in which they are seen as a "jacket" or "bastard" (Blackford 2015). In the period prior to the advent of the Michael Manley administration in the 1970s, the "outside child" was legally illegitimate and was referred to as a "bastard". Although today more rights are afforded to the "outside child", the term is still used as a pejorative, denoting otherness and a lesser or marginal status.

When my father died, for instance, my mother refused to demand, on my behalf, her due of my father's estate, for which he left no will. His wife or children made no attempts to include me. Therefore, I, his biological child, was left outside of his legacy. Through civilized sharing, children like myself would not have to suffer the shame and stigmatization that comes with this "marginal" status. Furthermore, no "little white lies" would be needed to cover up the secret of a child's true paternity, which often happens when a woman knows she risks losing her economic and social stability if she admits that the child she is pregnant with does not belong to her primary partner.

By advancing a critique of uncivilized sharing, Stephens urges us to investigate how oppression is rooted within the fabric of the romantic and domestic relationship structures that we practise. She challenges the status quo "wifey-matey" dynamics as they occur in Jamaican society and which, as I have argued, often occur as women as an economically disempowered group try to eke out material gains or social mobility through romantic or sexual relationships with men. This often leaves the women involved in precarious positions and at times, contributes to incidents of intimate partner violence and covering the true paternity of children born out of relationships deemed errant. In response to this, Stephens's vision allows us to dream of other ways of organizing ourselves as a society; ways premised on equity, transparency and mutual consent. By starting this conversation, she "redefine[s] our [social] geography, to re-create and remove the lines of impossibility in which we exist" (Boyce Davies 1994, 23).

NOTES

1. In Patwa, "buddy" is a word used to describe the penis. It is often used as a metaphor for the economic and social opportunity that is represented in a sexual liaison with a prospective lover.
2. Special thanks to my mother for correcting my misunderstanding of the terms man-sharing/swapping while I thought through this piece.
3. In Jamaican Patwa, the term "giving bun" means to cheat on one's primary partner.
4. The word "jacket" is used in Patwa to describe a situation where the paternity of a child is attributed to another man who is not the biological father.

REFERENCES

Blackford, Richard. 2015. "Michael Manley and the 'Smadditisation' of Jamaica". *Jamaica Observer.* 13 December. http://www.jamaicaobserver.com/columns/Michael-Manley-and-the--smadditisation--of-Jamaica_45525.

Boucher, Lisa. 2003. "Respectability and Reputation: A Balancing Act". *Totem: The University of Western Ontario Journal of Anthropology* 11 (1): 85–87. http://ir.lib.uwo.ca/totem/vol11/iss1/12.

Boyce Davies, Carole. 1994. *Black Women, Writing, and Identity: Migrations of the Subject.* London: Routledge.

Clarke, Paul. 2019. "Review Equal Pay Laws, Gender Advocate Urges". *Gleaner.* 9 March. http://jamaica-gleaner.com/article/lead-stories/20190309/review-equal-pay-laws-gender-advocate-urges.

Maddox, Britney. 2018. "The 'Ride or Die' Narrative Is Too Often Code for an Unhealthy

Kind of Black Love". *Afropunk*, 4 May. http://afropunk.com/2017/07/ride-die-narrative-often-code-unhealthy-kind-black-love.

McMayo, Andrena. 2014. "Gender Inequality: A Practical Perspective". *Gleaner*, 13 March. http://jamaica-gleaner.com/gleaner/20140313/letters/letters7.html.

Perkins, Anna Kasafi. 2008. "Tasting Tears and [Not] Admitting Defeat: Promoting Values and Attitudes through the Music of Tanya Stephens". Inaugural Lecture of the Centre for Social Ethics, St Michael's Theological College, Kingston, Jamaica, 12 January.

———. 2013. "Love the Long Ding Dong: Tanya Transgresses Christian Sensibilities?" In *International Reggae: Current and Future Trends in Jamaican Popular Music*, edited by Donna Hope, 94–123. Kingston: Pelican.

Russell, Heather. 2010. "Man-Stealing, Man-Swapping, and Man-Sharing: Wifeys and Mateys in Tanya Stephens' Lyrics". In *Caribbean Erotic: Poetry, Prose and Essays*, edited by Opal Palmer-Adisa and Donna Aza Weir-Soley, 276–91. Leeds, UK: Peepal Tree Press.

Whyte-Smith, Oberlene. 2017. "'Is She Cause It!' Domestic Violence and Human Rights Abuse in the Jamaican Context Part 1". *Gleaner*, 5 March. http://jamaica-gleaner.com/article/news/20170305/she-cause-it-domestic-violence-and-human-rights-abuse-jamaican-context-part-1.

DISCOGRAPHY

Stephens, Tanya, vocalist. 2004. "It's a Pity". MP3 audio. Track 7 on *Gangsta Blues*. VP Records.

———. 2004. "Tek Him Back". MP3 audio. Track 8 on *Gangsta Blues*. VP Records.

———. 2006. "Home Alone". MP3 audio. Track 19 on *Rebelution*. VP Records.

———. 2006. "Still a Go Lose". Track 5 on *Rebelution*. VP Records.

CHAPTER 11

Power and the Construction of the Erotic

KAREN CARPENTER

Ave yuh eva stap to tink wa mek a gyal cheat?
Ave yuh eva ask ar if she like ow yuh dweet?
Yuh need fi check yuhself before yuh start kiss yuh teet
Cuz
Yuh nuh ready fi this yet, bwoy!

(Have you ever stopped to think what makes a girl cheat?
Have you ever asked her if she likes how you do it?
You need to check yourself before you start to kiss your teeth
Cuz
You are not ready for this yet, boy!)
(Stephens 1997)

IN THIS CHAPTER, I SET OUT TO CHALLENGE the intentionality expressed in Tanya Stephens's female and male stereotypes by interrogating the female to male sexual dynamic, the female to female power dynamic and by comparing these to earlier empirical data from Jamaica on sex-role stereotypes. I was first drawn to the project of critically examining the lyrical content of Stephens's songs by the well-known choruses and the responses of her fans to her songs on YouTube. Fans both praised Stephens's lyrical genius and showed that they identified with the portrayals of women in the songs. Some identify with the intrigue of the love situations she portrays, while others see the situations she describes as an opportunity for their alter ego to be expressed through the artiste. In analysing the lyrical content of some of Stephens's catalogue, I have adopted a phenomenological perspective as a sex and relationship therapist. I am interested in how others make meaning of their world, how this worldview helps them to achieve their relational goals and the ways in which their intentionality is directed at each other in pursuit of the erotic. The selected lyrics are treated as social commentary on relationships in Jamaica in general, rather than an autobiography of the artiste herself. Of course, the characters only exist within the one-dimensional world of Stephens's lyrics; therefore, any analysis is necessarily limited to the intentions presented in these songs. It is for this reason that it is psychologically more appropriate to examine the protagonist rather than the artiste. The artiste herself cannot be fully known from the projected alter ego of the female stereotype she plays on stage or in her lyrics. There is no assumption that the female protagonists in Stephens's songs reflect her own lived experiences. While social and cultural scholars to date have focused their attention on gendered and unequal sociopolitical exchanges in Stephens's work, little consideration has been given to the realm of the emotional and psychological.

THE PSYCHOLOGY OF RELATIONSHIPS

The science of relationships has a short history relative to the lifespan of the science of psychology. Currently, the interest in the areas of romantic, erotic relationships has exploded (Sternberg and Sternberg 2019; Fisher 2017; Jonasdottir and Ferguson 2014; Barriteau 2012; Friday 2012; Perel 2007). We want to know what makes relationships work, how the romantic fire can be kept alive and what creates the magic between sexual partners. Human erotic behaviour and the mental processes that direct these behaviours have been dissected and analysed for the better part of eighty years. The purpose of relational psychology is to understand the elements of human interaction necessary for supporting and encouraging healthy sexual and non-sexual relationships between individuals. The intentionality of positive psychology is not to impose value judgements about behaviours that are right or wrong but rather to enhance people's abilities to engage in relationships that promote good mental and emotional health (Slade 2010). This is the lens that is employed in examining Stephens's lyrics. The intent is to create a gestalt (Wertheimer 1938), with the lyrics appearing in relief against the background of the social expectations of male-female romantic relationships in Jamaica. The lyrics reflect the protagonists' socio-erotic behaviour, viewed in relief against the kinds of contexts that positive psychology would consider supportive of healthy relational interaction. The space between these two understandings provides insight into the Jamaican psychosexual landscape. One definition of the healthy erotic relationship can be seen in psychiatrist M. Scott Peck's (1978) description of love as the willingness of one individual to extend him or herself, in the service of both his or her own psychosexual growth and development and the growth of another person.

Robert Sternberg and Karin Sternberg (2019) famously carried out studies of thousands of couples to determine the secret ingredients to healthy, long-term love, and discovered that the essentials were intimacy, passion and commitment. Further, he conducted groundbreaking research confirming that there are at least eight different types of love between partners. Hendrick and Hendrick (2006) examine the ways in which individuals exchange sexual and relational pleasure and the stories that they create for themselves and their partners in pursuit of romantic passion. Despite the many approaches to sex research cited earlier, there are some common principles shared by researchers in the area as to what constitutes healthy exchanges between sexual partners and how these can be enhanced and managed for mutual benefit. There is no denial in the fields of relationship research and psychotherapy that sex and the erotic are essential elements of romantic love; indeed, these are central for human growth and development. However, what we consider erotic is highly subjective and there are clear differences between what one person considers erotic and the desires of another. Additionally, there is a difference between the erotic and that which may be seen as predictive of healthy psychosexual development between partners. Notwithstanding these differences, we acknowledge that there is a wide range of core erotic themes that drive passion for particular individuals, and that consent to any participation in the sexual dynamics of multiple partnerships is healthier than deception (Morin 1996). In the study of psychosexual behaviour, we have over one hundred paraphilia and fetishes on record, and yet less than a handful of these incur any social or legal sanctions. Invariably, psychology places hard boundaries around behaviours that cause harm to the self and others and behaviours that exclude the ability to consent. The erotic, therefore, is supported within the boundaries of consenting adult exchanges that do no harm.

PHENOMENOLOGICAL PSYCHOLOGY AND THE SELF

Through the lyrical content and performances of artistes such as Stephens, we can observe models of sociosexual engagements that reflect the society in which we live. We can know what behaviours are applauded, supported and encouraged through the acceptance of her protagonists' behaviour. What we cannot know is her motivations and her private thoughts. We have access to the stories she tells in song and though her stage persona. Even if we consider any public confessions and interviews that reveal glimpses of her private self, we know little from the songs selected here of the psychology of the real Vivienne Stephenson. I would, therefore, be wary of ascribing motives to her protagonists that are not described in the lyrics. The catalogue of songs serves as a kind of Rorschach Test,[1] in that we learn more about the listener's psychological views of relationships through their responses than we do about the lyricist's internal state. It is an abstraction, a random inkblot on paper, which we interpret according to our own interior lives. The inkblots themselves are neither menacing nor friendly; they allow us to experience emotions and responses and free the creative mind, thereby projecting from our own experiences onto the actors in the songs. Songwriters, painters and artistes alike hold up a mirror to society, but it would be amateur to suggest we can know the artiste from the works she presents. We imbue the artistes' performances with our own stories in much the same way art lovers imagine they can read the motivation of the artist in the renditions of his paintings. Psychology also accepts that we exist at various levels of self-disclosure and that what constitutes the private self is often not for public viewing. The personality is the composite of all the selves, private, public, ideal and real, while the persona is the perceived self. It is a form of representation of self in everyday life (Goffman 1959), a set of on-stage performances that provides a mask for the private self. Human interaction is largely a performative task, and the extent that we can integrate the many selves is the degree to which we can maintain healthy self-esteem and self-affirming relationships with others (Branden 2001).

If we accept that much of human interaction is performative in nature (Goffman 1959), we can easily understand that our performances are motivated by three simple factors related to context and audience. Maurice Merleau-Ponty (2005) describes these motivations as *intentionality*. He describes authentic action that is intrinsic to your personality as the *en soi*; while expressions that are intended to create an impression on others are described as *pour soi*; and those behaviours with the intentionality of giving pleasure to others reside in the *pour l'autre*. Merleau-Ponty's phenomenology of intentionality is concerned with the purpose of the action and sees intentionality as a kind of arrow, directing action either towards maintaining the presentation of the self to others or towards the fulfilment of the needs of others. Within the therapeutic environment, "the term phenomenology denotes a method of study, biasless, reflective examination of experience" (Meacham 1971, 4) that demands the use of scientific modalities for optimal mental and interpersonal health. It is predictive of behaviour, not prescriptive or value laden. No one behaviour is better than another within the boundaries of doing no harm; however, a behaviour is considered appropriate and effective if it is based in reality and research and can achieve the desired outcome. A behaviour then must be consistent with the intentionality of the individual and must support the mental well-being of those involved in the exchange.

The songs included in the analysis below speak to romantic engagements, whether fleeting or long term. The term "romantic relationships" signals a sexual engagement, rather than the lay understanding of romantic gestures, such as gifts and poetic expression. Therefore, for a relationship to be romantic it must necessarily include a sexual exchange. Sex can also be understood in its purely biological sense of male and female, but again that is not what is intended here. Sex in and of itself in the psychological sense means much more than intercourse and refers to a cycle of behaviour that begins with desire and culminates in orgasm. In this chapter, sex refers to all erotic acts between all partners, from intentionality – as in desire – to actuality, from sexual satiation to the sexual climax. Stephens's songs are replete with explicit sexual imagery and provide a rich source for examining female to male, and female to female sexual exchanges. It is in these exchanges that we can see the parallel in the commodification of sex to the Marxist value system (Marx and Engels [1867] 1909).

SEXUAL ENCOUNTERS AS EXCHANGE

One perspective on sexual exchange is that of Karl Marx. However, he has been criticized for the incompleteness of his economic exchange theory. In its original conceptualization, Marxian classical economic theory (theory of labour and work value) has been criticized for being "gender blind" (Brown 2014). The theory has subsequently been co-opted by feminist theorists and adapted to address issues of patriarchy and women's subjugation. The Marxist-feminist approach is outside the scope of the present work and is not the focus of the classical exchange theory. Rather, the focus here is the original philosophical argument, which positions human interaction in an equation of exchange and suggests how value is determined. These centre around use value and exchange value. Marx considers labour as the social substance that makes up value (Marx and Engels [1867] 1909). However, the work we put into a service or product cannot be seen in the item or service itself. We can only see the material value of the item through its exchange, whether for money or for other goods. We might also consider its exchange value as its worth – what we are willing to pay for receiving this item or service to satisfy a human need. He further states that a commodity "in the language of the English economists, is anything necessary, useful or pleasant in life, an object of human wants, a means of existence in the widest sense of the term" (1). Pleasure, therefore, is recognized as an important aspect of exchange. All commodities, says Marx, have two values, use value and exchange value. We might consider use value as the properties of the commodity or experience. Sexual experiences, for example, generally have an inextricable pleasure associated with them. Their exchange value is dependent on the participants involved in the activity, whether it comes as expressions of love, affection or goods and money. Sex is not only useful and pleasant but is also a necessary means of continuing the species. Sex also fulfils the other characteristics of a commodity, such as being an object of human want. Stephens's songs are replete with sexual activities that display these characteristics of the use and exchange value.

THEMES IN THE PLAYBOOK

"Yuh nuh ready fi dis yet bwoy" is a sentiment echoed throughout Stephens's extensive catalogue of musical hits and is perhaps one of the most memorable lines from her songs. The essence of these songs, which speak to female erotic desire, loudly declares the incompetence of men in the bedroom and their general mistaken assumptions about their ability to please women. Stephens derides the sexual prowess of men and chastises them for falsely boasting about their abilities in bed. A song such as "Tek Him Back" also exposes men as financial frauds who only look good when they are on the arm of another woman. Stephens continually calls into question male sexual supremacy and challenges male dominance. Additionally, the artiste's rather extensive catalogue of over two hundred singles and EPs, more than thirty-four of which she has either written or arranged herself, can be summarized as follows: contestations of sexual power, unrequited love, getting the upper hand in sexual relations and love triangles. The protagonists in the songs battle over sexual dominance, be it female–male or female–female. There are always winners and losers in the mix, and sometimes one protagonist can play a dual role, as they lose in the very act of winning.

Her song "Can't Breathe" is a bitter lament of a rejected lover. It may in fact provide a realistic look at the inability of so many, within the local context, to grapple with and accept rejection. Everyone experiences rejection at some point, we also reject others. This realization can often give us some perspective in dealing with a partner's desire to leave. Not so the protagonist in "Can't Breathe":

> You want me to take it like a man, but I'm a girl who cries
> So if I puncture your tires, don't be too surprised
> And while I'm at it, hell, I may as well key up your car
> 'Cause what you did to my heart that's an act of war.

"Can't Breathe" encourages the listener, in Stephens's own words, to "keep it real". Yet, in the Jamaican common parlance, it can also be viewed as a ballad of "bad mind".[2] The female protagonists in the songs do not believe they should ever be rejected. They do not want to experience the give and take of romantic relationships. They are either interlopers or "hard done by", and can justify any malicious action. It is not a play book for the faint of heart. Indeed, it is somewhat heartless. On the other hand, we might argue that this is a pragmatist's point of view which reflects the reality of male-female relationships, especially in Jamaica. I would, however, argue that it is a pessimistic view of relationships in which the very act of inter-relating becomes a futile "fuck them and leave them" emotional battle zone. Indeed, this is the reality for some men and women. To that extent, Stephens's body of work does honour those voices. Indeed, every fan page is replete with positive comments lauding her lyrical genius. A sample of viewer comments on YouTube below the video for the song "Can't Breathe" shows just this:

> bernard karathe: "tanya stephen is one of the illest out there . . . heavy vocals and lines . . . respect"
>
> liquidgoldeyes: "I concur!"
>
> Miaa430: "This song is straight SAVAGE!! I'm pretty sure every female can relate to this song. I know I can. Love this song."

These are only a few of the comments supporting Stephens's protagonists. The issue here for the psychologist is not whether the stated view is wrong or right but, more importantly, whether it leads to good mental and relational health. A common theme in the Jamaican and indeed other popular music landscapes is the inability to accept the other person's right of refusal. There is a general superficial assumption that if two or more persons engage in a relationship, they are bound to each other regardless of the changes in their personalities and their lives. The reality is that love does die, and people do leave relationships and go on to be happy in other partnerships. This idea that our former lovers are often happier with someone new is not the stuff that sells music or movies and the drama is part of the formula for appealing to fans. Rejection is an experience that we must learn to manage. It is painful, but it is temporary and can be resolved without keying cars and puncturing tyres. Drama is an essential component of the television soap opera and its appeal translates into the world of popular music.

FEMALE-MALE AND FEMALE-FEMALE DYNAMICS

Stephens's songs that appear to be in the vein of sentimental love songs invariably express some regret, tragedy or unfulfilled wish. Songs such as "Take Good Care of My Man" (2020), "It's a Pity" (2004) and "Little White Lie" (2004) present women who have suffered at the hands of love and are forced by life's realities to make hard concessions. In "Take Good Care of My Man", the wife proceeds to school the matey (the female he is having the affair with) as to the proper care her husband should receive. The protagonist, who in other songs such as "Still a Go Lose" is dissed (shown disrespect) by the side chick (fleeting lover on the side), now turns around and humiliates the matey, since she has assumed the role of wife, or "wifey" to use Jamaican parlance. Perhaps this is an attempt to show both sides of the coin, although I rather doubt it, as there is no call-response intended in these two songs. What becomes clear is the female archetype presented in Stephens's songs must win, even if winning means a pyrrhic victory.

The construction of the female-male dynamic in the songs included here is primarily one of the woman in charge and free from relational commitments, which places her in the position of being free to roam, to choose and to dismiss men and women alike. The other is the dissatisfied woman, whether the dissatisfaction is with the performance of the man or with his absence and neglect, in a song such as "These Streets". In her 2004 rendition of "It's a Pity", the main character is already in a relationship which she values, but she can see herself happily involved in a deep relationship with another man she can only fantasize about, because he too is in a committed relationship. These are real issues that face men and women alike and this is perhaps where Stephens's greatest appeal lies. Men and women relate to the situations the lyrics describe, even if a great portion of these descriptions is couched in competing for men and their validation. The value of these engagements to the individual's psycho-sexual growth is debatable, particularly as the protagonists seek to debase other women and devalue the men they engage with, as highlighted in the lines of "Put It on You" (2006):

> If even a wuk pon di side was taboo
> Tell dem seh tonight we ago set it off back
> If wifey no like how mi put on a bruise pon you
> Wen mi done she fi tek it off back
> Wen mi put a likkle extra glue inna di Stickkity
> Bet any money she cyaa get it off back, woah

> (Even if being on the side was taboo
> Tell them tonight we are going to set if off back
> If your wife doesn't like how I put on a bruise on you
> When I am done with you, she should take you back
> When I put a little extra glue in my vagina
> Bet you any money she can't get it off of you, woah)

The lines above speak of a degree of stealth, clandestine hook-ups and casual encounters, regardless of the fact that a condom is referred to multiple times, in an acknowledgement perhaps of the need for safe sex encounters. The scenarios described in the songs included in the present work create an erotic image of the female who embodies what is considered traditionally male sexual risk-taking and promiscuity. The themes in Stephens's catalogue repeatedly present a protagonist who not only gets what she wants but also takes whatever and whoever she pleases. Many of her songs boast of conquests over a man who has already committed to another woman. Yet the protagonist is not to be mistaken with the now popular matey who is also in a one-down relationship with the man. In Stephens's lyrics, the female protagonist is a chauvinist, the female counterpart of the misogynistic male. The man is prey and she is the arch predator, dominatrix and the subject, not object of desire. This in turn sets up female to female competition, also echoed in a number of Stephens's songs, such as "Unapologetic":

> A suh mi still a ride, mi still a bum pon the side, still a ding a guy in the middle the night
> Still a moon light, nah apologize fi no gyal, wi no feel me them gyal dem no real
> Mi nuh play wid dem, mi nah look nuh friends, mi nuh parr again, nuh mix up an blen,
> Stan far again from the ole cribbit dem
> Mi rada trade wid a ting weh long till it ben
>
> (So I am still riding, I am still bumming on the side, still ringing guys in the middle of the night
> Still moonlighting, not apologizing for any girl who doesn't get me; those girls aren't real
> I don't play with them, I am not seeking any friends, I am not fraternizing with those washed-up women
> Standing far again from those undesirables
> I would rather trade with a phallic object/penis that is long until it bends)

In this song, "Miss Unapologetic" has no time for the consideration of the other woman's feelings, nor is she generally concerned if the other woman sees evidence of her man's infidelity, such as marks on his body as she proclaims in "Put It on You".

WOMAN IN CONTROL OF SEXUALITY AND REPRODUCTIVE CAPACITY

The sexual power and control that the female characters demonstrate are not only in the area of sex for pleasure but also in reproductive sex, where the woman holds the power of the truth of paternity. The song "Little White Lie" tells the story of a woman who is in a committed relationship but secretly has a child with another man. The secrets and lies keep her tied to both the absent father and the committed partner, whom she loves. It is another everyday story that is rationalized in reality, and in Stephens's song, by accepting that the woman has made a hard, but just choice. In "Still a Go Lose", Stephens returns to her female stridency and harsh pragmatism through another "tracing" (cursing out) song, with the "wifey" as the butt of her criticism. The female-female relations in her songs are competitive for the most part and combative. The usual accusation is that men stray because their regular partners no longer please them sexually and do not give them the attention they require. This is part of the common "wifey-matey" rhetoric in Jamaica and is not particularly novel, but sure to have wide appeal among the wider fan base. Sadly, it also furthers the male myths of sexually boring women and insatiable men. This dynamic is reversed in "Take Good Care of My Man", in which Stephens not only accepts the inevitability of a matey, once she is the "wifey", but also feels the necessity to "school her":

> I seh wen yuh secure yuh nuh war, you live way above dat
> An any wife a go fight wid a matey is a bait or a crook dat
> If yuh gonna be my understudy you gotta learn yuh lines
> You've got to improve
> What looks bad on him looks even worse on me
> As long as im safe

> Im wort more dan a couple a grand weh im put inna yu han
> or pon di night stan afta di slam
> Come on
> You gotta take good care of my man

> (I say, when you are secure, you don't war, you live way above that
> And any wife who is going to fight with a matey is a bait or a crook
> If you are going to be an understudy, you gotta learn your lines
> You've got to improve
> What looks bad on him, look even worse on me

> (He's worth more than a couple thousand dollars that he puts in your hand
> or on the night stand after sex
> Come on
> You gotta take good care of my man)

This song reproduces a hierarchy among women, where a matey is below a wifey in knowledge, self-care and worldliness. The first line above is ironic in that Stephens's songs never miss the opportunity to "dis a gyal" (show disrespect to a girl). Here, she does it through disdain for her understudy. Again, the negotiation with the other female is one of assessing the man's use value (Marx and Engels [1867] 1909) and carving out a memorandum of understanding regarding the wife's standards for the interloper – not the husband's. It is possible that such arrangements do indeed exist where the wife can instruct the outside lover and keep her in check. However, the reality of such situations is far more complex and fraught with resentments and deception than any three-minute song can outline.

FEMALE-FEMALE OWNERSHIP OF MALE DESIRE

In "Still a Go Lose" and the ever popular "Tek Him Back", the women are the ones who contest over male ownership and not the other way around. The man is on the chopping block and can be parcelled out for a schedule of encounters subject to the negotiation between the women. The matey argues that the man she has stolen from the wife is really unsatisfactory, and since he has not lived up to his promise, she wants to invoke the return policy and ask the wife to "tek him back" (take him back). The protagonist in "Still a Go Lose" points out that even if she sends the man back home to the wife, there is always another woman who will take her place. It is the man who is being passed around in a game of "reverse sexism", and the conversations in these songs are directed at women, by women. The man is rendered voiceless. There appears to be an unstated rule of the jungle in the descriptions of erotic exchanges that if men have done this to women in the past then women simply do the same to men and the balance is restored. This argument only perpetuates the unacceptable structures of patriarchy. Men and women possess the same psychological needs, even where society mediates the expression of these through gendered channels. The rejected and shamed male partner suffers the same emotional wounds as the rejected female. However, there is no evidence in Stephens's catalogue of a recognition of universal psychological needs of both genders, beyond the momentary erotic exchange. In "Still a Go Lose" she sings:

> Well if im waan fi stray
> im will find a way
> Nuh matter how much yuh move like mange
> Cuz if him leave me alone or me send him back home
> An nutten inna yuh house nuh change
> You know you still a go lose him
> A worry bout me suh much you nah see wen a
> Next gyal a groove him

(Well if he wants to stray
He will find a way
No matter how much you seek to restrict the man's sexual behaviour
Because if he leaves me alone or I send him back home
And nothing in your house changes
You know you're still gonna lose him
You are worrying about me so much you're unable to see when
Another girl is sleeping with him)

When examined through the lens of Marxist exchange theory, it is easy to see how Stephens's protagonist commodifies men's sexual value and converts its use value into an exchange between women and for women's pleasure. The use value of the male partner is that he can provide intense sexual pleasure, as demonstrated in the song "Boom Wuk" (2004). The whole basis of Marxist exchange theory lies in the exchange of something or someone through a social exchange. The female protagonists in Stephens's lyrics exchange sex with men, thereby commodifying them and even returning them when they do not live up to the expected function. It is the ultimate objectification of the male and his use value. The sexual politics embodied by Stephens's catalogue operates in much the way women have been de-personalized, objectified and commodified by men. In more recent times, Arjun Appadurai (1986) explains how social embodiment becomes attached to commodities, whether they be persons or things. He tells us that "economic exchange creates value. Value is embodied in commodities that are exchanged ... what creates the link between exchange and value is politics, construed broadly. This argument ... justifies the conceit that commodities, like persons, have social lives" (Appadurai 1986, 3). The point here is not a judgement about whether the females in Stephens's songs are wrong or right to exert this form of female power. The matter is somewhat more nuanced than that. Additionally, psychology does not seek to determine right or wrong but rather what is healthy and unhealthy and for whom. Further, in its most basic element, exchange theory asserts that all interactions and exchanges are transactions that rely on the desire of one and the willingness of the other to supply that desire. This idea is reinforced by Simmel (1978, 79) who reminds us that "every interaction has to be regarded as an exchange: every conversation, every affection (even if it is rejected), every game, every glance at another person".

The essential element in any exchange is reciprocity. We engage with others with the intentionality of sacrificing something for the gaining of something else. Even where one party appears to be in charge, they depend on the reciprocal cooperation of the other individual for the exchange to occur. Exchanges by their very nature create objectification (Simmel 1978). The simple fact is that if the elusive reciprocal and healthy relationships that men and women seek with each other rely on mutual respect, intimacy, vulnerability and trust, then Stephens's lyrics are not the place to look for guidance, because according to her, "It's all about the sex." "Don't Play" and "Put It on You" exhort the man to demonstrate his sexual skills, and in the process, there is the obligatory "diss" (disrespect) to the other woman, again in this instance, the wife. Her man is of a lower social class than the protagonist and so is his woman, as she has settled for a broke man. The intrinsic value of man as a person – his personality, his character – is entirely ignored, and the arena in which men have traditionally dominated women – money – is taken out of the equation, because this man has none. A complete emasculation is achieved in which the man only gets any sense of status, of meaning through his sexual exchange with the more powerful woman, who is not his "wifey". In "Boom Wuk" she sings:

> It's not di way yuh waak
> An' it's not di way yuh taak
> An' it's not your beat up car
> Yuh definitely ain't no movie star
> It's not the clothes you wear
> An' it's not your nappy hair
> It's not your gangsta flex
> Baybee, it's all about di sex
>
> (It's not the way you walk
> And it's not the way you talk
> It's not your beat up car
> You definitely ain't no movie star
> It's not the clothes you wear
> And it's not your nappy hair
> It's not your gangsta flex
> Baby, it's all about the sex)

Stephens's protagonists defy the norms of sex between a man and his woman as strictly private – between them – and places it in the public domain for negotiation with other women. In "Boom Wuk", for instance, the sexual space becomes one is which the man as object is still necessary to establish his exchange value:

Me nuh even andastan a why yuh wife a bruck war
Yuh mighta love me but to me is jus a jook star
Me jus a cut an' guh chru
Fling me kitty pon u
An' if de claw dem hol' u good luck star

(I don't even understand why your wife is warring
You might love me but to me it's just a sex man
I am just cutting and go through
Fling my vagina on you
And if the claws hold you
Good luck man)

The love triangle places the man in the centre of the two women, and erotic use value and desire are converted through the exchange of pleasure into erotic transactions, negotiated in the public arena by women. Here, the objections of the "wifey" are dismissed as foolish and futile, in light of the superior sexual power of the protagonist.

THE EROTIC SELF AS PLEASURABLE

The existential question arising from these selected examples of Stephens's work is: Who calls the shots? Undoubtedly, the female protagonist of the songs is in charge. The scenarios constructed on the basis of female power and sexual politics portray a series of interactions designed for conquest. The female is the subject of all actions, as she directs and empowers the male through her objectification of him. He is a tool used for her pleasure – not an equal partner – and sex is a battlefield, with the male organ as a weapon. His limits and boundaries are set by the female who demands a performance when she sings in "Don't Play": "Me expec fi get ravaged the whole night, nothing less" (I expect to be ravaged the whole night, nothing less). Stephens's lyrics describe an intentionality on the part of her female protagonists that is not pleasure in her own body, in her own erotic or self-pleasure. It communicates a model where the female erotic for itself (*en-soi*) is missing. The erotic transaction depends on the perception of the object – the other individual (*pour-soi*) – and the pleasure and desire are directed at the other (*pour l'autre*). Stephens's work denies the interdependence, give and take, of sexual encounters by privileging relations in which top-down power is exercised.

However, sexual intentionality as expressed through the body as a "vehicle of being in the world" (Merleau-Ponty 2005, 94) accepts that there can be no real dichotomy of desire; rather, we are both subject and object at the same time. If we are the body-subject as Merleau-Ponty would have us consider ourselves, then we necessarily have various ways of perceiving ourselves when we act in the world. When we engage sexually, we both give up and gain power and control through the body as "the pivot of the world" (94), which the partner encounters in the subject-object interchange. This is neither a negation of power nor of dominance or any exchange value that we may want to place on human sexual interaction. Equally, the "side-chick", "matey" and wife can only be in contention where they both perceive themselves to be in a clash over the sexual spoils of war. Simply thinking oneself to be in the dominant sexual position, therefore, does not make it so. Merleau-Ponty rejects the notion that the body directed at an intention can be purely subject or object. There can be no victor unless the object agrees to be vanquished, sexually or otherwise. If we follow this phenomenological thread to its natural conclusion, we see that the dominance, command and control that Stephens's female protagonists claim require the cooperation of the submissive male and his committed female partner. Romantic relationships in the real world rarely play out in the ways described in Stephens's "playbook". Nevertheless, there are those who receive the lyrics as a prescription for relationships and who certainly attempt to emulate the "dis a gyal" (disrespect a girl) culture. The litmus test for the stereotype presented in Stephens's lyrics is the reality that we face in everyday life.

LYRICS VERSUS LIFE

The female stereotype presented in Stephens's body of work moves through the cut and thrust of sexual politics with little real consequences, and that is where the fantasy ends. In the real world, far from the lights of the stage, there is a price to pay, often an emotional and psychological one. The way we see male and female sexual stereotypes has implications for what we expect of each other in relationships. In an earlier study designed to test Jamaican men and women's beliefs about gender stereotypes, an adjective list of one hundred items was designed and tested for cultural validity (Carpenter and Walters 2011). A second study was later conducted yielding fresh data which were examined against ten years of dancehall music, from 1998 to 2008 (Walters and Carpenter 2017).

Randomly selected male and female respondents from the generation influenced by the music of this period were also asked to choose adjectives they felt described men and women in Jamaica. Respondents described Jamaican men as: coarse, reckless, aggressive, lazy, tough, arrogant, stern, disorderly, robust, rigid, autocratic, courageous and hard-headed. At the same time, Jamaican women were seen as complaining, fussy, sexy, emotional, worrying, affectionate, sensitive, soft-hearted, sophisticated, fearful, excitable, warm and cautious. Stephens's female protagonists, by this standard, embody the male sex-role stereotype of being coarse, reckless, aggressive, tough, arrogant, stern, disorderly, robust, rigid, autocratic, courageous and hard-headed. In fact, they manifest all the male attributes, with the exception of lazy. However, her love songs also depict women who are stereotypically complaining, fussy and sexy. What comes through is a characterization that represents a role-reversal for the traditional male and female gender roles held by the population at large, suggesting that, to embody Stephens's female sexuality, women will have to be more like the stereotypical Jamaican man. Interestingly, this is an image that has been widely rejected by men and women alike, across the globe, who strive for gender equity and equality (Walker 1995; Barriteau 2012, Jonasdottir and Ferguson 2014; hooks 2014). There has existed throughout history an ever-growing number of male feminists (Jardine and Smith 1987), not to mention the many scholars, writers and speakers who have declared themselves pro-feminist, womanist, gender-sensitive and gender-inclusive. Noah Berlatsky (2014) gives a brief, but comprehensive, account of some of the more notable male feminists in history. Similarly, Schacht and Ewing (1998) present some of the leading modern writers in the area who see the deconstruction of traditional female roles as beneficial not only to women but also to men's lives. Feminist scholar Peter F. Murphy (2004) provides an informed view of the role of men in feminism spanning over twenty-five hundred years and in the Caribbean, philosopher Earl McKenzie (2008) is among the self-declared men who are feminist. Yet, here we are in 2018, still "unapologetic".

CONCLUDING THOUGHTS

To be fair, the depictions of erotic love, relationships and power in the Stephens's catalogue reflect a social reality for many men and women in the Jamaican society. Stephens's female protagonists often turn the tables on their male objects of desire, they control and use men's sexuality for their own pleasure in ways that many women would like to. We began with her fans and their applause for her lyrical talent and her performances. Clearly, the thousands who flock to her concerts identify with the ethic of the heartbreaker, cold, "love them and leave them style" that Stephens's female characters display, as is evidenced in comments on her YouTube video for "Pon di Side":

> islandgal319: Put it on me like a man from de side!!! Raaaay!!
> That's the way to keep it interesting
> ~ I love you Tanya Stephens!!!!
>
> jcansweetsap: love this song and the video, Tanya never disappoints :) and this is no less. She makes me love feeling guilty ;)
> LMAO. Tanya! Video concept shatttt!! Love it. Put it on like a man pon di side. Lol. #weak
>
> Stacy C: I love tanya more and more each time I listen to her
>
> Steve Powell: My favorite song on the album guilty

True, such reactions are counterintuitive for the individual seeking reciprocity, respect and mutuality, but there is the other need that some individuals have for an erotic experience that leaves them feeling more powerful, if even for a few minutes. As Hendrick and Hendrick (2006, 153) point out, "Love is a game to be played with a diverse set of partners over time. Deception of the partner and lack of disclosure about self and other partners are prime attributes of ludus."

This form of love is primarily practised during early adulthood, in the experimental stage of sexual development, and often includes a steady stream of new partners. With maturation, most young adults find ludus less attractive and seek out cohabiting partners and raise families. Ludus relies heavily on deception and having the upper hand while treating sexual partners as disposable. Ironically, while the partners in a game of ludus deceive others, they rarely themselves tolerate being deceived. The game comes to a screeching halt when the counterfeit lover is on the receiving end of being duped. Yet Stephens's songs reflect a reality common to many Jamaican intimate relationships far into late adulthood. While islandgal319 and jcansweetsap are thrilled at the descriptions of sex on the side and delicious guilt, there is another reality to the "cut and go through" lifestyle that Stephens's protagonists display.

There is the opposite tendency on the part of the politically correct members of the society, who do not support the messages in Stephens's music to attempt to hold artistes accountable for supporting such sexual practices in the rest of the population. However, artistes can rarely be held responsible for reflecting society as it is; instead, they hold up the proverbial mirror to society. Further, if we find this image of our sexual selves disturbing, then we must find ways of engaging with each in the kinds of relationships we actually value. Such relationships can hardly be identified if we continue to be ignorant about what motivates us towards unsatisfying romantic relationships and why sex has become more about power and transaction than mutual satisfaction. The very restrictions that distil sex, the erotic and pleasure into one silo, and being emotionally healthy and caring into another, make it difficult to conceive of good sexual partners who could "put it on like a man/[woman] pon di side". However, we rarely speak about sexual pleasure, the erotic and relationships with an understanding of what these mean to us psychologically.

A psychosexual, relational perspective demands an understanding of the subject-object dynamic and how power constructs notions of the erotic. When partners share the erotic power, they open themselves to experiencing sexual satisfaction as both subject and object, without yielding power in the relational space through both the dynamic of the entreaty and the satisfaction of yielding. We also find erotic pleasure in the body itself and its own existence, without the demand and cravings of another. In this way, we come to a full understanding of our own power to pleasure and satisfy our interior erotic needs without the other. Erotic power ceases to be power over and becomes a power for itself, within itself, the erotic of being *en-soi* and recognizing being as an end in itself. The erotic imagination has as its intentionality the experience of transcendence, which we imagine must be experienced through power over another body. Yet we often miss the transcendence in the chase to satisfy our erotic desires, because desire on its own has no end. It only has an intentionality towards sexual satisfaction through transcendence. Desire, raw desire, is just an arrow pointed at an object, any object of desire. When we examine relationships in which partners experience ludus, there is a recurrent feeling of emptiness, shortly after the most erotic of experiences, despite the passion, despite the chase, despite the power of being the subject of the erotic and not the object. Psychologically, the insufficiency is not in the exterior experiences of the body, but rather in the interior life of the individual.

As psychologists, we look for antecedents of insufficiency, perhaps in early childhood and other pivotal moments of transition from the safety of home as private to the public space of sexual relationships with others. There is a sense in which the vulnerable pleasure of childhood has been lost in translation for the adult who longs for mutual eroticism. It is this lack that drives the power dynamic between lovers when one controls the sexual pleasure and the other is reduced to an object of their desire. The power over the erotic self becomes one in which an object must be de-personalized and sacrificed on the altar of the ego. It is ultimately a win-lose erotica. If indeed it is "all about the sex", then the relational aspects become subsumed and the erotic becomes a transaction, which requires little more than a fleeting sense of winning before the desire returns and once again seeks to satisfy itself, using the other – *l'autre* – as a substitute for what it cannot find in itself. Again, this is not to argue that either type of power or pleasure is better or worse. I argue, simply, that the reciprocity of desire that is so rare, but so sought after, is to be found in the interchange, not exchange of erotic power, where we can be expressed as both subject and object simultaneously, through our own volition. In this way, healthy relationships become a well-choreographed flow of sexual energy between equals rather than a battle of unequally matched sexual warriors.

NOTES

1. The inkblot test created by Swiss Freudian Psychoanalyst Hermann Rorschach in 1921.
2. In Patwa, "bad mind" is used to describe a person who harbours feelings of envy, grudge or who wishes others ill.

REFERENCES

Appadurai, Arjun. 1986. "Introduction: Commodities and the Politics of Value". In *The Social Life of Things: Commodities in Cultural Perspective*, edited by Arjun Appadurai, 3–63. New York: Cambridge University Press.

Barriteau, V. Eudine. 2012. *Love and Power: Caribbean Discourse on Gender*. Kingston: University of the West Indies Press.

Brown, H. 2014. "Marx on Gender and the Family: A Summary". *Monthly Review* 66 (2). https://monthlyreview.org/2014/06/01/marx-on-gender-and-the-family-a-summary/.

Berlatsky, Noah. 2014. "A Short History of Male Feminism". *Atlantic*, 12 July. https://www.theatlantic.com/politics/archive/2014/06/a-short-history-of-male-feminism/372673/,2014.

Branden, Nathaniel. 2001. *The Psychology of Self-Esteem: A Revolutionary Approach to Self-Understanding that Launched a New Era in Modern Psychology*. San Francisco: Jossey-Bass.

Carpenter, Karen, and Gavin Walters. 2017. "Gender-Role Stereotypes and Culture in Jamaica and Barbados". In *Interweaving Tapestries of Culture and Sexuality in the Caribbean*, edited by Karen Carpenter, 15–34. Gewerbestrasse: Palgrave Macmillan.

———. 2011. "A So Di Ting Set: Conceptions of Male and Female in Jamaica and Barbados". *Sexuality and Culture* 15 (4): 345–60.

Fisher, Helen. 2017. *Anatomy of Love: A Natural History of Mating, Marriage, and Why We Stray*. New York: Norton.

Friday, Nancy. 2012. *Women on Top*. New York: Gallery Books.

Goffman, Erving. 1959. *The Presentation of Self in Everyday Life*. Hamburg: Anchor.

Hendrick, Clyde, and Susan Hendrick. 2006. "Styles of Romantic Love". In *The New Psychology of Love*, 2nd ed., edited by Robert Sternberg and Karin Weis, 149–70. Cambridge: Cambridge University Press.

hooks, bell. 2014. *Feminist Theory: From Margin to Center*. New York: Routledge.

Jardine, Alice, and Paul Smith. 1987. *Men in Feminism*. New York: Routledge.

Jonasdottir, A.G., and A. Ferguson. 2014. *Love: A Question for Feminism in the Twenty-First Century*. Routledge Advances in Feminist Studies and Intersectionality. Abingdon, UK: Routledge.

Marx, Karl, and Friedrich Engels. (1867) 1909. *Capital: A Critique of Political Economy*. Volume 1: *The Process of Capitalist Production*. Translated by Ernest Unterman and Edward Aveling. Chicago: Charles H. Kerr. https://oll.libertyfund.org/titles/marx-capital-a-critique-of-political-economy-volume-i-the-process-of-capitalist-production.

Meacham, W.P. 1971. "A Phenomenological Description of the Self". PhD dissertation, University of Texas at Austin. https://www.researchgate.net/publication/318699546.

Merleau-Ponty, Maurice. 2005. *Phenomenology of Perception*. Translated by Colin Smith. Taylor and Francis e-Library. http://alfaomnia.com/resources/Phenomenology+of+Perception.pdf.

McKenzie, Earl. 2008. *Philosophy in the West Indian Novel*. Kingston: University of the West Indies Press.

Murphy, Peter F. 2004. *Feminism and Masculinities*. Oxford Readings in Feminism. Oxford: Oxford University Press.

Morin, Jack. 1996. *The Erotic Mind: Unlocking the Inner Sources of Passion and Fulfillment*. New York: Harper Perennial.

Peck, M. Scott. 1978. *The Road Less Traveled: A New Psychology of Love, Traditional Values, and Spiritual Growth*. New York: Simon and Schuster.

Perel, Esther. 2007. *Mating in Captivity: Unlocking Erotic Intelligence*. New York: Harper Collins.
Schacht, Steven P., and Doris W. Ewing. 1998. *Feminism and Men: Reconstructing Gender Relations*. New York: New York University Press.
Slade, Mike. 2010. "Mental Illness and Well-being: The Central Importance of Positive Psychology and Recovery Approaches". *BMC Health Services Research* 10 (26). doi: 10.1186/1472-6963-10-26.
Sternberg, R.J., and K. Sternberg. 2019. *A New Psychology of Love*. Cambridge: Cambridge University Press.
Simmel, G. Georg. 1978. *The Philosophy of Money*. Edited by David Frisby and translated by Tom Bottomore and David Frisby. National Library of Australia. https://catalogue.nla.gov.au/Record/401104.
Walker, Rebecca. 1995. *To Be Real: Telling the Truth and Changing the Face of Feminism*. New York: Anchor Books.
Wertheimer, Max. 1938. "The General Theoretical Situation". In *A Source Book of Gestalt Psychology*, edited by W. D. Ellis, 12–16. London: Kegan Paul.

DISCOGRAPHY

Tanya Stephens, vocalist. 1997. "Yuh Nuh Ready fi Dis Yet". MP3 audio. Track 1 on *Too Hype*. VP Records.
———. 2004. "Boom Wuk". MP3 audio. Track 3 on *Gangsta Blues*. VP Records.
———. 2004. "Can't Breathe". MP3 audio. Track 13 on *Gangsta Blues*. VP Records.
———. 2004. "It's a Pity". MP3 audio. Track 7 on *Gangsta Blues*. VP Records.
———. 2004. "Little White Lie". MP3 audio. Track 6 on *Gangsta Blues*. VP Records.
———. 2004. "Tek Him Back". MP3 audio. Track 8 on *Gangsta Blues*. VP Records.
———. 2006. "Don't Play". MP3 audio. Track 20 on *Rebelution*. VP Records.
———. 2006. "Put It on You". MP3 audio. Track 3 on *Rebelution*. VP Records.
———. 2006. "Still a Go Lose". MP3 audio. Track 5 on *Rebelution*. VP Records.
———. 2006. "These Streets". MP3 audio. Track 18 on *Rebelution*. VP Records.
———. 2014. "Unapologetic". MP3 audio. Track 15 on *Guilty*. Sanctum Entertainment/VPAL Music.
———. 2020. "Take Good Care of My Man". MP3 audio. Track 1 on *Tanya Stephens Exclusive*. NODOPROD Records.

Epilogue
"A Bunch of Righteous Freaks..."
Tanya, God, Christians and the Bible

ANNA KASAFI PERKINS

THIS CHAPTER OFFERS THE BEGINNINGS OF A CARIBBEAN theological reading of selected tracks from Tanya Stephens's repertoire, particularly focusing on three key theological concepts: discipleship (Christians living Christianity), God (concept/doctrine of the existence, nature and purpose) and the Bible (inspired writings for Christian faith and life). In so doing, it acknowledges that it is in the music of the Caribbean that the cutting edge of theological reflection is evident (Copeland 2004a) and that Stephens, therefore, functions as an unwitting thea-logian – a theologian who takes seriously the concerns of women of African descent (Perkins 2011). The title of the chapter comes from her song "What a Day", in which she blends well these three themes – God, Christians and the Bible, supported by others such as social justice, improved human relationship and "men finally liv[ing] what they teach in law". She dreams of a day when myriads of global problems – hunger, racial animosity, corruption, "pricks with money but no social graces", war and the like – no longer exist. Stephens specifically laments the behaviour of certain Christians whom she labels "a bunch of righteous freaks extorting worse than the mob". She criticizes them for causing her, among other things, to leave church feeling like she has just been robbed. Her words are trenchant and offensive to some, but undoubtedly Stephens cares little for those who do not like her because, as she so pugnaciously informs us in "Who Is Tanya", "dem no hafi laik har but dem hafi rispek [har] skilz".

CULTURAL INTERTEXUALITY

In reading the text of Stephens's songs, which are formed and informed by "religious belief and practice, cultural sensibility, economic opportunity and exploitation, and material culture" (Cowan 2008, 13), it is possible to draw the outlines of the Jamaican and global society from which her songs emerge and at which they are directed. Stephens, like other cultural artistes and producers, depends on cultural intertextuality to deliver her message. Certainly, the religious or rather the Christian saturated context of Jamaica, as it is described by Latoya Lazarus (2012), acts as an important frame for her discourse so not requiring any deep excavation to arrive at meaning by her primary audience. Cowan (2008, 11), in his discussion of the use of religion in horror films, defines cultural intertextuality as "a set of conventions – social norms, religious practices, artistic products, folk wisdom, different parts of the taken for granted information . . . that are available for [artistes] to exploit as a kind of cultural shorthand to make specific points in their work". Stephens can count on certain references to resonate with her Jamaican audience without having to spell everything out. She deploys this well in her references to the King James Bible, Negro spirituals, sankeys, and local and international incidents on her tracks. Her language often reflects the quotidian ways in which Jamaicans deploy exclamations that many would consider taking the Lord's name in vain, as illustrated in songs like "Saturday Morning" (she exclaims, "God Almighty"), or in "Spilt Milk" where she demands divine retribution ("Do it Jah"). In "Cherry Brandy" she critiques deeply Christian notions like "living in sin". In other songs, such as "No Strings Attached", she begs for forgiveness as she contemplates adultery.[1]

CHURCH AND ONE-DAY-CHRISTIAN DISCIPLES

Christian believers are a special target for Stephens's critical commentary on faith, faithfulness and discipleship. She is highly critical of Christian believers, some of whom, as mentioned previously, she describes as a "bunch of righteous freaks extorting worse than the mob" ("What a Day") or whom she describes as "dirty niggas" in "Mi and Mi God". These miscreants engage in harsh judgement, "sidong an a joj mi" [sit in judgement]), that "condemns [others] to the pits of hell". Indeed, Christians rank beside politicians as one of Stephens's least favourite kinds of people. She speaks scornfully about both politics and religion, oftentimes in the same breath. She disdains organized religion and tribal politics, which she clearly sees as sharing similar traits when she pairs them in "To the Limit": "some people spend a lifetime, only experience politics and religion". From her Jamaican experience, where religious faith and political allegiance can be sources of division, to only participate in those two divisive activities does little to recommend a person. Ironically, both are powerful forces that can work to bring about change. At the same time, both can be sources of oppression and limitation for their passionate adherents as well as those they oppose and judge harshly. She is forthright in telling us why.

Stephens takes her most powerful broadside at Christians in "Sunday Morning" on the album *Rebelution*, which follows a piece entitled "Cherry Brandy". "Cherry Brandy", which extols the value of very friendly alcohol to dull the pain of love lost, is preceded by – while extending the sound effects-filled lament called "Saturday Morning" – phone ringing, dishes splattering, moaning and groaning, and drinks pouring. The context is unmistakable. "Saturday Morning" is what results from a "little [too much] Cherry Brandy". It tells the sadly humorous tale of a woman who awakens to find herself having to deal the consequences of liaisons with Smirnoff and "Mr Barcadi" the night before – an ugly sexually satiated stranger lying in her bed. She laments,

> this happened before
> this wasn't the first
> but I gotta admit, this one is the worst
> And where were my friends, didn't anybody see?
> God Almighty, this one is ugleee.

Despite vowing to change "her philandering ways", the unnamed woman finds herself requesting a beer even as she dismisses her unknown yet errant lover. (He rebuffs her with a very Jamaican kiss teeth and rejoinder, "Tek man fi blodklaat iidiat"! [Treating me like an (expletive) idiot!].) Very human weakness is on display in the unnamed's actions in a manner that is more often associated with men. And in the usual fashion of her homeland, God the Almighty is called to witness her weakness.

"Sunday Morning", a spoken word piece delivered in solemn tones, opens with organ music and is accompanied by a chorus of voices of a congregation who responds with laughter and shock at appropriate points. In this sermon, Stephens reprises the age-old critique that Christians are hypocrites and "one day Christians". She is directing her ire specifically at Christianity as it is manifested in its Sunday church-going variety. The Christianity that she rejects is the one embodied in imperfect Christians whom she describes, as we heard in "What a Day", as "a bunch of righteous freaks extorting worse than the mob". She rejects the toxicity of the Christian message, delivered by some Christians, who, in her decided opinion, suffer from psychoses (perhaps delusions of grandeur or superiority complexes). Her dismissal of certain forms of Christianity is almost Freudian as she too sees madness and schizophrenia lurking behind such toxic fervour. The Christians whom she challenges act superior to others during the week, only deigning to invite them to church on Sundays. Their weekday behaviour involves looking down at others from a pedestal on which they "so superficially perch". It would take very little to knock them off such a pedestal, it seems. In her usual satirical way, she charges in "Sunday Morning" that:

> The same set of people who say God lives in the sky
> Is the same set of people who criticize me anytime I get high
> And they even have a problem with my drinking
> And I say fine
> But if Jesus had a problem with drinking
> Would he turn water into wine?

Here, Stephens pokes fun at the contradictions in one-day Christianity.[2] For her, getting "high" should be the right thing to do as it should bring her closer to God, whom Christians believe lives in the sky. Her biting statement finds a certain resonance in the practices of Rastafarians, an indigenous Jamaican religious group who smoke marijuana as holy sacrament, which brings them to a spiritual plane wherein they can communicate with Jah and reason together (Chevannes 1994). Rastas reject notions that God lives in the sky; rather Jah is "earth's rightful ruler" in the manifestation of the Godman Emperor Haile Selassie I of Ethiopia.[3] Stephens's critique of Christianity is resonant of the Rastafari livity, whose adherents charge that true religion has been falsified by Christians. And to complicate matters quite a bit, Christians who themselves accuse each other of being hypocrites and one-day believers charge that one or the other rival denomination has falsified the Christian religion by even worshipping on the wrong day. No wonder she is ready for "a new religion".

Her biting sarcasm seems aimed at Christians who attack consumption of alcohol in any form. The importance they give to such behaviour appears contradictory to her in the face of Jesus's consumption and mass production of wine (the wedding at Cana, John 2:1–11). She seems to believe that Christians have a tendency to incorrectly "major in the minors".[4] Interestingly, Stephens's points of contact with the radical Rasta critique of Christianity parts company here, as most Rastas do not advocate the consumption of any form of alcohol. Of course, many would find her seeming to equate recreational drug use with drinking somewhat disconcerting. However, she may well be giving expression to a Jamaican folk attitude towards marijuana, which is not viewed as a hard drug as is cocaine and heroin. Rather, ganja is "natural" and wholesome, having numerous medicinal uses. Recall her statement in "Welcome to the Rebelution" that wholesome values like "curling up with a good book and a bong" have gone out of fashion. She is, of course, being a bit contentious when she tars every Christian who disagrees with that potentially harmful and seemingly contradictory lifestyle choice as being "too busy feeling sorry for her soul instead of seeking help for their psychosis".

Still, it is clear in "The Other Cheek" that Christians too often fail to "practise what they preach" (an allusion to Matthew 7:24–27; James 1:22–25; Romans 2:21). The centrality of this to Christian discipleship is emphasized by Burchell Taylor, Jamaican Baptist pastor and theologian: "The moral attitude with which you preach, teach, speak, counsel, advise, instruct, and interpret must be kept free from flippancy, hypocrisy, falsehood, evasion and deceit. No doubt this seems obvious, but in practice the temptations are great, the failure rate is by no means low and the consequences for the Christian community in its witness to the wider community are more than disastrous. They are absolutely tragic" (Taylor 1983, 66).

Sadly, many Christians do not contribute to the life and health of the people and society they are called to serve (Taylor 1983). In the name of God, Christians are called to play a healing[5] role in a sick society. Unfortunately, some are making it sicker. The tragedy of such behaviour is the cartoonish image of the Christian that Stephens both paints and rejects.

A NEW RELIGION

In "Sunday Morning", Stephens laments, "I am looking for a new religion / for God's sake I feel like I am in prison". She rightly decries the suffocating feel that some forms of conservative Christianity may have for those who want to be truly religious. She, therefore, dismisses what she considers to be the tyranny of conservative authoritarian Christian doctrine and morality. Her challenge to the Church demonstrates that "the church, a long-standing source and centre of moral authority and influence, can no longer take for granted that it has any special right or privilege to be heard and to have its dictates respected and followed" (Taylor 1992, 4). In fact, Taylor, in his 1992 GraceKennedy Foundation Lecture, presents some convincing arguments that there are areas of Jamaican social, cultural and political life in which the church is no longer considered to have the competence or right to comment or to offer counsel and advice. Taylor (1992) lists among these areas of social life which are often considered outside the church's competence: gambling, attitudes to holy days and seasons, forms of entertainment and revelry, the content of popular music or the morality of male-female relationships, and the quality of family life. These are the very areas in which conflicts arise between many conservative Christian churches and the masses.

Nonetheless, any phenomenon described as a religion is often offered a certain legitimacy and cultural acceptance (Cowan 2008). As such, many other expressions of faith are dismissed as false and misleading as happens with the treatment of non-Christian or African-derived religions like Revival and Rastafari in Jamaica. William James (2012) presents the classic definition of religion, which sees it as belief in an unseen order and the need to order our lives to live in harmony for our supreme good. Such a definition does not restrict religion to officially sanctioned groups and practices but opens the way for marginalized beliefs and practice like Revival, which was counted in the Jamaica census for the first time in 2010. At the same time, as Cowan (2008) argues, James's definition avoids the "good, moral, and decent fallacy" which is often on display in Jamaica where assumptions are made that only religious people or believers are moral. This popular misconception that religion is good or should always be good ignores the fact that negative social effects may result from religious faith and the actions of persons sincerely living it out. At the same time, "religious experience and reflection have always engendered poetry and literature, prompting the imagination and moving beyond speculative thought" (Detweiler et al. 2000, xi). Behold . . . Tanya!

NO TO CLERGY

Some people say no to drugs; Stephens says no to clergy in "Sunday Morning" in a two-pronged "apology" – "Sorry, pastor, bishop, I mean deacon". She rejects the claim to a special mediatory role for members of the clergy, effectively putting them out of work. In her eyes, they act as an obstacle to her relationship with God. She does not spare them "the length of her tongue" or the mark of her "favourite utensil" – the pen. In "What a Day" she declares herself

> tired of leaving church feeling like I've just been robbed
> two hours of rambling not much mention of God
> The richest man's the only one who does not have a job.

Evidently, attending church, in her experience, does not live up to expectations. Here, there is a play on the word "robbed": she is robbed of her money by the preacher, whom, as is discussed further below, she accuses of extortion, perhaps for using scare tactics or false promises to relieve her of her hard-earned money. She also feels robbed because she did not receive what she expected – important words about God. This is more than a critique of bad preaching. The "richest man" – the pastor – is the one who does not have a job (and by her telling – ought not to have a job). This reinforces that his riches must have been gained illegally, by extortion (or as Jamaicans say, "hol dong and tek wey" [restrain and rob]). Interestingly, the very focus on material goods and conspicuous consumption that Stephens excoriates for being present in church also is alive and well in dancehall. The correlate of wealth and prosperity in church is "bling" and "flossing" in the dancehall.

Dancehall and church may not be such distinct and opposing realities in Jamaica, as is often supposed. Rather, there may be a more complex and complicated interrelationship than is often recognized. There is no escaping the cultural reference to megachurches and the (mainly) men who pastor them globally and locally, who are notorious for their extreme wealth and luxurious lifestyles. With the focus of so many pastors being on wealth, the church experience does not speak of God. Undoubtedly, in "What a Day", Stephens is expressing her distaste with certain ways of being religious that focus on prosperity and wealth without addressing the real social concerns of "life and death being sold as a pair". Even within the wider church community, there are ongoing discussions about the falsity of such prosperity theology. The behaviour she finds so unsavoury has also been rejected by Burchell Taylor (1983, 65), who warns against the very serious fault of manipulating God's power and authority for our own selfish ends – that is, "taking God's name in vain". He cautions, in speaking to graduates of the United Theological College of the West Indies, future clergymen and women:

> You will be wise and careful, therefore, not to invoke the name of the Lord merely for the purpose of gaining special favours and privileges for yourself. You will be wise and careful not to invoke the name of the Lord merely to gain the confidence of others that you may exploit them. You will be wise and careful not to invoke the name of the Lord to gain respect; you have not earned and respect you do not deserve. You will be wise and careful not to invoke the name of the Lord merely as a means of protection or mischief.

Many of us are still not heeding Taylor's admonition.

THE BIBLE

Stephens professes both knowledge of and respect for the Bible, particularly the King James Version, which, like many Jamaicans, she believes to be in the original language. She confesses in "Sunday Morning",

> and is not even like mi a shot up di Bible
> See mi have a King James yah
> an mi even a look inna it.

To this end, she maintains the fiction that the Bible was originally written by King James, whom she addresses directly, for not having included any writings from a woman therein. While her conclusion follows from an incorrect premise, she is on to something in seeking out the woman's voice in sacred scripture. She therefore boldly and consciously sets up her work as the answer to the excluded voice of the female in the Bible. Hence, her concluding statement in "Sunday Morning": "not to worry, Behold the Chronicles of Tanya" (echoes of the *Chronicles of Narnia* or the *Chronicles of Riddick*). Her womanist credentials are unwittingly on display. She will not let the existing situation remain unchanged. The woman's voice seems to be chronicled in "You Keep Looking Up", which follows immediately upon "Sunday Morning". This is the track where she describes the nature and presence of God and claims a space for her voice as one from the margins, whose knowledge has been subjugated. She forthrightly places her experience and interpretation of the Scriptures as equally valid alongside the normative masculine perspectives that pervade the Caribbean biblical and theological enterprise. She rejects notions that such male perspectives are universal and normative. The authority to interpret scripture has been invested in men and the views of women have been deemed to be unimportant, even sinful. Not so for Stephens.

GOD ACCORDING TO TANYA STEPHENS

According to Middleton (2008, 22), "Centuries of serious and detailed readings of the Christian Bible . . . has led to what scholars now recognize as the traditional doctrine of God." Among the traits that are conceived as properly belonging to God alone are the following: God is One, the Supreme, eternal being at the centre of the universe. God is holy and a person, able to enter into relationship with Creation. "God possesses mind, will, and feelings, attributes made positively manifest through equitable, tender, and beneficent means." God is the creator/originator and sustainer of creation in which God immerses Godself (immanence) while remaining separate from it (transcendence). God is omnipresent, omniscient and omnipotent while constantly seeking to reveal Godself to human beings, as demonstrated in the pages of the Bible. "Countless theologians across the centuries have shaped, evaluated, rejected, reshaped, and demonstrated" this doctrine of God. Stephens is simply one of them, unwittingly.

Stephens has no need of classical and modern proofs of God's existence, such as those framed by medieval theologians Thomas Aquinas or Anselm. Like many Jamaicans, she takes the existence of God as a given. For her, God's nature and activity are not "deeply inscrutable" or a "theological mystery" (Middleton 2008, 21). Rather this "rough rider" expresses a deep yearning after God, whom she depicts as not simply being the God of Moses – the one who preaches love but has Christians carrying out war in his Holy name. She identifies the inherent contradiction in holding such a position and again challenges the myth of redemptive violence. According to "You Keep Looking Up", God is not to be found in the sky; a transcendent being that is so far away from humanity. No, God is to be found in and around us: "I am everywhere. . . . I am now." Her repetition of the "I am" alludes to the divine name as it is revealed to Moses in Exodus (Yahweh = "I am who I am"). Similarly, it recalls the "I am" statements of Jesus in John's Gospel, which themselves echo and indicate Jesus's divinity.

"You Keep Looking Up" is a paean to the omnipresent universally loving Divine. Stephens's intention, therefore, seems to be that "You Keep Looking Up" present her feminine view of divine reality which is lacking in the Bible. Quite an ambitious proposal. Without knowing it, Stephens is taking a very clearly womanist line in her reading and writing of sacred text, although her reading is still tied to masculine images of the divine as she always calls God "Father". "You Keep Looking Up" continues the theme of her concern for a concrete and contextual spirituality rooted in the experience of a divine being who is present among us. She challenges us:

> You keep looking up, why don't you look around you?
> I am everywhere, yes I am now
> I am the flowers, I am the trees
> I am the song floating in the breeze ...
> I am even your enemies
> I am the rock, I am the sand
> I am the girl I am the man
> I am the river flowing through the land
> I am everything and I am everyone

At first glance, her vision appears to be pantheistic. In her words, God is everything. God is everything, therefore, logically everything is God. The logic is similar to the Rasta syllogism that says God is a black man (Selassie), therefore black man is God (no mention of black woman). Such a pantheistic vision, of course, raises questions about the way Creation should be treated. Should worship be offered to the seas and the breeze because they are God? Such a perspective does not hold to the presence of a Creator God and would seem to go hand in hand with Stephens's rejection of conservative Christianity as she defines it. Yet, one suspects her vision is a much more panentheistic one, which accepts that everything that is, is in God, but God is somehow beyond everything that exists. This is so because her other pieces make it clear that she believes in a personal Creator God with whom she yearns to be in relationship. In one instance, in "Spilt Milk", she calls upon the universe or Jah to "punish him who left her when she needed him most". Another time, in "Damn You", she calls upon God for a "little reciprocity; nothing major, just equal pain" for the lover who jilted her. Similarly, in "Can't Breathe" she admits to not being able to say the words "God bless you" to someone who has hurt her. As she says, she's "keeping it real". Her very human petticoat is showing.

God is not only in the flowers and trees but is the personal being, who cares for individuals and to whom account needs to be given at some point. Stephens's venturing into the realm of panentheism is unwitting, however. Interestingly, in the modern theological and philosophical discourse around God, there has been a rejection of classical theism ("God of the philosophers"). Classical theism asserts that God is transcendent, self-sufficient, eternal, and immutable, omniscient, and omnipotent in relation to the world. God neither changes through time nor is affected by Creation. However, this God of classical theism has been challenged by contemporary theologians from both biblical and philosophical perspectives (Cooper 2010). Challengers like Cooper present various relational alternatives, from minor modifications, to major revisions, to varieties of panentheism, to new versions of naturalistic pantheism. He tells us that although God and the world are ontologically distinct, and God transcends the world, the world is "in" God ontologically. Classical theism, on the other hand, presents an unqualified distinction between God and Creation. Although related, God and Creation are always different from the other. Cooper argues convincingly that because there are such widely differing understandings of panentheism, some theologians are panentheist and are not aware of this (implicit panentheists). In his eyes, various kinds of panentheism inform much liberation, feminist, and ecological theology: "This is so because in different ways these theologies emphasize the liberation of specific groups of people as part of the reconciliation and communion of the whole cosmos in God" (Cooper 2010, 19). Cooper further claims that understanding panentheism is necessary for anyone who is theologically literate. Even a theologically unschooled Jamaican singjay can call us to a reflection on such weighty matters.

Of course, Stephens cannot be expected to see the philosophical or theological implications of her panentheistic position on the traditional belief in an omniscient and impassible creator. She is unaware that her reflections join those of many scholars in deepening our understanding of the divine. Undoubtedly, her implicit panentheism is aimed at calling us to more deeply value all of creation and each other. She is simply telling us that in our search for divinity, we are looking in the wrong place. If we really recognized that God is present in "the girl, woman, man ... even our greatest enemy ... in every bum and every king", our response to the world would very different. We would "look with love at whatever we see". Such love would abhor any form of oppression or injustice. Her perspective intersects unwittingly with the ideas of Methodist biblical theologian Walter Wink, who speaks of "the enemy as gift". Wink calls us to question whether the enemy does not tell us something about ourselves. Our enemies gift us with the ability to see aspects of ourselves that we would not be able to see any other way. According to a passage worth quoting in full:

> The enemy is ... not merely a hurdle to be leapt on the way to God. The enemy can be the way to God. ... How wonderfully humiliating: we not only may have a role in transforming our enemies, but our enemies play a role in transforming us. ... As we

become aware of our projections on our enemies, we are freed from the fear that we will overreact murderously toward them. We are able to develop an objective rage at the injustices they have perpetrated while still seeing them as children of God. The energy squandered nursing hatred becomes available to God for confronting the wrong or transforming the relationship. (1998, 171)

In light of Wink's challenge, the care and respect that Stephens calls for in "What a Day" becomes more intelligible.

HUMAN-DIVINE CONNECTION

In "You Keep Looking Up", Stephens literally speaks in the voice of God and assures us that God loves us all the same: "I love you the same whether you rich or broke / You're still my child whether you sniff or you smoke". Our status – moral or otherwise – does not truly alienate us from God. God is a God of mercy and compassion who continually reaches out to Creation, especially sinful human beings. Stephens believes in the possibility for the human connection to God to bring about conversion/change. Again, we see that thread of hope that runs through her unwitting theology. At the same time, this means that we will hear the admonition to "practise what you preach" repeatedly in several of her songs, examples of which include "The Other Cheek" and "Still Alive". For while she acknowledges human weakness and our fallible nature, this ought not to be used as an excuse for wrongdoing. She recognizes that this fallible nature is often expressed in a certain judgemental stance that is quick to condemn and prescribe. In "Mi and My Gad" she rejects the idea that any human person has the power to "bind and loose". She chastises us for a certain presumptuousness in telling God who should be saved and who not. That decision is not ours to make, and God, being a God of surprises, always turns our expectations upside down. Thus, she says very forthrightly in "Mi and Mi God":

> A no dem hol di kii to di pramis lan
> Dem kyaan shut mi owt a di purli manshan
> Caa mi fada se comemi faitful survant
> Mi waan dem com tel di fada se im wrang
> Som gyuys a gwaan laik dem own di privilig
> Fi tel ada piepl ow dem supuose fi liiv
> Mi naa watch no fais an lisen to no chat
> Mi unuo a jost one man perfek an a Jisaaz dat

So ef mi waan fi brok owt an galang bad
Dat's jos bitwiin mi an mi gad
An if mi waan fi skin out an ack laik mi mad
Dat's jos op to mi.

(They do not hold the key to the Promised Land
They can't shut me out of the pearly mansion
Because my father said come my faithful servant
I want them to tell the father that he's wrong
Some guys behave as if they own the privilege
To tell other people how they are supposed to live
I am not watching any face or listening to any talk
I know that there's only one perfect man, and that is Jesus
So, if I want to behave badly
That's just between me and my God
And if I want to expose my body and act like I am mad
That's just up to me.)

It is worth considering that her perspective in "Mi and My Gad" can be seen to be in direct opposition to positions she holds in other pieces. She appears to be rejecting any concern with certain dancehall behaviours such as "skinning out" and "galanging bad", where female revellers behave in a fashion that may expose much of their bodies for public consumption or participate in moves that too closely simulate the sex act. (Of course, "galang bad" can also refer to disorderly public behaviour that is expected of the so-called lower classes). Perhaps she is saying that even in the face of such publicly disruptive behaviour, which may be deserving of social opprobrium, the final judgement on the person's character and morality has to be left to God. Some may judge her position as bordering on a kind of amorality, in which everything goes, since morality is an individual matter or only to be worked out between her and God (and God knows). Of course, we know that is not the case as she has a clear sense of right and wrong and some evident norms guide her vision of a better world. For example, she takes on the painful topic of the discrimination against people living with HIV in "Still Alive". She calls on the employer who decides to fire the recently diagnosed Johnny, because of the fear his presence causes among his co-workers, to remember the biblical injunction to "judge not and you will not be judged". Stephens chastises the boss man for refusing to follow the teaching of the very Bible that he holds so dear but really did not understand.

She calls upon the employer to practise what he preaches as he is a model for others to follow. The Bible forms a source of moral authority for her that shapes how she perceives the world and the actions of others. The question is what is the basis for interpreting the injunctions of Scripture? Clearly, the key values for scriptural interpretation are love and brotherhood. Love being a verb not a noun, she tells him.

Returning to "Mi and Mi God", we see her rejecting judgements about her action as being sinful in a fashion that alludes to Jesus's response in the story of the woman taken in adultery (John 8:1–11) when she sings,

> So doan priich to mi bowt sin
> Or morals of self rispek
> So doan yu spiik to mi a ting
> Show mi a man ou neva sin yet.
>
> (So don't preach to me about sin
> Or morals of self-respect
> So don't you speak to be about any thing
> Show me a man that has never sinned.)

Here, she refuses to accept stoning from beings that are as sinful as she is herself. No one is in a position to judge her, or so she claims. This sounds like the same kind of rejection of traditional morality that is at play in the dancehall. But perhaps in this piece she is engaging in a bit of exaggeration for effect. In her very rejection of norms and values, she is reinforcing the need for such norms. Even as we struggle in our humanity to live morally, our judgment of others must always be tempered by compassion and our own sense of unworthiness.

EVIL ACCORDING TO TANYA STEPHENS

Stephens rephrases the age-old question of theodicy by stating that the God of some Christians sits idly by while we do wrong to each other and blame it on the Devil. In her eyes, such a being cannot be divine. She exclaims for "God sake", but her travails are intended for God's sake. She aims at releasing God from the captivity in which God has been kept by Christians, who do not really know him. The presence of Satan or Lucifer in the religious drama of Jamaican people is exposed for what it is: an excuse for us doing evil. Stephens is also alert to the divine sanction that many claim for their deeds and she rejects that wholeheartedly as well. In "Intro-spection" from her album *Infallible*, she reflects on the human condition wherein mistakes and sins are repeated. Again, she laments that Lucifer is the patsy for our wrongdoing. In this lyrical spoken word piece, she accuses us in our human condition of "mess[ing] up repeatedly and still show[ing] no contrition". She continues:

> And if it's bad enough just blame it on Lucifer
> Use him for the excuse that you didn't act of your own volition
> Go ahead rob, cheat, lie
> Remember Satan is the perfect alibi
> And all you have to do is repent before you die
> You'll still be accepted at that mansion in the sky
> Fret not thyself that your morals be mall[e]able
> For that's what makes you infallible

She claims that many of us feel we can get away with having lived a life of sin with a simple deathbed act of repentance. Such a morality is malleable – changing to suit the circumstances and the situation. That is to her the nature of infallibility. Happily, she does not reprise the well-known misunderstanding of the notion of infallibility that is so prevalent among many Jamaicans. Some Jamaicans see infallibility as referring to the pope and his being unable to sin. Her concern with such malleability directly addresses a strong cultural practice among many Jamaican, especially men, who reject the call of evangelical Christianity to be "saved", get baptized and give their lives to Jesus until they are quite elderly or next to death. The usual reason for such unwillingness is the depth of lifestyle change that such an acceptance of Jesus entails; born again Christians are expected to have the morality of saints – no drinking, cursing, carousing, or fun. Life in the world is sinful and must be rejected.

Again, we return to the question of sin. Anglican Caribbean theologian Kortright Davis asks the question, "What is the nature of Caribbean sin?" (1990, 77). Davis, of course, rejects the traditional "missionary" answer, which was sexual immorality that produced many children born out of wedlock. This is the morality that Stephens and other dancehall artistes reject, albeit in very different fashions. As Davis is clear, therefore, "sex is not where we need to look for the Caribbean sin. We need to look in the area of non-responsibility, for that is the area that touches every class of Caribbean citizenry" (77–78). It would be a mistake to simply focus on personal sin as has often been the case.

Davis argues also that Caribbean people, like the rest of humanity, live in a sinful world, a world deeply structured by sin. The structures of sin are deeply rooted in the ways of social intercourse, and only someone like Jesus Christ can rise above them and deliver those under the sway of sin. He emphasizes that no human agency is untouched by sin; no one is exempt from the need to be set free from sin. As Stephens taunts: "Show mi a man dat neva sin yet". In light of the peculiarities of the Caribbean situation, Davis sees the task of the Caribbean theologian as demonstrating systematically that to be of African descent is not the result of a divine mistake, and that the lingering sin of self-contempt no longer finds justification in the devices of former rulers. We have no excuse not to love ourselves. Davis identifies the major manifestations of sin in the region as racism, classism, self-contempt, non-responsibility and exploitation. All of which are challenged in Stephens's unwitting theological enterprise.

A NEW DAY, A NEW RELIGION

Having rejected all that is at variance with the divine presence in Jamaica, Stephens in "What a Day" presents a vision for a new day which is decidedly and frighteningly apocalyptic:

> I got a vision of a whole other plain
> Where the spiritual can flourish again
> I'm just waiting for the fire to rain
> Burn dung everything and start clean.

Apocalyptic visions of the world are not new to the West and certainly not new to the Caribbean. Stephens's vision of a new world may be influenced by a strand of Christianity that welcomes the destruction of world as a sign of the end times and the return of Christ. Such Christians find their vision of the end of the world in particular ways of reading the Apocalypse. Revelation 11:18 – "the time has come to destroy the destroyers of the earth" – is often read as a destruction of the earth in some kind of cosmic conflagration at the hands of a wrathful God. This is the fire that she is waiting to rain down and burn up everything. Her fiery vision also echoes the Rastafarian proclivity for "burning" of all things Babylon. Rastas see the current social order as ripe for chanting down – that is, subject to prophetic denunciation and cursing. Among their favourite targets for denunciation ("bun") is Rome (representing the Roman Catholic Church) and the Babylonian system of politics and economics in which the American imperium is deeply implicated. A strong sense of an impending end pervades much of the apocalyptic discourse of the New Testament, as Lutheran theologian Barbara Rossing reminds us. Rossing (2008) is clear, however, that for the most part early Christian texts do not primarily envision the destruction of the earth or the created world. Rather, in proclaiming the dawning of a new age in Christ, they were envisioning the end of the Roman imperium based on oppression and injustice. The apocalyptic language is deliberately chosen to counter Rome's imperial and eschatological claim to eternal hegemony and to underscore the urgent coming of a new age. The fiery imagery reflects the conviction that the old imperial order is passing away and that the reign of God is taking root. The expectation is both destruction and regeneration. Stephens's dream of a better day can only result from the destruction of the destructiveness that is at play now. There is a real paradox here. The power of fire to destroy and cleanse lies behind Stephens's vision of a new day, a new religion. It is a hope-filled theological vision.

CONCLUSION

The Caribbean does itself a disservice if it attempts to draft an agenda for the theological enterprise within the Caribbean region without paying attention to the peculiar contribution of the region's popular music. Dancehall, the music form of the Jamaican masses, while being particularly troubling with its rampant "slackness", commodification of women, worship of the gun and bling, contains an important strand that bears some attention. The unwitting theological enterprise of Stephens challenges the belief that theology properly resides within church and seminary and is the purview of trained theologians. Rather, theology arises from the very bowels of the Jamaican Caribbean people as they attempt to discern what the Divine is doing with, in and through us in our current circumstances. In so doing, we will come to see how those among us whose voices have been subjugated find within dancehall a space to give voice to their sense of betrayal by religious and political leadership, the oppressive nature of traditional orthodoxies that serve to continue to subjugate and silence them. Stephens's extensive discography points us to live questions about the nature of God, the human-divine relationship, the role of church, and the human call to change the world in the face of discrimination, economic exploitation and human frailty. We all look forward to that day.

NOTES

1. Of import here is the fact that "Sintoxicated" is the name of one of her earlier albums (Warner Music Sweden 2001).
2. Stephens is not alone in this. Listen, for example to Lovindeer's "One Day Christian" on the album *The Best of Lovindeer* (2009).
3. Listen, for example, to Jimmy Cliff's "The Harder They Come" on the soundtrack of the 1972 movie *The Harder They Come*.
4. For those who miss the irony in her claim, Stephens may be criticized for falling into the trap of a form of "proof texting" where her drinking habits are sanitized by appealing to Jesus's turning water into wine.
5. Of significance here is that the word "healing" is the root meaning of the word salvation (*salvus*).

REFERENCES

Chevannes, Barry. 1994. *Rastafari: Roots and Ideology*. Syracuse, NY: Syracuse University Press.

Cooper, John W. 2010. "Panentheism: The Other 'God' of the Philosophers': An Overview". *American Theological Inquiry* 1:11–29.

Copeland, Shawn M. 2004a. "Black Political Theologies". In *The Blackwell Companion to Political Theology*, edited by Peter Scott and William T. Cavanaugh, 264–79. Malden, MA: Blackwell.

Copeland, Shawn M. 2004b. "Living Stones in the Household of God". In *Living Stones in the Household of God: The Legacy and Future of Black Theology*, edited by Linda E. Thomas, 183–88. Minneapolis: Fortress Press.

Cowan, Douglas E. 2008. *Sacred Terror: Religion and Horror on the Silver Screen*. Waco, TX: Baylor University Press.

Davis, Kortright. 1990. *Emancipation Still Comin': Explorations in Caribbean Emancipatory Theology*. Maryknoll, NY: Orbis.

Detweiler, Robert, David Jasper, S. Brent Plate, and Heidi L. Nordberg. 2000. *Religion and Literature: A Reader*. Louisville, KY: Westminster John Knox Press.

James, William. 2012. *Varieties of Religious Experience: A Study in Human Nature*. Kindle edition. Amazon Digital Services.

Lazarus, Latoya. 2012. "This Is a Christian Nation: Gender and Sexuality in Processes of Constitutional and Legal Reform in Jamaica". *Social and Economic Studies* 61 (3): 117–43.

Middleton, Darren JN. 2008. *Theology after Reading: Christian Imagination and the Power of Fiction*. Waco, TX: Baylor University Press.

Perkins, Anna Kasafi. 2011 "Carib-being and Theo-logy these days: The Unwitting Theological Enterprise of the Music of Tanya Stephens". Augustus Tolton Lecture, Catholic Theological Union, Chicago, 2 March.

Rossing, Barbara. 2008. "Hastening the Day When the Earth Will Burn: Global Warming, 2 Peter, and the Book of Revelation". In *The Bible in the Public Square: Reading the Signs of the Times*, edited by Cynthia Briggs Kittredge, Ellen Bradshaw Aitken, and Jonathan A. Draper, 25–38. Minneapolis, MN: Fortress Press.

Taylor, Burchell. 1992. *Free for All? A Question of Morality and Community*. GraceKennedy Lecture. Kingston: GraceKennedy Foundation.

Taylor, Burchell. 1983. "Taking God's Name in Vain". In *The Caribbean Pulpit: An Anthology*, edited by Gayle Clement and William Watty, 63–69. Kingston: C.H.L Gayle.

Wink, Walter. 1998. *The Powers That Be: Theology for a New Millennium*. New York: Doubleday.

DISCOGRAPHY

Stephens, Tanya, vocalist. 1997. "Mi and Mi God". MP3 audio. Track 4 on *Too Hype*. VP Records.

———. 2004. "Can't Breathe". MP3 audio. Track 13 on *Gangsta Blues*. VP Records.

———. 2004. "Intro". MP3 audio. Track 1 on *Gangsta Blues*. VP Records.

———. 2004. "The Other Cheek". MP3 audio. Track 15 on *Gangsta Blues*. VP Records.

———. 2006. "Cherry Brandy". MP3 audio. Track 11 on *Rebelution*. VP Records.

———. 2006. "Damn You". MP3 audio. Track 7 on *Rebelution*. VP Records.

———. 2006. "Saturday Morning". MP3 audio. Track 10 on *Rebelution*. VP Records.

———. 2006. "Spilt Milk". MP3 audio. Track 9 on *Rebelution*. VP Records.

———. 2006. "Sunday Morning". MP3 audio. Track 12 on *Rebelution*. VP Records.

———. 2006. "To the Limit". MP3 audio. Track 17 on *Rebelution*. VP Records.

———. 2006. "Welcome to the Rebelution". MP3 audio. Track 1 on *Rebelution*. VP Records.

———. 2006. "What a Day". MP3 audio. Track 16 on *Gangsta Blues*. VP Records.

———. 2006. "Who Is Tanya". MP3 audio. Track 2 on *Rebelution*. VP Records.

———. 2006. "You Keep Looking Up". MP3 audio. Track 13 on *Rebelution*. VP Records.

———. 2012. "Intro-spection". MP3 audio. Track 1 on *Infallible*. Tarantula Records.

———. 2012. "No Strings Attached". MP3 audio. Track 3 on *Infallible*. Tarantula Records.

———. 2012. "Still Alive". MP3 audio. Track 10 on *Infallible*. Tarantula Records.

Appendix

The following is the text of a citation presented to Vivienne Tanya Stephens by the Institute for Gender and Development Studies at the 2017 symposium in her honour:

> The Institute for Gender and Development Studies, University of the West Indies, recognises the contribution of Tanya Stephens (born Vivienne Tanya Stephenson), reggae artiste extraordinaire, to discourses on gender, social justice and human rights for the people of Jamaica and beyond.
>
> In over two decades of lyrical and creative leadership, Tanya Stephens, 'rebelutionary' critic, has unwaveringly challenged the inequities that have pervaded Jamaican society and the entertainment industry in particular. She is not hesitant to critique through her music and lyricism, injustices rooted in classism, racism, sexism and homophobia; the false holiness of missionary heterosexual monogamy, or to talk about the joys of sexual expression. She demands that "a woman's worth is not to be judged by the length of her skirt". Her music pushes us to answer the question: What and how can we be better human beings for this Jamaica land we are supposed to actually love?
>
> By her stance, she has over and over again demanded respect for women as women while ensuring that men are themselves respected. This did not prevent her from ridiculing the self-praising man, who "nuh ready fi dis yet". Her constant pleas for the renewal and recommitment of men and women to their intimate relationships in the face of the temptations of "these streets" cannot be dismissed. Her personal challenge at being a good parent and the need to form bonds of affection with her own offspring can serve as a lesson for us. Hers is an honest admission of not possessing infallibility as a parent, but wanting only what is best for her child. She humourously throws light on the pain of the woman who makes the decision to name the wrong man as the father of her child. Such a white lie is not little and she makes it clear that such fairytale living is fraught from pain for all involved.
>
> The Church is a foundational institution in Jamaica and many persons profess religious faith to which they are not faithful. The contradictory way that many Christians live their faith has caused her to call for a "new religion" where people no longer kill each other and give Satan the blame or wage war in God's holy name.

She has even been so bold as to deliver chastisement to pastors and other spiritual leaders whose leadership may well be blocking many from a true faith experience.

The socio-economic inequality which marks the lives of many Jamaicans living in the inner city and the role of our political leadership in fostering this unending poverty elicits her tears as she cries out on behalf of the disenfranchised. Her successful forays into entrepreneurship both in the record industry and in tourism serve as an inspiration to women. She is a dedicated and relentless human rights advocate; especially for the rights of women and children in her lyrics, her speeches, and her interviews. Jamaica is lucky to have to you. We are honoured to embrace you and we are humbled by your warrior woman strength. We are grateful for your critical and bold voice.

Tanya, we salute you. Intellectual, survivor, mother, entrepreneur, lyricist. You're still a number one with your number two pencil!

Contributors

ADWOA NTOZAKE ONUORA lectures in the Institute for Gender and Development Studies, the University of the West Indies. She is the author of *Anansesem: Telling Stories and Storytelling African Maternal Pedagogies*.

ANNA KASAFI PERKINS is a senior programme officer in the Quality Assurance Unit, the University of the West Indies, Jamaica. Her publications include *Quality in Higher Education in the Caribbean* and *Justice and Peace in a Renewed Caribbean*.

AJAMU NANGWAYA is a former lecturer in the Institute of Caribbean Studies, the University of the West Indies, Mona, Jamaica. He is co-editor (with Michael Truscello) of *Why Don't the People Rise Up? Organizing the Twenty-First Century Resistance* and (with Kali Akuno) of *Jackson Rising: The Struggle for Economic Democracy and Black Self-Determination in Jackson, Mississippi*.

TANYA BATSON-SAVAGE is publisher and editor-in-chief of Blue Banyan Books and its imprint Blouse and Skirt Books. She is the author of *Pumpkin Belly and Other Stories*.

ELSA CALLIARD-BURTON teaches French at Ardenne High School, Kingston, Jamaica.

KAREN CARPENTER is the director of the Caribbean Sexuality Research Group Sexology Clinic, University Hospital of the West Indies, and lecturer at the Institute of Gender and Development Studies, the University of the West Indies, Mona, Jamaica. Her publications include *Questioning Caribbean Jewish Identity*; *Interweaving Tapestries of Sexuality and Culture*; and *Love and Sex: The Basics*.

MELVILLE COOKE lectures in the Bachelor of Arts in Communication Arts and Technology programme at the University of Technology, Jamaica.

ALPHA OBIKA lectures in communication studies at the Caribbean School of Media and Communications and at the Institute of Caribbean Studies, the University of the West Indies, Mona, Jamaica.

NICOLE PLUMMER lectures in the Institute of Caribbean Studies, the University of the West Indies, Mona, Jamaica.

CHAZELLE RHODEN is a doctoral student in anthropology at Columbia University, New York.

SARA SULIMAN is an infectious disease scientist at Harvard Medical School, Boston.

www.ingramcontent.com/pod-product-compliance
Lightning Source LLC
Chambersburg PA
CBHW031708230426
43668CB00006B/151